ANTICHRIST AND APOCALYPSE

THE 21 PROPHECIES OF REVELATION
UNVEILED AND DESCRIBED

A COMMENTARY ON
THE BOOK OF REVELATION

BY
TAYLOR R. MARSHALL

SAINT JOHN PRESS
MMXXII

Sacred scripture citations generally from the 1899 edition of the Douay-Rheims (Challoner) Bible or alternatively are English translations by Taylor Marshall based on the Latin, Greek, or Hebrew.

A special thanks to David Garcia, Selina Davis, Michael McCann, Donna Lehr, Mary Marshall, and Steven Scheerbaum with their help on the text and formatting.

Marshall, Taylor
Antichrist and Apocalypse / Taylor Marshall
1st ed. 220923
Includes bibliographical references and index
ISBN:
1. Roman Catholicism. 2. New Testament. 3. Theology. I. Title.

Published by
Saint John Press
Box 1765 Colleyville, Texas 76034

Printed in the United States of America

Please visit on the web at:

www.taylormarshall.com

I dedicate this book to my confirmation saint,

The Apostle John

"the disciple whom Jesus loved"

"The Antichrist will not be so called; otherwise he would have no followers. He will not wear red tights, nor vomit sulphur, nor carry a trident nor wave an arrowed tail as Mephistopheles in Faust. This masquerade has helped the Devil convince men that he does not exist. When no man recognizes, the more power he exercises. God has defined Himself as 'I am Who am,' and the Devil as 'I am who am not.'

"He will set up a counterchurch which will be the ape of the Church, because he, the Devil, is the ape of God. It will have all the notes and characteristics of the Church, but in reverse and emptied of its divine content. It will be a mystical body of the Antichrist that will in all externals resemble the mystical Body of Christ."

-Archbishop Fulton Sheen

"Outside the Church, the world will not recognize the Antichrist as the Antichrist. They will wrongly recognize him as 'our Christ' and as the head of his false church."

-Taylor R. Marshall

CONTENTS

Part I: Who and What is Antichrist?

> "How can you be a Christian? There are so many fake and evil pastors, evangelists, priests, cardinals, and popes. It's a scam."

Every Christian has heard the objection above. The answer is quick and simple: the presence of wicked and false leadership was foretold by Christ before He died on the cross, and He repeated this teaching throughout His ministry. The story of creation includes the betrayal by Satan. The history of Christianity begins with the internal betrayal by Judas Iscariot. This pattern of infiltrating betrayal, says Christ, will continue until the end of the world—and climax with the final betrayal by the Antichrist.

Christ teaches us that evil is always an inside job. Like cancer, it falsely mimics our real cells and then seeks to kill the entire body. Evil is a parasite living off its host body. The principal cause of this cancer is Satan, and the final manifestation of this infection is the arrival of the Antichrist as Satan's chief and final antagonist opposing Jesus Christ. Before we get to the end, we must reach back to the beginning of the cancer. How did Satan enter in?

A BOOK OF HOPE

The last book of the Bible is the most hopeful and joyous of the entire Bible. How can that be when it details plagues, disease, wrath, the Antichrist, wars, tribulation, starvation, and damnation? This final book of the New Testament is called "Apocalypse" or *Apokalypsis* in the original Greek. The prefix *apo* means "away," and the verb *kalypso* means "to veil or cover." The Apocalypse is literally "taking away the veil." It is the "revelation" of what God has done, is doing, and will do to finally redeem and restore the creation that He initiated in Genesis.

People, often, wrongly speak of the book of Revelation*s*. But it's not plural; it's singular. There is one single Revelation. One Apocalypse. We are allowed to sit in heaven and watch the one plot in one screening. The veil is taken away, and we see human history and its climax *from God's point of view*. I will refer to the last book of the Bible as the book of the Apocalypse to remind us of this reality and to be more faithful to the original Greek.

The book of Genesis begins with the Trinity. There is God the Father, speaking the Word, who is the Son of God, and the Spirit hovering over the waters. If we are to understand the ending (Apocalypse), we must understand the beginning (Genesis). This is why Christ calls himself Alpha and Omega—the first Greek letter and the last Greek letter.

The story of humanity begins on the sixth day of creation. On day six, God creates land animals: "And God said: Let the earth bring forth the living creature in its kind, cattle and creeping things, and beasts of the earth, according to their kinds. And it was so done" (Gen 1:24).

As you will learn, the Antichrist in the Apocalypse is specifically described as a "beast of the earth," and his number is 666. But we will get to that in more detail in chapters to come. Adam and Eve are also created on day six along with these land beasts:

And he said: Let us make man to our image and likeness: and let him have dominion over the fishes of the sea, and the fowls of the air, and the beasts, and the whole earth, and every creeping creature that moveth upon the earth. And God created man to his own image: to the image of God he created him: male and female he created them. (Gen 1:26–27)

The characters of the Apocalypse are coming alive. We have the beasts, the man, and the woman. Next, we see the villain. Chapter 3 of Genesis introduces the antagonist who will play a major role in the Apocalypse.

And they were both naked: to wit, Adam and his wife: and were not ashamed. Now the serpent was more subtle than any of the *beasts of the earth* which the Lord God had made. And he said to the woman: Why hath God commanded you, that you should not eat of every tree of paradise? (Gen 2:25–3:1, emphasis added)

The serpent is Satan, the former high angel of light who led an angelic rebellion against God. Satan and one-third of the angels rebelled and transformed into demons. Why did they rebel? The twelfth chapter of the Apocalypse reveals why, but we are not there yet.

Eve ate the fruit and gave it to Adam. They fell into sin and death and realized they were naked. They hid and clothed themselves. Then God sought them out.

Man, Woman, and the Devil (Gen 3:9–13)
[9] And the Lord God called Adam, and said to him: Where art thou?

[10] And he said: I heard thy voice in paradise; and I was afraid, because I was naked, and I hid myself.

[11] And he said to him: And who hath told thee that thou wast naked, but that thou hast eaten of the tree whereof I commanded thee that thou shouldst not eat?

¹² And Adam said: The woman, whom thou gavest me to be my companion, gave me of the tree, and I did eat. ¹³ And the Lord God said to the woman: Why hast thou done this? And she answered: The serpent deceived me, and I did eat.

Adam blames the woman and God: "The woman, whom thou gavest me." The woman blames Satan: "The serpent deceived me." And then God metes out punishment upon all three—first, the serpent:

Satan Becomes a Land Beast (Gen 3:14–15)

¹⁴ And the Lord God said to the serpent: Because thou hast done this thing, thou art cursed among all cattle, and beasts of the earth: upon thy breast shalt thou go, and earth shalt thou eat all the days of thy life. ¹⁵ I will put enmities between thee and the woman, and thy seed and her seed: she shall crush thy head, and thou shalt lie in wait for her heel.

Satan was once a high angel. Then he is cast down to crawl upon the earth on his belly. He eats earth and becomes a lowly beast of the land. Moreover, he is now made a perpetual enemy of the Woman (Mary) in particular. Enmities are placed between Satan and the Woman. In both the Hebrew and Greek Septuagint version of Genesis 3:15, the words for *enmity* refer to deep hatred, animosity, or a state of opposition. Satan and the Woman are totally opposed to one another, and this opposition is also between his seed and her Seed. Her Seed, as we shall see, is Jesus Christ and all those that belong to Him. Satan's seed is the Antichrist and all who belong to him.

The next half of the verse describes the protoevangelium, or proto-Gospel. It is the proclamation of God to Adam and Eve that he will save them from Satan, sin, and death. He says, "she shall crush thy head, and thou shalt lie in wait for her heel" (Gen 3:15). Historically, there has been debate over how to translate this verse and render it from the Hebrew. The debate centers on whether God says "he" shall crush Satan's head or whether "she" shall crush Satan's head. Now, it does not much matter since either reading is orthodox and true.

"He" means Christ crushes the head of Satan absolutely, and "she" means the Woman (Mary) crushes the head of Satan by virtue of her role as the Mother of Jesus, and as New Eve. For Catholics, the "she" reading is the traditional reading of the Latin Vulgate, and it is important because it highlights the importance of the Woman (Mary) in human salvation. In other words, the "she shall crush" reading supports the Catholic argument that Mary's role is Mother of the Redeemer. The obvious solution to this problem is simply to look at the original Hebrew. But that is where the problem begins. The Hebrew texts are divided on the issue. The Hebrew Masoretic manuscripts say, "he shall crush." However, there are two Hebrew manuscripts that read, "she shall crush." Our three best and oldest Jewish witnesses to Genesis 3:15 interpret the passage as "she shall crush." These are Philo Judaeus (d. c. AD 50), Josephus the Roman historian (d. AD 100), and the great medieval Jewish commentator Moses Maimonides (d. AD 1204). Philo argues that the Hebrew parallel poetry of Genesis 3:15 demands the reading of "she shall crush."[1] Josephus, also writing in Greek, describes the passage for us as reading "she shall crush."[2] Then, last of all, Maimonides also states that Genesis 3:15 teaches that the Woman shall crush the head of the serpent.[3]

---

[1] Cited by Cornelius a Lapide in his *Comentaria in scripturam sacram, Tomus I In Genesin. I–III.*

[2] Josephus, *Antiquities*, lib. I, cap 3, 4.

[3] Maimonides, *More nebochim*, P. II, cap 30. These three great Jewish scholars testify to the traditional Catholic reading of the Latin Vulgate's "she shall crush." Why are the Hebrew manuscripts that we have today different from these ancient Jewish witnesses? The answer is that the Masoretic manuscript tradition has been corrupted—something claimed by both the Eastern and Western Fathers throughout the centuries.

As we shall see, Chapter 12 of the Apocalypse depicts a war between "the Woman" and an enormous "red dragon." This is a reference to the "enmities between the serpent and the Woman." Next, God judges the Woman and then the Man. Their punishments relate to birth labor, crop labor, and the tree of life:

Punishment of Woman (Gen 3:16)

To the woman also he said: I will multiply thy sorrows, and thy conceptions: in sorrow shalt thou bring forth children, and thou shalt be under thy husband's power, and he shall have dominion over thee.

Punishment of Man (Gen 3:17–19)

[17]And to Adam he said: Because thou hast hearkened to the voice of thy wife, and hast eaten of the tree, whereof I commanded thee that thou shouldst not eat, cursed is the earth in thy work; with labour and toil shalt thou eat thereof all the days of thy life.
[18]Thorns and thistles shall it bring forth to thee; and thou shalt eat the herbs of the earth.
[19]In the sweat of thy face shalt thou eat bread till thou return to the earth, out of which thou wast taken: for dust thou art, and into dust thou shalt return.

Christ will be the "New Adam" and will redeem us by wearing the sign of Adam's curse. He will wear a crown of thorns (not gold) to reveal himself as the Son of Man—the Son of Adam and the Seed of the Woman.

Adam & Eve Expelled (Gen 3:20–24)

[20]And Adam called the name of his wife Eve: because she was the mother of all the living.
[21]And the Lord God made for Adam and his wife, garments of skins, and clothed them.
[22]And he said: Behold Adam is become as one of us, knowing good and evil: now, therefore, lest perhaps he

put forth his hand, and take also of the tree of life, and eat, and live forever.

²³And the Lord God sent him out of the paradise of pleasure, to till the earth from which he was taken.

²⁴And he cast out Adam; and placed before the paradise of pleasure Cherubims, and a flaming sword, turning every way, to keep the way of the tree of life.

God has promised a future Redeemer to crush the head of the serpent. He has clothed Adam and Eve with animal skins. Animal skins mean that animals were killed in atonement. God covers their shame, but He also locks them out of Paradise and places cherubim guarding the way with flaming swords. We will not see this tree again (still guarded by living cherubim) until the taking away of the veil in the Apocalypse. The Apocalypse is the map on our quest for that Tree of Life.

BRIDE OF CHRIST OR WHORE OF SATAN?

The Old Testament contains peoples, places, and things that foreshadow the reality of the New Testament. For example, Saint Peter says that Noah inside the ark foreshadows salvation through baptism (1 Pet 3:20–22). Saint Paul writes that Israel passing through the Red Sea foreshadows baptism (1 Cor 10:2). Similarly, the Passover Lamb foreshadowed the Eucharist (1 Cor 5:7). Adam, Moses, Joshua, David, Daniel, and Jonas foreshadow Jesus Christ in various ways. Jerusalem as a city signifies the Church and points to Heaven as the heavenly City of God.

In the New Testament, the Church is called the Bride of Christ, and Christ is the Groom. They are married together through the New Covenant. This image was foreshadowed in the Old Testament. God was Groom and Israel was Bride. The prophet Osee's[4] message relates the story of God as a husband betrayed by the infidelity of his wife—the nation of Israel. The prophets Isaias, Jeremias, Ezechiel, Daniel, and the twelve Minor Prophets play the roles of judges, lawyers, and accusers in a trial between God and His unfaithful wife. God is calling for his wife, but she runs away to pursue foreign kings and the gods of other nations. Idolatry is repeatedly associated with infidelity and adultery toward God.

This produces the archetype of "two women" that appears throughout the Bible. The unfaithful woman is the archetype associated with Eve, Delilah, and Jezebel. She is the harlot found throughout the book of Proverbs. The faithful woman is associated with Judith and Mary. She is the woman of valor in the final chapter of Proverbs:

---

[4] The prophet Hosea is also Osee. I am generally following the Greek and Latinate spellings of biblical names. Osee is Hosea. Jeremias is Jeremiah. Elias is Elijah, and so on. I use these spellings because these spellings were used by the apostles in the New Testament.

The Faithful Wife of Valor (Prov 31:10–31)

[10] Who shall find a valiant woman? far and from the uttermost coasts is the price of her.

[11] The heart of her husband trusteth in her, and he shall have no need of spoils.

[12] She will render him good, and not evil, all the days of her life.

[18] She hath tasted and seen that her traffic is good: her lamp shall not be put out in the night.

[19] She hath put out her hand to strong things, and her fingers have taken hold of the spindle.

[20] She hath opened her hand to the needy and stretched out her hands to the poor.

[23] Her husband is honourable in the gates, when he sitteth among the senators of the land.

[26] She hath opened her mouth to wisdom, and the law of clemency is on her tongue.

[27] She hath looked well to the paths of her house, and hath not eaten her bread idle.

[28] Her children rose up, and called her blessed: her husband, and he praised her.

[29] Many daughters have gathered together riches: thou hast surpassed them all.

[30] Favour is deceitful, and beauty is vain: the woman that feareth the Lord, she shall be praised.

[31] Give her of the fruit of her hands: and let her works praise her in the gates.

In the Apocalypse, we will find these two women once again. To which woman do you belong? The Whore of Babylon belongs to the Antichrist. The Bride of Christ belongs to Jesus Christ. The devil will have his false prophets. He will have his false kingdom. He will have his false bride, who is a harlot. He will have the mark of the beast. And he will have his false Antichrist as king. But God also has His prophets. He has a true kingdom without end. He has a true bride who is pure. He has a baptismal mark of the Trinity. And He has committed it all to His Divine Son, who is the true King and Christ.

The Apocalypse takes away the veil by showing us twenty-one prophetic events as three cycles of seven prophecies: seven seals, seven trumpets, and seven plagues. In this life, we see things as jumbled and mixed; but, when we remove the veil, we see God against Satan. Kingdom against Kingdom. Bride against Harlot. Christ against Antichrist.

up to oppose a real pope. And so on. By combining the two terms, we have three potential meanings for "antichrist":

1. Against Christ
2. Opposite of Christ
3. In the place of Christ

The popularity of the term "Antichrist" over "pseudochrist" probably arose because "Antichrist" has multiple levels of meaning. The Antichrist is not just a false messiah—he is against Christ, opposed to Christ, and makes himself stand in the place of Christ.

The word "antichrist" appears only five times in the Bible. Only Saint John the Apostle uses the term "antichrist." Here are the first two occurrences of "antichrist":

1st & 2nd Antichrist References (1 Jn 2:18)
Little children, it is the last hour: and as you have heard that Antichrist cometh, even now there are become many antichrists: whereby we know that it is the last hour.

Saint John's very first mention of Antichrist is singular and is accompanied by "as you have heard that Antichrist cometh." Here Saint John presumes that his Christian audience already knows of the final end times of the Antichrist. But John's second reference to antichrists (plural) also indicates that there are many other antichrists. This conforms to Christ our Lord warning us of a plurality of pseudochrists.

3rd Antichrist Reference (1 Jn 2:22)
Who is a liar, but he who denieth that Jesus is the Christ? This is Antichrist, who denies the Father, and the Son.

Saint John's third reference provides a theological definition of Antichrist as "one who denies the Father and the Son." In Saint John's time, this would include Greek, Roman, and Syrian idolaters. It would also include all Jewish people who denied the Father and Son. In the context of this epistle, John is especially warning Christians of infiltrating heretics who deny that Jesus is the Son of the Father.

4th Antichrist Reference (1 Jn 4:2–3)
²By this is the Spirit of God known. Every spirit which confesseth that Jesus Christ is come in the flesh, is of God: ³And every spirit that dissolveth Jesus, is not of God: and this is Antichrist, of whom you have heard that he cometh, and he is now already in the world.

John expands the meaning of Antichrist. He has told us there is a single Antichrist to come at the end of time. He has told us that there are currently many antichrists who deny the Father and Son. Here he reveals the "spirit of the Antichrist," which is both coming in the future and is already present in the world as of AD 90. He contrasts the Spirit of God with the spirit of the Antichrist. He further defines the heresy of the Antichrist as every spirit that does not confess Jesus as coming in the flesh.

5th Antichrist Reference (2 Jn 1:7)
For many seducers are gone out into the world, who confess not that Jesus Christ is come in the flesh: this is a seducer and an Antichrist.

This fifth and final reference to Antichrist reveals that many Antichrist "deceivers" have gone out into the world, and their Antichrist heresy is that they do not confess that "Jesus is come in the flesh." The apostle John here refers to the Docetic heresy of the early church that taught that Jesus was an archangel (not the eternal Son of God) who pretended to be a human, but never was incarnate of the Virgin Mary. The early presence of this heresy, even in the time of the apostles, is likely why Saint John included the historical story of the apostle Thomas literally placing his fingers into the physical wounds of the resurrected Jesus Christ. Moreover, Saint John describes the presence of the biological mother of Jesus Christ at the foot of the cross and that Christ appointed John to care for her. In conclusion, we learn from Saint John that:

1. Christians under the apostles had been instructed to expect a final Antichrist.
2. There were many deceiver Antichrists already trying to trick early Christians. (These are the pseudochrists that Jesus Christ spoke about.)
3. These deceiving Antichrists were inspired by the "spirit of Antichrist," which is opposed to the Spirit of God.
4. The heretical doctrine of Antichrist is the denial of at least three dogmas:
    i. The Father and the Son
    ii. That the Son is from God
    iii. That Jesus Christ has come in the flesh

We will return to the teaching of Saint John about the Antichrist as the beast in the Apocalypse, but before we do, let us examine how Saint Paul's doctrine of Man of Sin conforms with Saint John's doctrine of Antichrist.

"MAN OF SIN" & *KATECHON* IN SAINT PAUL

The apostle Paul does not use the term "pseudochrist" (Christ's term) or Antichrist (John's term), but he does use the terms pseudo-apostles[6] (false clergy) and pseudo-brethren[7] (false laymen) to describe those who have infiltrated the one true Church of Christ. When he speaks of Antichrist, he refers to him as the "Man of Sin" and the "Son of Perdition." We find this teaching in one of Paul's earliest epistles:

Paul Describes Man of Sin (2 Thess 2:3–5)

[2] That you be not easily moved from your sense, nor be terrified, neither by spirit, nor by word, nor by epistle, as sent from us, as if the day of the Lord were at hand.
[3] Let no man deceive you by any means, for unless there come the apostasy[8] first, and the Man of Sin be revealed, the Son of Perdition,
[4] Who opposeth and is lifted up above all that is called God, or that is worshipped, so that he sitteth in the temple of God, shewing himself as if he were God.
[5] Remember you not, that when I was yet with you, I told you these things?

Saint Paul is writing to these early Christians about what he has already taught them (v. 5) concerning the final Day of the Lord (v. 2) and the coming of the Man of Sin (v. 3). Saint Paul describes a prophetic sequence of events that we later see in the vision of Saint John's Apocalypse. First comes the *apostasia*, or "apostasy." This apostasy will be the great revolt and falling away of professed Christians from Christ. Theologians call this the Great Apostasy. Next, the

---

[6] 2 Corinthians 11:13. "For such false apostles (ψευδαπόστολοι) are deceitful workmen, transforming themselves into the apostles of Christ."
[7] Galatians 2:4. "But because of false brethren (ψευδαδέλφους) unawares brought in, who came in privately to spy our liberty, which we have in Christ Jesus, that they might bring us into servitude."
[8] The Douay-Rheims translation has it as "unless there come a revolt." But the Greek word is αποστασια, or *apostasia*. So I have translated it literally "apostasy."

Man of Sin, also known as the Son of Perdition, will be revealed. When Paul says the Man of Sin is "revealed," he uses here the Greek verbal form of "apocalypse."[9]

Paul details how this Man of Sin will oppose and exalt himself above all that is called God. From this we learn that he will oppose all other false gods, idols, false religions, and also the true God and true religion, as we shall examine in future chapters. He will also enthrone himself in the temple of God and demand that he be recognized and worshipped as the only god. The question of whether this temple is the temple in Jerusalem or the temple of the Church is examined in future chapters.

Saint Paul then continues his discourse with more details:

Paul Describes the *Katechon* (2 Thess 2:6–7)

⁶ And now you know what withholds (κατεχον, or *katechon*), that he may be revealed in his time.

⁷ For the mystery of iniquity already works; only that he who now holds (κατεχων, or *katechōn*) does hold, until he be taken out of the way.

Saint Paul introduces the end times concept of *katechon*, which in Greek means "withhold, restrain, bind, or secure." The power of the Antichrist is somehow restrained by something *and* someone. In verse 6, Paul speaks of a neuter *katechon*—a restraining *thing*. But in verse 7, Paul speaks of a masculine *katechōn*—a restraining *person*.[10] Many early Christians taught that the restraining *katechon* thing is the Roman Empire and the restrainer *katechōn* person is the Roman emperor. Cardinal Manning cites Tertullian, Lactantius, and John Chrysostom as believing that the

---

[9] Saint Paul says the Man of Sin will be αποκαλυφθη (aorist, passive subjunctive, third-person singular of αποκαλύπτω). This Greek verb is related to the Greek noun apocalypse.

[10] The difference between the two forms of *katechon* is that the masculine version *katechōn* has the long final omega (mega *o*) and the neuter version *katechon* has shorter omicron (micro *o*).

Roman Empire was the *katechon* preventing the Antichrist.[11] Later authors say that the *katechon*, or the Roman Empire, is transformed into the *katechon* of the Roman Church. The restraining *katechōn* person is the Pope of Rome who holds the "binding" power of the keys of Christ.[12] This is the precise position of Cardinal Manning, who draws on the work of Saint Leo the Great, Saint Thomas Aquinas, and Dominic Soto:

> Saint Thomas [Aquinas], resting upon this passage, says that the Roman Empire has not ceased, but is changed from the temporal into the spiritual, *commutatum de temporali, in spirituale.* Dominic Soto holds the same opinion. It was then, the Apostolic Church which, spreading throughout all the nations, already combined together by the power of the heathen empire of Rome, quickened them with a new life, penetrated them with a new principle of order, with a new spirit of unity, consecrated and transfigured the unity of the material forces by which they were held together, gave them one mind, one intelligence, one law, one will, one heart, by the faith which illuminated the intelligence of all nations to know God, by the charity which bound them together in the unity of one family, by the one fountain of jurisdiction which sprang from our divine Lord, and through His Apostles governed the whole earth.[13]

As we shall shortly see, the prophet Daniel does see the fourth beast (Rome) as the most vicious pagan kingdom, which is then handed over and given to the Son of Man

---

[11] Henry Cardinal Manning, *The Present Crisis of the Holy See: A Warning about Antichrist* (Coppel, TX: Christ the King Library, 2021), 67–69. See also Pseudo-Methodius, Apocalypse, cap 10 (ca. AD 690) for Roman identity of katechon.

[12] Christ to Simon Peter: "whatsoever thou shalt bind upon earth, it shall be bound also in heaven: and whatsoever thou shalt loose upon earth, it shall be loosed also in heaven" (Mt 16:18).

[13] Manning, *A Warning about Antichrist*, 71–72.

(Christ). Cardinal Manning is correct when he remarks, "The Church of God rests upon the basis of natural society, on the foundations of the old Roman Empire."[14]

Saint Paul then explains in verse 7 that at the end of time, the *katechōn*-restrainer, whoever he is, will "be taken out of the way." This suggests that the Church and Roman Empire (or the integration thereof) and the papacy and monarchy (or the integration thereof) would be "taken away" before the arrival of the Antichrist. The Marian apparition of our Our Lady of La Salette in 1846 to two French children, Maximin Giraud and Mélanie Calvat at La Salette, France, told of a coming "eclipse of the church" and persecution of the papacy. Cardinal Manning was writing in 1861 as Europe was dissolving the union of the Catholic Church and the state. In 1870, the Papal States were lost. The apparition of Our Lady of Fatima happened in 1917, and by 1918 the last Habsburg Emperor was deposed from the imperial throne. These political events and the subsequent apostasy of the faithful from the Church are certainly worth our attention.[15]

---

[14] Manning, *A Warning about Antichrist*, 81.
[15] See *Infiltration: The Plot to Destroy the Church from Within* for a full historical account of the events in the 1800's leading up to the erosion of faith and morality among the clergy and laity during the 1960's to our time.

JESUS CHRIST SLAYS THE ANTICHRIST

Saint Paul then describes how our Lord Jesus Christ will kill the Antichrist:

The Death of the Antichrist (2 Thess 2:8–11)

[8] And then that wicked one shall be revealed whom the Lord Jesus shall kill with the spirit of his mouth; and shall destroy with the brightness of his coming, him,

[9] Whose coming is according to the working of Satan, in all power, and signs, and lying wonders,

[10] And in all seduction of iniquity to them that perish; because they receive not the love of the truth, that they might be saved. Therefore, God shall send them the operation of error, to believe lying:

[11] That all may be judged who have not believed the truth but have consented to iniquity.

Our Lord Jesus Christ will kill the Antichrist Man of Sin with the Spirit of His mouth. Prior to this, the Man of Sin, who operates by the power of Satan, will work fake signs and false miracles. Finally, Christ will judge not only this Antichrist but all those that supported and dedicated themselves to Satan and his Antichrist. They shall perish in the pool of fire. We will revisit the details and various accounts of the death of the Antichrist when we study Apocalypse chapter 20.

It's remarkable that the apostles Paul and John already had a vivid account of the final Antichrist or Man of Sin. How did the apostles receive these details? Three sources are probable. First, Jesus Christ directly taught many details of sacred tradition to the apostles that were not written down.[16] Secondly, the apostles were given the spirit of prophecy and likely received infused knowledge or foresaw the end times, as was certainly the case with Saint John's

---

[16] John 21:25. But there are also many other things that Jesus did; if they were written every one, the world itself, I think, would not be able to contain the books that should be written.

28

Apocalypse. Thirdly, many of the details of the final Antichrist are revealed in the Old Testament through the prophets Isaias, Ezechiel, Daniel, and others.

ANTICHRIST IN THE OLD TESTAMENT: SEVEN EPOCHS

When therefore you shall see the abomination of desolation, which was spoken of by Daniel the prophet, standing in the holy place: he that readeth, let him understand.

—Our Lord Jesus Christ, Matthew 24:15

The Prophet Daniel is the most apocalyptic prophet of the Old Testament. He was allowed to see the pre-incarnate Jesus Christ as the Son of Man destroying Satan's four pagan kingdoms. In order to better understand the Antichrist as Satan's puppet and Christ's destruction of the kingdom of Satan, we must review the story of the Bible up until this point. We must also understand the role of covenants in God establishing His kingdom against the kingdoms of Satan.

As we know, the first man and woman fell from their original state of righteousness by the agency of Satan. However, God promised that the Woman and the "Seed of the Woman" would strike the head of Satan and bring about a reversal of the curse of sin (Gen 3:15). The Seed is a poetic term describing a child or heir. The Old Testament is a series of covenants and curses regarding the coming of Christ, the Seed of the Woman. The lineage of that Seed begins with Adam and threads through Abraham, Isaac, Jacob, Judah, Jesse, David, and so on, to the Virgin Mary. The prophetic story of the Old Testament falls into seven epochs:

1. Adam to Noah
2. Abraham, Isaac, Jacob, and the patriarchs
3. Moses and the exodus to Judges
4. David and the kings
5. Babylonian exile
6. Restoration to Jerusalem
7. Christ and the New Covenant

Around two thousand years before Christ, God chose a man named Abram and called him out of Babylonia. In the twelfth chapter of Genesis, God promised three things to Abram: (1) a Promised Seed, or Heir of Blessing; (2) a Promised Land; and (3) the Universal Blessing to All Nations (Gen 12:1–3). Next, God changed his name from Abram, meaning "Exalted Father," to Abraham meaning, "Father of a Multitude." This threefold promise is the Abrahamic Covenant. God established circumcision as a sign of His covenant with Abraham. In a certain sense, circumcision pointed toward the Seed—the future biological heir of the promise. God promised that this covenant would one day "bless all the families of the earth."

Abraham never fully possessed the Promised Land, but he and his wife, Sarah, did conceive a promised child in their old age. His name was Isaac. Isaac in turn was the father of Jacob, who wrestled with God and consequently received the name Israel ("He-Who-Wrestles-God"). Israel had twelve sons for whom the twelve tribes of Israel were named. When the Promised Land experienced a severe famine, these twelve sons of Israel went to Egypt and prospered there until a new Pharaoh arose to the throne of Egypt. This Pharaoh enslaved the Israelites.

The Israelites remembered that they were supposed to be the great heirs of Abraham and possess the Promised Land. Instead, the Israelites had become slaves in Egypt. God heard their prayers and raised up a prophet around the year 1490 BC. His name was Moses, and God commissioned him by speaking to him through a burning bush.

Moses went before the Pharaoh, repeatedly proclaiming the command of God: "Let my people go!" Pharaoh hardened his heart, and so God brought ten terrible plagues. The final plague was the death of each firstborn son. Through Moses, God instructed the Israelites to keep the first Passover meal so as to exempt themselves from this final plague against the firstborn sons of Egypt. In the morning, having lost his firstborn son, the troubled Pharaoh told the Israelites to get out. The Israelites packed up and left Egypt, but before they had exited the borders of Egypt, the Pharaoh had a change of mind. With the Israelites trapped between the Red Sea on one side and the Pharaoh on the other, God miraculously opened the Red Sea, and the Israelites escaped. This is the exodus.

Once the Israelites were safely in the wilderness of Sinai, Moses ascended Mount Sinai to receive the Ten Commandments. While Moses was on Mount Sinai, the Israelites rebelled against God by crafting a golden calf, with which they committed idolatry. In response to Israel's infidelity, God cursed Israel to roam the wilderness for forty years. At Mount Sinai (Exodus–Leviticus) and then later in Moab (Deuteronomy), Moses mediates a covenant of probation for the newly redeemed but idolatrous Israelites. This covenant mediated by Moses is the Mosaic Covenant.

The Mosaic Covenant consisted of 613 laws that established the moral, ceremonial, and civic code of Israel. The Mosaic law prescribed the kosher food laws, described the construction of the ark of the covenant that housed the tablets of the Ten Commandments, and established the system of animal sacrifice at the tabernacle that functioned as a moveable cloth Temple.

After forty years of roaming in the wilderness, Moses appointed his successor, Joshua, to lead the next generation of Israelites into the Promised Land. Moses died, and tradition holds that an angel hid his body (Jude 1:9). Joshua led the Israelites across the Jordan River and into the Promised Land that had been promised to Abraham. They began to conquer the region's seven Canaanite nations, which were known for their idolatry, child sacrifice, and sexual immorality.

The Israelites battled these Canaanite peoples for hundreds of years. In about 1020 BC, God chose a shepherd boy named David (after God rejected the disobedient King Saul) to establish a permanent monarchy for Israel. Out of love for God, David expressed his desire to build a permanent house of worship for God. In response to David's faithful love, God established David as the anointed king of Israel. God made three promises in this Davidic covenant in 2 Samuel 7:9–16. First, David's son would build a house for God's name—that is, God's permanent temple in Jerusalem (7:13). Second, God would establish the throne of his kingdom forever (7:13, 7:16). Third, God would be his father, and David would be His son (7:14). Thus, King David and his royal line of descendants became known by the title "Messiah," meaning "Anointed One."

King David chose the city of Jerusalem as his capital. He ruled from Jerusalem, and God revealed to him plans to build a permanent temple in Jerusalem that would replace the cloth tabernacle that housed the ark of the covenant. During the time of his son Solomon, the Israelites completely conquered and possessed the entire Promised Land, as far as the Euphrates River.[17]

This was the Golden Age of Israel, which included a united kingdom under David's son Solomon, a glorious temple, and a fully possessed Promised Land. One thousand years had elapsed since God first made His promise to Abraham. At last, the Abrahamic Covenant had finally come to fulfillment: the Seed (the Davidic Messianic lineage), the Land (the conquered Promised Land), and the Universal Blessing to All Nations. Recall that Solomon consecrated the temple as "a house of prayer for all nations" (Isa 56:7).

Then it all fell apart. God had appointed Israel to be a holy nation set aside to bless all the nations. Yet Israel did not fulfill this vocation. Just as Israel began to have international influence, King Solomon the Wise allowed idolatry to flourish in the land of Israel. Solomon also

---

[17] The Euphrates River becomes an important sign in the book of the Apocalypse, particularly with the number six, as we shall see.

receives 666 talents of gold every year as tribute (3 Kings 10:14). As we shall see when we study Apocalypse 17 and the Whore of Babylon, Solomon's idolatry and relationship to gold and 666 teach us about the nature of the Antichrist as an "Anti-David" and "Anti-Messiah."

After Solomon died, Israel fell into civil war, and the ten northern tribes of Israel revolted against Solomon's heir in Jerusalem. These ten northern tribes established their own monarchy in the city of Samaria and built two new idolatrous temples in the north for worship of golden calves—revealing that Israel's affection for "holy" cows had not yet been eradicated.

This division of Israel after the death of Solomon led to the establishment of two kingdoms infected with idolatry. There was the northern kingdom of Israel, with its capital in Samaria, and the southern kingdom of Judah, with its capital in Jerusalem. The northern kingdom was idolatrous from its inception, and God chastised the northern kingdom of Israel by sending them into exile under the Assyrians in 722 BC. These northern Israelites mingled with the Assyrians and were lost. They are the so-called ten lost tribes of Israel.

The southern kingdom of Judah was more faithful to God, but it also succumbed to idolatry. God led them into exile under the Babylonians in 587 BC. This era is known as the Babylonian exile. The Israelites of the southern kingdom of Judah became known as Jews since they belonged to the tribe of Judah. Incidentally, the word "Judaism" derives from this usage.

The Babylonian exile was a bleak era in the history of redemption, but God had not abandoned the children of Abraham. God sent prophets who reassured his people of God's covenants to Abraham, Moses, and David. The prophets announced that God would bring about redemption through the Promised Seed, the descendent of Abraham and David—the Messiah. The Messiah would restore them in the Promised Land and bring about the Universal Blessing to All Nations.

During this era of exile in Babylon, God established a prophet named Daniel. Recognizing the inherent talents in Daniel, the Babylonians chose the astute young man to be a servant of King Nebuchadnezzar of Babylon. Daniel was the king's good servant, but God's first. He faithfully served King Nebuchadnezzar but also religiously observed the law of Moses. Instead of eating the sumptuous food of the king's table, he consumed only water and vegetables because he was certain that the king's food was not prepared according to the kosher laws given by Moses.

DANIEL ON FOUR PAGAN KINGDOMS

It is in the prophecies of Daniel and the other prophets that we begin to see God preparing the world for the coming of the Messiah. Daniel describes two different visions that reveal a succession of four earthly kingdoms climaxing in the advent of God's Messianic kingdom of heaven. Daniel's prophecies foretell that there would be four Gentile (non-Jewish) kingdoms that will reign over the Jewish people until the coming of the Messiah and the restoration of the kingdom of God.

The first vision is found in the second chapter of Daniel. It describes a dream that Nebuchadnezzar had about an enormous statue composed of four different materials. First, the head was of gold. Second, the chest and arms were silver. Third, the belly and thighs were bronze. Fourth, the legs and feet were of iron and clay. According to the vision, a stone would be hewn from a mountain without human hands and cast into the statue. This small rock would smash against the statue's iron and clay feet, which would cause the entire statue to crumble. Then the small rock would become a great mountain and fill the entire earth.

Daniel interpreted the dream in the following way. First, the golden head was Nebuchadnezzar and his Babylonian Empire. Next, an inferior kingdom would then follow the Babylonian Empire, as silver is inferior to gold. Then, a third kingdom would arise—one inferior to the second kingdom, as bronze is inferior to silver. Lastly a fourth kingdom would arise that was different than the previous three. As for the small uncut rock cast down from heaven, Daniel explains:

The Uncut Stone Breaks the Pagan Kingdoms (Dan 2:44–45)
[44] But in the days of those kingdoms the God of heaven will set up a kingdom that shall never be destroyed, and his kingdom shall not be delivered up to another

people, and it shall break in pieces, and shall consume all these kingdoms, and itself shall stand for ever. [45] According as thou sawest that the stone was cut out of the mountain without hands, and broke in pieces, the clay, and the iron, and the brass, and the silver, and the gold, the great God hath shewn the king what shall come to pass hereafter, and the dream is true, and the interpretation thereof is faithful.

The stone from heaven in the days of the fourth kingdom signifies that "the God of heaven will set up a kingdom that shall never be destroyed."

Looking back, we understand the prophecy as corresponding to the following historical chronology when heathen kingdoms ruled over the Jews:

1. Babylonian Empire (ca. 587–539 BC)
2. Medo-Persian Empire (ca. 539–331 BC)
3. Greek Empire (ca. 331–168 BC)
4. Roman Empire (ca. 63 BC–AD 70)

It was, in fact, in the days of the fourth kingdom, the Roman Empire, that God established His Messianic Kingdom:

Jesus Born in 4ᵗʰ Kingdom—Rome (Lk 2:1,4–6)

[1]In those days a decree went out from Caesar Augustus that all the world should be enrolled. . . . [4]And Joseph also went up from Galilee, from the city of Nazareth to Judea, to the city of David, which is called Bethlehem: because he was of the house and lineage of David, [5]to be enrolled with Mary, his betrothed, who was with child. [6]And while they were there, the time came for her to be delivered.

It is also common knowledge that Christ was crucified under Pontius Pilate, the Roman governor of Judea. From a historical point of view, we see that the rock of ages came crashing into the Roman Empire. The kingdom of Christ began precisely when Daniel predicted—during the era of the fourth kingdom, the kingdom of Rome.

Before moving on, it is important to note here that the four kingdoms of the Gentiles also began to anticipate a Messiah in their own way. Ezechiel and Daniel called King Nebuchadnezzar of Babylon the king of kings (Eze 26:7; Dan 2:37), a title given subsequently to Jesus Christ. Isaias called King Cyrus of Persia the Messiah (Isa 45:1), a surprising use of the term for a Gentile king! Alexander the Great of Greece united the Mediterranean world, proclaimed himself the Son of God, and died at the age of thirty-three. The Greco-Syrian ruler Antiochus IV later ruled the Promised Land, desecrated the temple, and in turn became a type of the false messiah or Antichrist.

THE 4ᵀᴴ BEAST & THE SON OF MAN

In the seventh chapter of Daniel, the prophet records a related dream that he experienced concerning four beasts coming from the Great Sea. He sees

1. A lion with eagle wings (Dan 7:4).
2. A bear raised up on one side with three ribs between its teeth (Dan 7:5).
3. A leopard with four wings and four heads (Dan 7:6).
4. A fourth beast, terrible and dreadful and exceedingly strong, and it had great iron teeth, eating and breaking in pieces, and treading down the rest with its feet: and it was unlike to the other beasts which I had seen before it, and had ten horns (Dan 7:7).

The winged lion, or lamassu, is a common Babylonian motif and stands for the Babylonian Empire. The bear "raised up on one side" is the Medo-Persian Empire, within which the Persian part was stronger and exalted. The three ribs in the bear's mouth represent the Medo-Persian Empire's victory over the alliance of Egypt, Lydia, and Babylon.

The four-headed and four-winged leopard stands for the Greek Empire, which experienced rapid expansion under Alexander the Great. The four heads represent the four generals who divided the empire into four provinces after Alexander's death in 323 BC. These four provinces were Macedonia, Asia Minor, Egypt, and Syria.

The fourth beast is not depicted as an animal, but as something "terrible and dreadful." Its "iron teeth" recall the iron of the fourth kingdom mentioned in the second chapter of Daniel. In fact, Daniel writes, "The fourth beast shall be a fourth kingdom upon the earth" (Dan 7:23).

As in the vision of the second chapter of Daniel, God intervenes supernaturally during the kingdom of the fourth beast:

Jesus Appears as Son of Man (Dan 7:13–14)

[13] I beheld therefore in the vision of the night, and lo, one like the Son of Man came with the clouds of heaven, and he came even to the Ancient of days: and they presented him before him.
[14] And he gave him power, and glory, and a kingdom: and all peoples, tribes and tongues shall serve him: his power is an everlasting power that shall not be taken away: and his kingdom that shall not be destroyed.

This vision of the Son of Man coming on the clouds is a vision of the Messiah, and Jesus Christ identifies the vision as a description of Himself just before the Jewish and Roman authorities condemn Him:

Jesus said to him, "You have said so. But I tell you, hereafter you will see the Son of Man seated at the right hand of Power and coming on the clouds of heaven" (Mt 26:64).

Once again, we find that Daniel rightly prophesies that the Messiah will arise in the time of the fourth kingdom. It is during the time of the fourth kingdom that the Messiah shall receive His own kingdom—the kingdom of God. Daniel states that the fourth kingdom of Rome will "persecute the saints" (Dan 7:25), and history testifies that Rome certainly persecuted not only Christ but also the early church. Next, Daniel explains:

Son of Man Defeats the 4th Beast (Dan 7:26–27)

[The fourth beast's] *dominion shall be taken away*, to be consumed and destroyed to the end. And the kingdom and the dominion and the greatness of the kingdoms under the whole heaven *shall be given to the people of the saints of the Most High*; their kingdom shall be an *everlasting kingdom,* and all dominions shall serve and obey them.

The kingdom is taken away from the fourth beast and given to whom? This final kingdom is granted to the people of the saints of the Most High! The four kingdoms culminate in the coming of the Messiah, and then the kingdoms are given over to the saints of the Most High—to the Church. The Lord Jesus Christ is the true King of kings, the true Messiah, the true Son of God, and the true ruler of all the nations. The culmination of Daniel's four kingdoms—the Roman Empire—is handed over to the people of Jesus Christ. The Church is not the Roman Empire, but it receives the Roman Empire.

Daniel spoke of this transferal before the coming of Christ, and the recorded history after Christ bears witness to this truth. This is why the theological concepts of the Apocalypse, such as the Son of Man, the Beasts, and the Antichrist centers on the friction between two historic cities: Jerusalem and Rome. Our Lord Jesus Christ was crucified outside Jerusalem on a Roman cross. And at the end of time, the Antichrist will reign in Jerusalem under the shadow of a renewed but broken Roman Empire. Before examining the Antichrist in the Apocalypse, let us first examine the biblical distinction between the many "antichrists" and the one final Antichrist of the final tribulation before the end of the world.

ONE ANTICHRIST OR MANY ANTICHRISTS?

The first question about the end-times Antichrist is whether he will be one man or more than one man.[18] The epistles of Saint John refer to many antichrists, and this causes confusion. The Apocalypse of Saint John also refers to the beast of the sea and the beast of the land. Are there twin antichrists? To add further confusion, many Christian theologians and saints have identified heretics such as Arius and Mohammad as antichrists. Martin Luther and early Lutheran apologists taught that the Antichrist was not one man but rather the succession of Popes in Rome, and this we will show to be false.[19]

The key here is the distinction already made by Saint John: "You have heard that the Antichrist cometh, even now there are become many antichrists" (1 Jn 2:18). In the Greek, John differentiates between the Antichrist and many antichrists. Mohammad, the founder of Islam, denied the Father and the Son, and so he is rightly called an antichrist and heretic. But Mohammad is not *the* Antichrist of the last days. And against the Lutherans, the Antichrist is a single man and not an office held over time by many men.

That the Antichrist will be one singular "Man of Sin"[20] is the plain reading of Saint Paul, but it is also the teaching of Christ our Lord. Saint Irenaeus of Lyons (d. AD 202), who was taught by Polycarp, who was taught by the apostle John, interprets Christ's words as a prophecy to the Antichrist:

---

[18] This section and the rest of Part 1 are generally dependent on Saint Robert Bellarmine's book 3 in his *De Contraversiis I, De Romano Prontifice*, Trans. Ryan Grant. Post Falls, ID: Mediatrix Press, 2016. In this section of *De Pontifice Romano*, he refutes the Lutheran attempts to identify the papacy with the Antichrist. However, it is useful because it provides a florilegium of Patristic sources on the topic of Antichrist. Most of the citations and refences that I use are dependent on the sources of Bellarmine in this section.

[19] Saint Robert Bellarmine refutes this Lutheran novelty of "string of popes as antichrist" in *De Romano Pontifice* lib 3, cap. 2. *De Contraversiis I, De Romano Prontifice*, Trans. Ryan Grant. Post Falls, ID: Mediatrix Press, 2016.

[20] Paul uses the singular Greek word for human person: ανθρωπος.

Saint Irenaeus of Lyons on the Antichrist

The Lord also spoke as follows to those who did not believe in Him: "I have come in my Father's name, and ye have not received Me: when another shall come in his own name, him ye will receive" (John 5:43), calling the Antichrist "the other," because he is alienated from the Lord.[21]

Tradition follows this interpretation, as Saint Ambrose,[22] Saint Augustine,[23] Saint Jerome,[24] and many others read John 5:43's "another shall come in his own name" as referring to the final Antichrist and his reception by the Jewish people.

---

[21] Irenaeus, *Adversus haereses,* lib. 5, 25.

[22] Ambrose, *in 2 Thess* cap. 2.

[23] Augustine, *Tract. in Joann,* 29.

[24] Jerome, *Epistle ad Algasiam.*

DID THE ANTICHRIST ALREADY COME?

Some teach that the Antichrist has already come and gone and that we live after his time. This is contrary to the plain reading of Scripture. Those who assert that the Antichrist has already lived are those who follow a strict preterist reading of the New Testament. The strict preterists hold that *all* prophecies of the New Testament have all been completed in full by the fall and destruction of Jerusalem in AD 70 when the Romans sacked and burned the city and its temple. This thesis derives from Matthew 24, where Christ seems to teach that the tribulation and end of the world are imminent and will accompany the destruction of the Jerusalem temple. The preterist says that the great tribulation was the martyrdom of the apostles from AD 63 to AD 70, and the Second Coming was Christ's spiritual judgment of Jerusalem in AD 70. Who, then, is the preterist Antichrist? They name Emperor Nero Caesar the Antichrist, who is now dead and gone.

Sacred tradition and the majority of Church Fathers see the preterist account as only partially correct. The orthodox reading is that the events in Matthew 24 and the Apocalypse are in the future but typologically revealed by a partial preterist reading. The destruction of Jerusalem in AD 70 foreshadows the final tribulation, which will once again happen in Jerusalem. The martyrs of AD 63–AD 67 in Jerusalem and Rome foreshadow the martyrs of the end of time. And Nero Caesar is a foreshadowing of the cruel Antichrist.

Other errors were made over time. Augustine and Jerome catalog the words of certain seers who claimed that the world would end 200, 300, 500, 666, or even 1000 years after Christ. They were false. Augustine rightly rebuked all those who claimed to know the end of the world: "It is not for us to know the time and the hour which the Father has placed in his power."[25]

Another early error, perhaps the very error condemned by Saint John, was the secret teaching of the Samosatan

---

[25] Augustine, epistle 80 in *ad Hesychium.*

heretics. They were the disciples of the heretical bishop of Antioch, Paul of Samosata (d. AD 275). They denied the Father and the Son (i.e., they were anti-Trinitarian) and taught that the original Jesus was not divine, but a pure man adopted by God. Their secret teaching was that the Antichrist appeared during the times of the apostles and went to Rome. From Rome, the Antichrist abolished the teaching that Jesus was just a man and exchanged it with the teaching that Jesus was the eternal Son of God.[26] This error is easily refuted because Paul says that the Antichrist will make himself into a god and not make Jesus into a god.

Lutherans have also sought to demonstrate the Antichrist appeared around AD 600 or in AD 666 in the person of the Bishop of Rome, often asserting that Pope Saint Gregory the Great was the first in a string of antichrists. Lutherans have claimed this because Pope Gregory promoted the invocation of saints and Masses for the dead.[27] The Lutheran claim can also be refuted by the hundreds of quotations in the Church Fathers prior to AD 600 attesting to prayers for the dead and the invocation of saints. Moreover, the string of antichrists theory does not fit the tight parameters established by Saint Paul and Saint John for the Antichrist. The Swiss Protestant Heinrich Bullinger (d. 1575) asserts the year of the Antichrist happened in AD 753, a year he arrived at by adding 666 years to the time of the apostles. The anti-Catholic writer Wolfgang Musculus (d. 1563) calculated that the Antichrist had already come in AD 1200.[28] These silly calculations are followed by no one because they fail to fit the features of the Antichrist, because none of them establish the biblical feature that the reign of Antichrist will be both obvious and short.

---

[26] See Robert Bellarmine *De Romano Pontifice,* lib. 3, cap 3.

[27] David Chytraeus (d. 1600) was the chief proponent of this Lutheran error of "string of Antichrist popes." Chytraeus was professor of the University of Rostock and one of the co-authors of the Lutheran Formula of Concord. Another part of his thesis was the convergence of Frankish power with the Catholic Church with Pepin I, who died in AD 640.

[28] Musculus, *De Ecclesia,* 24.

BEFORE THE REIGN OF ANTICHRIST

Two things must happen before the reign of Antichrist, which will last only three and a half years. First, all the nations must receive the Gospel of Jesus Christ:

Abomination of Desolation (Mt 24:14–15)

[14]And this gospel of the kingdom, shall be preached in the whole world, for a testimony to all nations, and then shall the consummation come.

[15]When therefore you shall see the abomination of desolation, which was spoken of by Daniel the prophet, standing in the holy place: he that readeth let him understand.

The Gospel must be preached in the whole world. The Gospel had not yet reached Japan, Australia, or Patagonia by AD 500, AD 666, or even AD 1200. It is only after the 1500's that one could say that missionaries were active on every habitable continent. In fact, today is a time in which we can honestly confess that the Gospel is available, if not preached, in every city on planet earth. Only after the universal spread of the Gospel will the consummation come. Part of the reason for this is that the great apostasy (all nations rejecting Christ) will be part of the manifestation of the Antichrist. Christ then warns that the abomination of desolation will stand in the holy place.

Secondly, the Roman Empire must be dissolved. Tertullian explained that Christians prayed for the Roman Empire's endurance because the supreme destruction of the world would be threatened when the Roman Empire was overturned.[29] Cyril of Jerusalem teaches, "The aforesaid Antichrist will come when the times of the Roman Empire have been completed."[30] Saint John Chrysostom teaches the same: "When the Roman Empire has been abolished from our

---

[29] Tertullian, *Apologeticus,* 32.
[30] Cyril of Jerusalem, *Catechesis,* 15.

midst, then Antichrist will come."[31] Saint Ambrose also teaches that the Antichrist shall emerge after the dissolution of the Roman Empire. Saint Jerome explains why Christians universally believed this:

Saint Jerome on Roman Empire

We should therefore concur with the traditional interpretation of all the commentators of the Christian Church, that at the end of the world, when the Roman Empire is to be destroyed, there shall be ten kings who will partition the Roman world amongst themselves. Then an insignificant eleventh king will arise, who will overcome three of the ten kings . . . after they have been slain, the seven other kings also will bow their necks to the victor.[32]

This is the little horn that emerges in Daniel's vision. Jerome also wrote, "Says the Apostle, 'Unless the Roman Empire should first be desolated, and the Antichrist proceed, Christ will not come.'" This is Jerome's interpretation of Saint Paul regarding the *katechon* as the legal order of the Roman Empire. The transformation of the Roman Empire under Constantine in the 300's into Christendom with a Supreme Roman Pastor in the Pope and a Holy Roman Emperor may account for how the "Roman Empire" as *katechon* continues. This raises a number of questions we previously touched on. Was the 1918 deposition of the last Emperor of Austria, Karl von Habsburg, the removal of the *katechon*? Will the eclipse or abolition of the Roman Papacy be the final removal of the Roman *katechon*? Will the Roman Apostolic See fall vacant? Will it be held by an imposter antipope? These are questions that I cannot answer, but the dissolution of all things Roman from Christendom (including the Latin language) in the last hundred years is perhaps a prophetic omen for our times.

---

[31] Cited by Robert Bellarmine, *De Contraversiis I, De Romano Prontifice*, Trans. Ryan Grant. Post Falls, ID: Mediatrix Press, 2016. Lib. 3, cap. 5.
[32] Jerome, *Commentarii in Danielem*.

IS THE ANTICHRIST THE SON OF SATAN?

A common misunderstanding is that the Antichrist is Satan. Others wrongly believe that the Antichrist will be Satan pretending to be a physical human. This error is easily refuted since the apostle Paul calls him the Man of Sin. In Greek, Paul uses the word *anthropos* for man, and this refers to a human person. Also, Apocalypse chapter 13 distinguishes between the dragon (Satan) and the beast of the sea (Antichrist) as two different persons.

A far more popular error is that the Antichrist will be the son of an impure union between Satan and a human mother. It is a matter of Christian dogma that Jesus Christ our Lord was virginally conceived by the Holy Spirit and born of the Blessed Virgin Mary. This virginal conception was foretold by the Hebrew prophets, and it is a sign that Christ is fully God, with God as His eternal Father. Since Satan seeks to mock and blaspheme Christ, many Christians have supposed that the Antichrist will also be conceived by Satan with a human mother. This mistake may be due to the fact that Saint Paul calls the Antichrist the Son of Perdition. But here the apostle poetically refers to the Antichrist's destiny to perish in the lake of fire. It does not mean that the Antichrist is literally and biologically the son of Satan. The theological problem is that Satan is incorporeal and cannot provide a human seed to produce a human child in the womb of a woman. Therefore, the Antichrist is not the offspring of Satan, but the Antichrist is perfectly possessed and ruled within by Satan. Saint John of Damascus explains that it is impossible for Satan to copy the miracle of the virgin conception of Christ. The devil himself, therefore, does not become man in the way that the Lord was made man. God forbid![33]

We believe, then, that the Antichrist will be conceived in an act of illicit sex, just as Solomon was born of

---

[33] John of Damascus, *De Fide Orthodoxa*, lib. 3, cap. 26. Translated by E.W. Watson and L. Pullan. From *Nicene and Post-Nicene Fathers, Second Series*, Vol. 9.

fornication. Saint John of Damascus continues his treatment of the conception and birth of Antichrist:

> But he becomes man as the offspring of fornication and receives all the energy of Satan. For God, foreknowing the strangeness of the choice that he would make, allows the devil to take up his abode in him. He is, therefore, as we said, the offspring of fornication and is nurtured in secret, and suddenly he rises up, rebels and assumes rule.[34]

The Antichrist, as the perfect servant of Satan, "receives all the energy of Satan" and is the perfect vessel of Satan. The private revelation of Melanie[35] states, "It will be during this time that the Antichrist will be born of a Hebrew nun, a false virgin who will communicate with the old serpent, the master of impurity, his father will be B."[36] The identity of the father is not known. Yet the role of the mother as a Hebrew deserves special attention.

[34] John of Damascus, *De Fide Orthodoxa,* lib. 3, cap. 26.
[35] For details on Melanie and the apparition of Our Lady of La Salette, see Taylor R. Marshall, *Infiltration: The Plot to Destroy the Church from Within* (Manchester, NH: Sophia Institute Press, 2019), 19-25 and the text of the apparition in the book's index at page 274.
[36] Taylor R. Marshall, *Infiltration: The Plot to Destroy the Church from Within* (Manchester, NH: Sophia Institute Press, 2019), 274-6.

THE ANTICHRIST AS AN ISRAELITE

All the earliest Christian writers teach that the Antichrist will be an Israelite and style himself as Messiah, Christ, and King of the Jews. Jerome says in his commentary on Daniel:

> The Antichrist will rise from a modest nation, that is, from the people of the Jews. He will be so lowly and despised that he will not be given royal honor, but he shall obtain rule both through treachery and deceit. He will do this because he will feign himself as the leader of the covenant, that is the law, and the covenant of God.[37]

The prophecy of the Antichrist as an Israelite goes back to the book of Genesis with the prophecies of Jacob, who was also called Israel. He prophesies over his twelve sons, but when he comes to Dan, he oddly prophesies evil over him:

> **Jacob Foretells the Serpent of Dan (Gen 49: 16–18)**
> [16] Dan shall judge his people like another tribe in Israel.
> [17] Let Dan be a snake in the way, a serpent in the path, that biteth the horse's heels that his rider may fall backward.
> [18] I will look for thy salvation, O Lord.

Dan is the snake or serpent who bites the heels of horses. And it leads Jacob to call out for "thy salvation, O Lord." The prophet Jeremias warns us of the tribe of Dan regarding idols and horses:

> For a voice of one declaring from Dan and giving notice of the idol from mount Ephraim. (Jer 4:15)

> The snorting of his horse was heard from Dan, all the land was moved at the sound of the neighing of his warriors:

---

[37] Jerome, *Commentarii in Danielem,* cap. 11.

and they came and devoured the land, and all that was in it: the city and its inhabitants. (Jer 8:16)

Dan is the serpentine warrior who will conquer the Holy Land and Jerusalem. And when Saint John lists the twelve tribes of Israel in the seventh chapter of the Apocalypse, he purposefully omits the tribe of Dan. Why?

The most famous person from the tribe of Dan was Samson and some believe Jacob was prophesying to this future long-haired hero, known for his strength (and fornication). Did Jacob prophesy that Samson (from the tribe of Dan) would be a serpent in the way of the Philistines? It's unlikely since the serpent is a negative symbol of sin and deception. Why would a father identify his son, or even Samson, with this evil analogy? The serpent of Dan points to someone gravely more dangerous and wicked than Samson.

The Church Fathers assert that the Antichrist will be an Israelite and will derive from the tribe of Dan or will be like Dan as the prophesied "serpent in the way." He will outwardly follow obedience to the law of Moses, in false imitation of Christ. He will be circumcised, keep the Sabbath, and outwardly obey the precepts given by Moses. That he will be an Israelite (but not of the tribe of Judah like Jesus Christ) is foretold by Christ: "I am come in the name of my Father, and you receive me not: if another shall come in his own name, him you will receive" (John 5:43). The people of Israel will receive the Antichrist as their Messiah in his own name. Jerome writes:

> The Antichrist will make all these things not by virtue, but from the concession of God on account of the Jews and because they refused to receive the love of truth, the Spirit of God through Christ, that having received a Savior, they would be saved. So then God will send upon them not an operator, but the operation itself, that means the font of error, that they would believe lies.[38]

---

[38] Jerome, *Quaest. 11 ad Albasiam.*

51

The Jewish nation, which still waits for the coming of a miraculous and powerful messiah, will be deceived and accept the Antichrist (Liar Messiah) as their own King of the Jews. The Antichrist will establish a false peace by bringing about global harmony with Jerusalem. That the Jewish nation will be deceived and receive the Antichrist as their messianic king is taught by Irenaeus,[39] Hippolytus,[40] Cyril of Alexandria,[41] Hilary of Poitiers,[42] Ambrose of Milan,[43] Augustine,[44] Jerome,[45] Cyril of Jerusalem,[46] John Chyrsostom,[47] Gregory the Great,[48] and John of Damascus.[49] Saint Ambrose teaches (as do the Church Fathers) that the Antichrist will be circumcised,[50] and he will enforce circumcision as a matter of law.[51] Gregory the Great teaches that the Antichrist will enforce a regime of Judaizing: "Because the Antichrist will compel the people to Judaize so that he might restore the rite of exterior law. He will want the Sabbath to be kept to place the faithlessness of the Jews in himself."[52] Cyril of Jerusalem also teaches that the Antichrist will be outwardly zealous for Jerusalem.[53] This brings us to the topic of the capital and throne of the Antichrist.

---

[39] Irenaeus, *Adversus haereses*, lib. 5
[40] Hippolytus, *De consummatione mundi*.
[41] Cyril of Alexandria, *in Joan*, cap 5.
[42] Hilary, *in Matth*, 25.
[43] Ambrose, *in Lucam*, lib. 10, cap. 21.
[44] Augustine, *in Joan*, cap. 5.
[45] Jerome, *in Daniel*, cap. 11.
[46] Cyril of Jerusalem, *Catechesis*, 15.
[47] John Chrysostom, *in Joan*, cap 5.
[48] Gregory the Great, *Moralium*, lib. 31.
[49] John of Damascus, *De Fide Orthodoxa*, lib. 4, cap. 28.
[50] Ambrose, *Comm. in 2 Thess. 2*.
[51] Martin of Tours, as found in Sulpitius, *Dialogue* lib. 2.
[52] Gregory the Great, *Moralium*, lib. 31.
[53] Cyril of Jerusalem, *Catechesis*, 15.

ANTICHRIST AS ENTHRONED IN JERUSALEM

The apostle Paul, as noted above, relates that the Antichrist "sits in the temple of God, showing himself as if he were God" (2 Thess 2:4). A similar picture is given by Christ: "the abomination of desolation, which was spoken of by Daniel the prophet, will be standing in the holy place" (Mt 24:15). Whether seated (Paul) or standing (Christ), the Antichrist will enthrone himself in the holy place, which is the temple of God.

Where is the temple of God that will be defiled by the enthronement of Antichrist? The most obvious reading is that this refers to the holy city of Jerusalem and a rebuilt temple in Jerusalem. This is the nearly unanimous teaching of the Church Fathers. But another popular reading is that the temple of God spoken of by Saint Paul is the one true Church. Elsewhere the apostle uses the same words: "Know you not, that you are the temple of God, and that the Spirit of God dwelleth in you?" (1 Cor 3:16). The apostle also teaches the church, "groweth up into a holy temple in the Lord" (Eph 2:21). Will the Antichrist sit in the Church of God as if he is God? Below are the early Bible commentators' readings of the meaning of "sits in the temple of God":

Antichrist in Jerusalem	Antichrist within Church
Irenaeus	
Hippolytus	John Chyrsostom*
Cyril of Jerusalem	Oecumenius
Hilary of Poitiers	
Ambrose	
Jerome	
John Chyrsostom*	
John of Damascus	

John Chrysostom finds himself in both columns. Regarding the Antichrist, he affirms that the Antichrist will sit in both places: "He will command himself to be worshipped as a god, and to be placed in the temple, not only in Jerusalem, but even in the churches."[54] Writing three centuries later, John of Damascus directly contradicts him: "In the temple, not ours, but in the old Jewish temple."[55] It may be that the Antichrist, who will abolish Christian worship, will have some sort of icon or image of himself in all former Christian churches. The only commentator to say that the Antichrist will *not* be seated in Jerusalem is Oecumenius of Trikka, who lived circa 990. He is the most recent of all and should be rejected. All the early Church Fathers are entirely united around the fact that the Antichrist will be seated in Jerusalem.

---

[54] John Chrysostom, *Homily 3 in 2 Thessalonians.*
[55] John of Damascus, *De Fide Orthodoxa,* lib. 4, cap. 28.

ANTICHRIST PROCLAIMS HIMSELF AS GOD

We have already seen that the Church Fathers are united in teaching that the Antichrist will teach that he, not Jesus Christ, is the true Christ. Ambrose states that the Antichrist will "argue from the Scriptures that he is the Christ."[56] But the Antichrist will go further to establish himself as a god alone. This is the reason why he will eventually ban all other religions, all other gods, and all idols. The Antichrist will tolerate only the worship of the Antichrist. "He shall not regard any gods: for he shall rise up against all things" (Dan 11:37). Paul tells us the Antichrist will oppose the worship of anyone or anything besides himself: "He opposeth and is lifted up above all that is called God, or that is worshipped, so that he sits in the temple of God, showing himself as if he were God" (2 Thess 2:4).

Many wrongly believe that the Antichrist will be an ecumenist who promotes all religions. Others wrongly suppose that the Antichrist will restore ancient Roman paganism—the worship of Jupiter and the pantheon. Nothing could be further from the truth. He will be jealous of *all* worship not directed at him. He will not tolerate the worship of Allah, Krishna, Buddha, totems, idols, ancestors, or other humans. As an Israelite who outwardly follows the rules of Moses, the Antichrist will abolish all idols. Paul explains how he will oppose "that which is worshipped." The Greek here is *sebasma*, which means "idols" elsewhere.[57] This is why Irenaeus taught, "He will indeed put away the idols and will lift himself up as the one idol."[58] Cyril of Jerusalem and John Chrysostom also teach that the Antichrist will abolish idols.

---

[56] Ambrose, *in Luc.*, cap. 21.
[57] σέβασμα. Wisdom 15:17 and Acts 17 refer to idols using his word: "For passing by, and seeing your idols (σεβασματα)."
[58] Irenaeus, *Adversus Haereses*, lib. 5.

THE GREAT TRIBULATION OF THE ANTICHRIST

The Church counts ten Roman persecutions, beginning with the persecution of Nero (AD 60's) and ending with the persecution of Diocletian (AD 299–305). But these persecutions will pale in comparison to the Great Tribulation warned of by Christ: "For there shall be then great tribulation, such as hath not been from the beginning of the world until now, neither shall be" (Mt 24:21). The idea of a "great tribulation" is spoken of in 2 Esdras (Nehemias) 9:37 and 1 Maccabees 9:27. It will be a time of horrible and painful martyrdom for those who love and serve Christ. Saint John sees these Great Tribulation martyrs filing into heaven: "These are they who are come out of great tribulation" (Apoc 7:14). It is the time when "Satan shall be loosed" (Apoc 20:7).

The nineteenth-century dispensational idea that true Christians will be "raptured" before the tribulation is utterly false. The Great Tribulation will "surround the camp of the saints and the beloved city" (Apoc 20:8). The Apocalypse of John also repeatedly refers to the martyrs who suffer under the Great Tribulation. Many early Christians say that the martyrs of the last days who are killed by the Antichrist will be more courageous than all the previous martyrs. It is estimated that seventeen thousand Christians were martyred under the Roman Emperor Diocletian from AD 299–305. The Great Tribulation will produce many times more martyrs in the final three and a half years of his wicked reign.

The Great Tribulation will also enforce the abolition of Sacred Scripture, baptism, the Eucharistic Sacrifice of the Mass, and the other sacraments for three and a half years: "And from the time when the continual sacrifice shall be taken away, and the abomination unto desolation shall be set up, there shall be a thousand two hundred ninety days" (Dan 12:11). Every early Christian biblical commentator teaches that the "continual sacrifice taken away" refers to the end of all Christian worship and especially the holy sacrifice of the Eucharist.[59] In 1 Maccabees, the persecution began with the burning of Scripture, the banning of circumcision, and the interruption of divine worship and sacrifice. This foreshadows the Antichrist's ban on Christian Scripture, baptism, and worship for 1,290 days, which is three and a half years.

The duration of the Great Persecution is undoubtedly three and a half years, as we have already seen many times. Saint Irenaeus writes, "He will reign for three years and six months, then the Lord will come from heaven."[60] Saint Jerome confirms: "The time means a year. The times according to Hebrew idiom means two years. The half a time means six months. This is the duration when the saints will be given to the power of the Antichrist."[61] Saint Cyril says, "The Antichrist will reign for merely three and a half years, which we know is not from spurious books, but from the prophet Daniel."[62] Saint Augustine says, "The reign of the Antichrist will be very savage. For time and times and half a time is one year, two years, and half a year."[63]

Why three and a half years? God established the seven-day week, and seven is the preeminent number of perfection and sanctity. A week broken in half is a sign of wickedness. The ministry of Christ on earth from his baptism in the Jordan until his crucifixion and resurrection was exactly three and a half years. So, it may be (as based

---

[59] Augustine teaches that the Antichrist will not allow baptism of adults or children in De civitate Dei, lib. 20, cap. 8. Robert Bellarmine catalogues the great number of early saints who taught that public prayer and the Eucharist sacrifice will be banned by the Antichrist in De Romano Prontifice, lib. 3, cap. 7. Trans. Ryan Grant. Post Falls, ID: Mediatrix Press, 2016. He lists Irenaeus, Jerome, Theodoret, and Hippolytus as early witnesses to the interpretation of Daniel 12:11:

"And from the time when the continual sacrifice shall be taken away, and the abomination unto desolation shall be set up, there shall be a thousand two hundred ninety days."

[60] Irenaeus, Adversus haereses, lib. 5, 5.

[61] Jerome, Commentarii in Danielem, cap. 7.

[62] Cyril of Jerusalem, Catachesis 25.

[63] Augustine, De civitate Dei, lib. 20, cap. 23.

on calculations from Daniel) that the final three-and-a-half-year bloody persecution of the Church by the Antichrist is the completion of the ministry of Christ. Christ preached for exactly three and a half years. Perhaps His ministry and passion will be completed by His Church's passion for another three and a half years under the Antichrist. This would establish the perfect "week" of seven years as foretold by Daniel.

THE ANTICHRIST SUMMARIZED

So far, we have established the following facts about the Antichrist and his coming:

1. He will be a true human man.
2. He will be conceived of fornication.
3. He will be an Israelite.
4. The Antichrist will keep the Sabbath and follow the Jewish laws of Moses, circumcision, and kosher living.
5. Before the Antichrist is revealed, the Gospel must be preached to all nations.
6. His coming will be signaled by the Great Apostasy—a mass falling away from Christ.
7. He will deny that Jesus is of the Father or of the flesh.
8. He will claim to be the true Messiah or Christ.
9. Christian worship and sacraments will be banned.
10. Idolatry will be banned.
11. He will appoint a False Prophet who will work three false miracles:
    a. He will apparently cause fire to come down from heaven.
    b. He will make the icon of the Antichrist speak.
    c. He will apparently resurrect the Antichrist from the dead.
12. The world will worship the Antichrist as the only god.
13. He will sit in the rebuilt temple in Jerusalem as a false messianic god.
14. He will reign in partnership with "ten kings."
15. With an enormous army, he will persecute Christians in the battle of Armageddon (Gog and Magog to come)
16. Jerusalem will be destroyed.
17. Jesus will slay the Antichrist.
18. The devil, the Antichrist, and the False Prophet will be cast into the lake of fire.

After the death of the Antichrist, Jesus Christ will judge the living and the dead.

Part II: Apocalypse Revealed

Now that we have established the existence of a final Antichrist who will arise after the removal of the *katechon* and Great Apostasy, let us begin with the first verses of the book of Apocalypse and read them line by line. A reader can only fully appreciate the Apocalypse and understand the role of the Antichrist if he reads through the eyes of the Old Testament prophets. Along the way, we will interpret each section of the Apocalypse not with speculation but by following the clues given to us by the Old Testament. After learning about seven churches, we begin our journey through the twenty-one prophecies of Apocalypse, arranged as a triple cycle of sevens: seven seals, seven trumpets, and then seven plagues. The Old Testament and the Church Fathers will unlock for us the mysteries of 666, the mark of the beast, the Whore of Babylon, Gog and Magog, the slain Lamb, the four living creatures, the robes, the armies, the seven trumpets, the seven plague vials, the seven-sealed book, the incense, 144,000, the thousand-year millennium, and much more.

Christ Revealed in Heaven (Apocalypse 1)

The book of the Apocalypse was revealed to Saint John, one of the twelve apostles. John was known as the beloved disciple, and he was part of Christ's inner three, consisting of Peter, John, and John's brother James the Greater.[64] According to tradition, Saint John wrote down the vision of the Apocalypse on a scroll while he was exiled on the island of Patmos.

John does not give us a date for when he received this vision and when he wrote it down. The vision and the writing of it may have been one event or two events separated by time. There is a tradition that John wrote it down toward the end of his life in the AD 90's. However, the text of the vision presumes that the temple in Jerusalem is still standing. The temple was destroyed by the Romans in AD 70. This points to the vision happening before AD 70.[65] Therefore, the earliest date would be the AD 60's, and the latest date would be in the AD 90's. Regardless of the date, tradition identifies the Apocalypse as being the last book written by the last living apostle. It is the final and last piece of public revelation given by God to mankind. It completes the Bible once and for all.

John's Apocalypse was originally a single scroll, and it also mentions a heavenly scroll with seven seals that only the Passover Lamb can open. The Passover Lamb is Christ. As we approach the Apocalypse, we must humbly admit that we cannot rightly interpret the vision without Christ. Yet we should not be afraid to read it. The first verse of the book explains that God the Father gave the vision to Jesus Christ to share it with His servants, Christians still on earth.

---

[64] There was another apostle named James who was the first bishop of Jerusalem. He is called James the Lesser.

[65] My personal view is that the Apocalypse was received and written by John before AD 70 while the temple was still standing. It also seems that the epistle to the Hebrews is directly dependent on the Apocalypse. It may be that John received it in the AD 60's and then published it in the AD 90's before his death as a final testament to the church.

Jesus Christ wants you to read the Apocalypse (Apoc 1:1–3)

¹ The Revelation of Jesus Christ, which God gave unto him, to make known to his servants the things which must shortly come to pass: and signified, sending by his angel to his servant John,

² Who hath given testimony to the word of God, and the testimony of Jesus Christ, what things soever he hath seen.

³ Blessed is he, that readeth and heareth the words of this prophecy; and keepeth those things which are written in it; for the time is at hand.

The Apocalypse is an inner-Trinitarian gift. God the Father gives this revelation to His Son Jesus Christ. The purpose is that Jesus Christ then will share it with all his servants (Christians). Jesus Christ accomplishes this by sending His angel to the apostle John as a guide.

The book of the Apocalypse is the only book in the Bible that begins with a note of promise: "Blessed is he that readeth and heareth the words of this prophecy; and keepeth those things which are written in it; for the time is at hand" (Apoc 1:3). If you read this book and keep what it teaches, you are guaranteed to be blessed.

Saint John Speaks to His Audience (Apoc 1:4–6)

⁴ John to the seven churches which are in Asia. Grace be unto you and peace from him that is, and that was, and that is to come, and from the seven spirits which are before his throne,

⁵ And from Jesus Christ, who is the faithful witness, the first begotten of the dead, and the prince of the kings of the earth, who hath loved us, and washed us from our sins in his own blood,

⁶ And hath made us a kingdom, and priests to God and his Father, to him be glory and empire for ever and ever. Amen.

John writes to seven churches. We will learn about these seven churches soon. He then sends grace from three sources:

1. "from him that is, and that was, and that is to come"
2. "from the seven spirits"
3. "And from Jesus Christ"

The first is God the Father. The second is the Holy Spirit. Why "seven spirits"? The prophet Isaias described the Holy Spirit as sevenfold:

> And the Spirit of the Lord shall rest upon him:
> 1) the Spirit of wisdom,
> 2) and of understanding,
> 3) the Spirit of counsel,
> 4) and of fortitude,
> 5) the Spirit of knowledge,
> 6) and of godliness. And he shall be filled with
> 7) the Spirit of the fear of the Lord. (Isa 11:2–3)

Seven is not referring to seven distinct persons, but seven is the holy number. The term "seven spirits" refers to the Holy Spirit.[66] The Catholic Church addresses the Holy Spirit as *Tu septiformis munere, dextrae Dei tu digitus*—"Thou Sevenfold Gift, Thou finger of the right hand of God." This hymn to the Holy Ghost was composed in the ninth century by Rabanus Maurus, Archbishop of Mainz (d. AD 856), and it is sung on the feast of Pentecost, before the election of a

---

[66] There are three other references to the Holy Spirit as sevenfold. Christ holds the seven spirits in 3:1. In 4:5, the seven lamps before the throne are the seven spirits. And in 5:6, the seven eyes of the Lamb (Jesus) are the seven spirits.

new Pope, at the consecration of bishops, the ordination of priests, the sacrament of confirmation, the dedication of churches, the celebration of synods or councils, and the coronation of monarchs, and also at the profession of members of religious institutes.

The third is God the Son, Jesus Christ. He has washed us and loved us and made us a kingdom and priests to God the Father. John then sees Jesus Christ arrive before him:

Jesus Comes on Clouds as Lord God (Apoc 1:7–8)
[7] Behold, he cometh with the clouds, and every eye shall see him, and they also that pierced him. And all the tribes of the earth shall bewail themselves because of him. Even so. Amen.
[8] I am Alpha and Omega, the beginning and the end, saith the Lord God, who is, and who was, and who is to come, the Almighty.

Christ coming on the clouds is a reference to the Son of Man coming as prophesied by the prophet Daniel. He is pierced because He was crucified. He is Alpha and Omega, beginning and end. The reference to him coming on clouds also points to His ascension into a cloud: "And when he had said these things, while they looked on, he was raised up: and a cloud received him out of their sight" (Acts 1:9). The book of Acts details the Church on earth after the Ascension. The Apocalypse begins with His ascension into the cloud but shows the action beginning in Acts from a heavenly point of view:

John on the Island of Patmos (Apoc 1:9)
I John, your brother and your partner in tribulation, and in the kingdom, and patience in Christ Jesus, was in the island, which is called Patmos, for the word of God, and for the testimony of Jesus.

Saint John indicates that he is not just their Apostle. He is their brother and partner in the tribulation. The tribulation has already begun in the first century with the first apostles. He is exiled to the island of Patmos for spreading the Word of God and testimony of Jesus. He suffers.

In the Spirit on the Lord's Day (Apoc 1:10)
I was in the Spirit on the Lord's day, and heard behind me a great voice, as of a trumpet.

The Lord's Day is Sunday. Christ died on Good Friday and rose three days later on Easter Sunday. Ever since, the day of rest and worship has shifted from the Old Covenant Sabbath on Saturday to the New Covenant Lord's Day on Sunday.[67] Saint John is worshipping "in the Spirit" on Sunday. The voice tells him to write to the seven churches:

7 Churches as 7 Candlesticks (Apoc 1:11–12)
[11] Saying: What thou seest, write in a book, and send to the seven churches which are in Asia, to Ephesus, and to Smyrna, and to Pergamum, and to Thyatira, and to Sardis, and to Philadelphia, and to Laodicea.
[12] And I turned to see the voice that spoke with me. And being turned, I saw seven golden candlesticks.

And then Jesus Christ appears in eternal glory to John, presumably for the first time since Christ's Ascension into heaven. He is standing among seven golden candlesticks—seven churches.

---

[67] The early Christians and apostles worshipped with a liturgical Eucharistic rite on Sunday and not Saturday. "And on the first day of the week, when we were assembled to break bread, Paul discoursed with them" (Acts 20:7). See also 1 Cor 16:2; Jn 20:1, 19.

APPARITION OF FIERY CHRIST

We rightfully remember our Lord Jesus Christ as the baby in the manger at Bethlehem, as walking on water, as crucified on the cross, and as risen from the dead. Recall, however, that after Christ rose from the dead, Mary Magdalene and the disciples had difficulty recognizing Him. If apocalypse means "take away the veil," then we need to remove the veil and see Christ as He is now:

White Hair & Fiery Eyes (Apoc 1:13–16)
[13] And in the midst of the seven golden candlesticks, one like to the Son of Man, clothed with a garment down to the feet, and girt about the chest with a golden girdle.

[14] And his head and his hairs were white, as white wool, and as snow, and his eyes were as a flame of fire,

[15] And his feet like unto fine brass, as in a burning furnace. And his voice as the sound of many waters.

[16] And he had in his right hand seven stars. And from his mouth came out a sharp two-edged sword: and his face was as the sun shineth in his power.

Our Lord Jesus Christ stands among the seven candlesticks as a bishop and wears vestments and a golden sash like a priest and king. His feet are smoldering brass. His hair and beard are white, not brown. His eyes burn like fire. His face is like the sun. His voice thunders. A sword extends from his mouth. This refers to the prophecy of Isaias: "The Lord hath called me from the womb, from the bowels of my mother he hath been mindful of my name. And he hath made my mouth like a sharp sword" (Isa 49:1–2). The apostle John walked with Christ for three years. He stood at the foot of the cross when He died. He spoke with the resurrected Christ. But now, this vision of Christ in heaven is so fearful that he seems to die:

John Falls as Dead (Apoc 1:17–20)

[17] And when I had seen him, I fell at his feet as dead. And he laid his right hand upon me, saying: Fear not. I am the First and the Last,

[18] And alive, and was dead, and behold I am living for ever and ever, and have the keys of death and of hell.

[19] Write therefore the things which thou hast seen, and which are, and which must be done hereafter.

[20] The mystery of the seven stars, which thou sawest in my right hand, and the seven golden candlesticks. The seven stars are the angels of the seven churches. And the seven candlesticks are the seven churches.

Verse 19 indicates that what we are about to see is both present day to John and in the future. This raises the problem of whether the Apocalypse is past, present, future, or all three. Did the Antichrist already come? Has he always existed? Or will he come in the future?

APOCALYPSE IN THE PAST OR FUTURE?

Christ told us explicitly that the Apocalypse shows us "things which are and which must be done" (Apoc 1:19). There are several schools of thought on how to date the events depicted in the Apocalypse. The futurist interpretation sees everything in the Apocalypse as in the future and at the end of time. The preterist interpretation sees everything in the Apocalypse as in the past. The preterist says that the Apocalypse mystically describes the persecution of the Church during Emperor Nero Caesar's reign in the AD 60's and the destruction of Jerusalem by the Romans in AD 70. A third interpretation, called historicism, asserts that the Apocalypse traces the history of Christianity from AD 33 until the arrival of the Antichrist and the end of time. Which school is correct?

A combination of all three is correct. The Apocalypse is a kaleidoscope and telescope of multiple events interlinked and overlayed with one another. As we examine the seven churches, we will see that there are seven actual churches under the apostle John in Asia Minor. But they also retell the seven epochs of the Old Testament. They may also tell of the seven epochs of the New Testament—from Christ to the Antichrist. We will also see that the Roman persecution in the AD 60's and the Destruction of Jerusalem in AD 70 foreshadow the final Great Tribulation, the Antichrist, and the final conflagration of the world at the judgment of Christ.

Seven Churches and Seven Ages
(Apocalypse 2 & 3)

The Apocalyptic Jesus Christ now gives seven messages to seven angels of the seven churches. Each of the seven churches is denoted by its geographic name:

1) Ephesus
2) Smyrna
3) Pergamos
4) Thyatira
5) Sardis
6) Philadelphia
7) Laodicea

The order of the cities on a map, beginning with Ephesus, creates an A-frame shape, with the island of Patmos off the coast nearby:

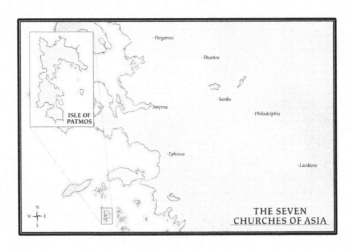

THE SEVEN
CHURCHES OF ASIA

WHY ASIA AND WHY PATMOS?

The seven churches are highly symbolic and follow the order of the seven Old Testament epochs. But why did God choose the Roman province of Asia for this vision? Today we think of Asia as encompassing as far as Russia and China. But during the time of Saint John, the province of Asia was the westernmost part of what we now call Asia Minor or Turkey. The Greek historian Herodotus (d. 440 BC) referred to the region as Asia. Asia is a female name, and legend associates it with the epic of Troy and the origin of the Trojan War.

The original geography of Asia, Greek legend says, was named after Princess Asione, who was a princess of the famous Asian city of Troy. Most students know that Homer's *Iliad* begins in Asia Minor, with the city of Troy as its chief city. King Menelaus of Sparta wages war against Troy because the Trojan prince Paris had abducted Queen Helen, the wife of King Menelaus. What many students don't know is that Prince Paris originally traveled from Troy to Sparta in order to restore the elderly Princess Asione to her home in Troy. Along the way, Paris gets sidetracked by Queen Helen's beauty and steals the king's wife.

According to Greek mythology, Apollo and Poseidon were angry with King Laomedon of Troy because he refused to honor the vow he made to them for building the strong walls of Troy. In retaliation, Apollo sent a plague on the city, and Poseidon sent a sea beast. Both of these details feature in the Apocalypse. King Laomedon was told the city would be spared if he exposed his virgin daughter Asione to the sea beast (*ketos* in Greek). King Laomedon obeyed the vicious gods and chained his daughter Asione to the rocks by the sea for the sea monster to devour her. Heracles happened to arrive just then on his return from the expedition against the Amazons. He saw the virgin princess Asione exposed on the crag. He promised to kill the sea monster on the condition that King Laomedon would give him the horses that he had received from Zeus. The king agreed, and Heracles battled the sea monster. The sea beast swallowed Heracles, but the hero hacked away at the interior of the sea beast for three days before it died. Heracles arose on the third day, having lost all his hair. Even worse, King Laomedon refused to give him the promised horses (just as he had refused to pay back the gods)!

Enraged by the king's trickery, Heracles attacked the city of Troy and killed King Laomedon. He took the king's daughter Asione, who had been rescued, and gave her to his friend Teleman (the father of Ajax in the Homer's *Iliad*) to be his wife. Heracles then conferred the kingship of Troy to Asione's brother Priam (father of Hector and Paris).

Many years later, when Asione was an old woman, King Priam asked his son Paris and Aeneas to bring his elderly sister Asione back to Troy. But on this occasion, Paris became distracted and brought home Queen Helen instead. This triggered the ten-year-long Trojan War. King Priam and the Trojans justified the abduction of Helen as retaliation for the Greek king refusing to return his sister Asione to Troy.

Given the mythological backdrop of Asione's story, the geography of Asia begins to make sense. Asia Minor, especially the island of Patmos, are geographically between Rome and Jerusalem, and the relationship between these two cities is a constant theme of the Apocalypse. But the newly baptized converts of the seven cities in Asia under the apostleship of Saint John would have known these Greek legends about a powerful hero saving a future queen from a sea beast. Apocalypse 12 tells of the sea beast coming out of the sea to devour the crowned Woman and her Child. Even the detail about Heracles fighting from within the belly of the sea beast for three days evokes the power of Christ emerging on the third day as victor over hell, death, and the dragon. As we will see, the visions of the Apocalypse are in complete concord with the visions of Daniel and Ezechiel, but they also have a relationship with the story of Asia and the region's namesake, Asione.

JESUS HAS 7 MESSAGES FOR 7 CHURCHES

The Lord Jesus Christ is directing a special message for each of the churches in Asia under the apostle John's care. He addresses the "angel" of each of these churches. The Greek word *angelos* literally means "messenger"—a likely reference to the human bishop as chief messenger of each community. We know nothing of the practical or pastoral conditions of the church in each of the seven cities beyond what Christ speaks to each church. There is no point speculating about the details of each historical community. Instead, let us examine the order of the seven churches as detailing two mysteries. The first mystery is the history of the seven epochs of the Old Testament. The second mystery is the history of the Church in the New Testament unfolding as seven epochs from Christ to the Antichrist. In these seven messages, we will find all the apocalyptic elements of tribulation, the Antichrist, false prophets, and the harlot.

7 Churches as Old Testament History

Our Lord Jesus Christ places hints within each of His seven messages to the seven churches that reveal a chronological pattern mirroring the story of the Old Testament. Here are the clues embedded in the seven messages to the seven churches in each Asian city:

1) Ephesus: "tree of life, which is paradise"
2) Smyrna: "those that say they are Jews and are not" and "tribulation of ten days"
3) Pergamum: "where Satan dwells," "Balaam and Balak," and "hidden manna"
4) Thyatira: "Jezebel," "authority over the nations," and "rod of iron"
5) Sardis: "alive but dead," "strengthen the things that remain," "thief," and "a few not defiled"
6) Philadelphia: "key of David," "synagogue of Satan," "pillar in the temple," and "New Jerusalem"
7) Laodicea: "lukewarm," "vomited out," "rich but naked," "I stand at the gate and knock," and "seated with the Father"

Christ as God is speaking to humanity and addressing them by epoch from Adam in paradise (Ephesus) until Christ rises again and is seated with the Father (Laodicea). The seven churches in chronological order establish the seven epochs from Adam to Jesus Christ.

1) Ephesus: Epoch of Adam
2) Smyrna: Epoch of Abraham and the Patriarchs
3) Pergamum: Epoch of Moses and Exodus
4) Thyatira: Epoch of King David and the Kings
5) Sardis: Epoch of Babylonian Exile
6) Philadelphia: Epoch of restoration to Jerusalem
7) Laodicea: Epoch of Christ and rejection by Jerusalem

Let's examine each message in detail.

First Message to the Church of Ephesus as the First Epoch of Adam

[1] Unto the angel of the church of Ephesus write: These things saith he, who holdeth the seven stars in his right hand, who walketh in the midst of the seven golden candlesticks:

[2] I know thy works, and thy labor, and thy patience, and how thou canst not bear them that are evil, and thou hast tried them, who say they are apostles, and are not, and hast found them liars:

[3] And thou hast patience, and hast endured for my name, and hast not fainted.

[4] But I have somewhat against thee, because thou hast left thy first charity.

[5] Be mindful therefore from whence thou art fallen: and do penance and do the first works. Or else I come to thee, and will move thy candlestick out of its place, except thou do penance.

[6] But this thou hast, that thou hatest the deeds of the Nicolaites, which I also hate.

[7] He, that hath an ear, let him hear what the Spirit saith to the churches: To him, that overcometh, I will give to eat of the tree of life, which is in the paradise of my God. (Apoc 2:1–7)

Christ walks in the midst of the candlesticks, just as God walked in the midst of the garden (v. 1). Christ rebukes them for losing their first love (v. 4). Then he says they have fallen (v. 5), just as Adam and Eve fell into original sin. If the church of Ephesus overcomes, Christ will let them "eat of the tree of life, which is the paradise of my God" (v. 7). Clearly, the church of Ephesus represents the first stage of humanity in Adam and Eve and their fall from the garden of paradise.

Second Message to the Church of Smyrna
as the Second Epoch of Patriarchs

⁸ And to the angel of the church of Smyrna write: These things saith the First and the Last, who was dead, and is alive:
⁹ I know thy tribulation and thy poverty, but thou art rich: and thou art blasphemed by them that say they are Jews and are not but are the synagogue of Satan.
¹⁰ Fear none of those things which thou shalt suffer. Behold, the devil will cast some of you into prison that you may be tried: and you shall have tribulation ten days. Be thou faithful until death: and I will give thee the crown of life.
¹¹ He, that hath an ear, let him hear what the Spirit saith to the churches: He that shall overcome, shall not be hurt by the second death. (Apoc 2:8–11)

This message begins with a warning about those "who say they are Jews and are not but are a synagogue of Satan" (v. 9). The second half of Genesis tells the story of the patriarchs and the problem of false brothers betraying faithful brothers. Abraham has two sons at enmity with one another: Isaac and Ishmael. Isaac has two sons at enmity with each other: Jacob and Esau. Jacob tricks Esau out of the covenantal blessing. Jacob has twelve sons by four women. Their story is one of fighting over their birthright and their jealousy over Joseph and his coat. Clearly, not all born under Abraham are of Abraham. The message warns of prison, a reference to Joseph being imprisoned. There is tribulation for ten days, just as God sent ten plagues for ten days in Egypt. This epoch begins with Abraham and ends with the exodus.

Third Message to the Church of Pergamus
as the Third Epoch of Moses

¹² And to the angel of the church of Pergamus write: These things, saith he, that hath the sharp two-edged sword:
¹³ I know where thou dwellest, where the seat of Satan is: and thou holdest fast my name, and hast not denied my faith. Even in those days when Antipas was my faithful witness, who was slain among you, where Satan dwelleth.
¹⁴ But I have against thee a few things: because thou hast there them that hold the doctrine of Balaam, who taught Balak to cast a stumbling block before the children of Israel, to eat, and to commit fornication:
¹⁵ So hast thou also them that hold the doctrine of the Nicolaites.
¹⁶ In like manner do penance: if not, I will come to thee quickly, and will fight against them with the sword of my mouth.
¹⁷ He, that hath an ear, let him hear what the Spirit saith to the churches: To him that overcometh, I will give the hidden manna, and will give him a white counter, and in the counter, a new name written, which no man knoweth, but he that receiveth it. (Apoc 2:12–17)

Christ warns of the teaching of Balaam and of Balak. Balak was a king who hated God's people. Balaam was a prophet hired by King Balak to curse them before they entered the Holy Land (v. 14). The name Balaam means "conquer people." These two foreshadow the Antichrist King and the False Prophet of Apocalypse 13 working together to condemn God's chosen people. He warns against idolatry and fornication (v. 14), which were the temptations of the people beginning with the golden calf incident. He warns of the Nicolaites. In Greek, the name Nikolaus means "conquer people"—the same as Balaam in Hebrew. Christ mentions the "doctrine of Balaam" in v. 14 and the "doctrine of Nicolaites" in v. 15. They are the same things. This teaching "conquers the people." Christ will make "war with the sword of my mouth" against them, and this refers to how the angel of the Lord countered Balaam with a drawn sword (Num 31:8). Those Christians that overcome will receive the hidden manna (v. 17), a clear reference to the heavenly bread (Ex 16:33–34) given to sustain the people in the wilderness under Moses. Paul teaches that some manna was hidden inside the ark of the covenant (Heb 9:4).

Fourth Message to the Church of Thyatira as the Fourth Epoch of Kings

¹⁸ And to the angel of the church of Thyatira write: These things saith the Son of God, who hath his eyes like to a flame of fire, and his feet like to fine brass.
¹⁹ I know thy works, and thy faith, and thy charity, and thy ministry, and thy patience, and thy last works which are more than the former.
²⁰ But I have against thee a few things: because thou sufferest the woman Jezabel, who calleth herself a prophetess, to teach, and to seduce my servants, to commit fornication, and to eat of things sacrificed to idols.
²¹ And I gave her a time that she might do penance, and she will not repent of her fornication.
²² Behold, I will cast her into a bed: and they that commit adultery with her shall be in very great tribulation, except they do penance from their deeds.
²³ And I will kill her children with death, and all the churches shall know that I am he that searcheth the reins and hearts, and I will give to every one of you according to your works. But to you I say,
²⁴ And to the rest who are at Thyatira: Whosoever have not this doctrine, and who have not known the depths

of Satan, as they say, I will not put upon you any other burthen.

²⁵ Yet that, which you have, hold fast till I come.

²⁶ And he that shall overcome, and keep my works unto the end, I will give him power over the nations.

²⁷ And he shall rule them with a rod of iron, and as the vessel of a potter they shall be broken,

²⁸ As I also have received of my Father: and I will give him the morning star.

²⁹ He that hath an ear, let him hear what the Spirit saith to the churches. (Apoc 2:18–29)

After the time of Moses and the judges, God chose David and his ancestral line to be the kings of Israel. In the previous epoch, Christ identified his enemies with Balaam the False Prophet and Balak the False King in the wilderness. Now Christ introduces the royal harlot named Jezebel—a prophetess who taught Balaam and Balak to commit fornication and eat things sacrificed to idols (verse 20). In the Old Testament, Jezebel was a Phoenician queen of the ninth century BC who introduced idolatry and pagan priests into Israel (3 Kings 16–21, 4 Kings 9:22). Christ is angry because they "tolerate" Jezebel in their midst. After the death of King David, his son Solomon, through his many wives, introduced idolatry and fornication into Israel. Idolatry was often imported by foreign queen consorts who brought their false religion with them. Christ promises to those who overcome "to rule the nations with a rod of iron as the vessels of a potter." This is a direct promise by God to King David and the messianic kings after him: "I will give thee the nations for thy inheritance, and the utmost parts of the earth for thy possession. Thou shalt rule them with a rod of iron, and shalt break them in pieces like a potter's vessel" (Ps 2:8–9).

Fifth Message to the Church of Sardis
as the Fifth Epoch of Exile

[1] And to the angel of the church of Sardis, write: These things saith he, that hath the seven spirits of God, and the seven stars: I know thy works, that thou hast the name of being alive: and thou art dead.
[2] Be watchful and strengthen the things that remain, which are ready to die. For I find not thy works full before my God.
[3] Have in mind therefore in what manner thou hast received and heard: and observe and do penance. If then thou shalt not watch, I will come to thee as a thief, and thou shalt not know at what hour I will come to thee.
[4] But thou hast a few names in Sardis, which have not defiled their garments: and they shall walk with me in white, because they are worthy.
[5] He that shall overcome, shall thus be clothed in white garments, and I will not blot out his name out of the book of life, and I will confess his name before my Father, and before his angels.
[6] He that hath an ear, let him hear what the Spirit saith to the churches. (Apoc 3:1–6)

After the kingdoms of Israel and Judah committed idolatry in spite of repeated warnings from the prophets, God handed them over to exile under the Assyrians and Babylonians. Their temple was destroyed, and they became slaves in foreign lands. Christ now turns his attention to this sad estate by calling His people "alive but dead" (v. 1). Since they are in exile, He tells them to "strengthen the things that remain" (v. 2). God punished the kings by having foreign kings steal their land and territories like a thief. Now Christ also "comes upon them like a thief" (v. 3). In the Old Testament, God left behind a remnant, and here Christ also speaks of "a few not defiled" (v. 4). During the exile, all the written records of genealogies and property were lost. Yet Christ here promises to those that overcome, "I will not erase your name from the Book of Life" (v. 5).

Sixth Message to the Church of Philadelphia as the Sixth Epoch of Restoration from Exile to Jerusalem

⁷ And to the angel of the church of Philadelphia, write: These things saith the Holy One and the true one, he that hath the key of David; he that openeth, and no man shutteth; shutteth, and no man openeth:
⁸ I know thy works. Behold, I have given before thee a door opened, which no man can shut: because thou hast a little strength, and hast kept my word, and hast not denied my name.
⁹ Behold, I will bring of the synagogue of Satan, who say they are Jews, and are not, but do lie. Behold, I will make them to come and adore before thy feet. And they shall know that I have loved thee.
¹⁰ Because thou hast kept the word of my patience, I will also keep thee from the hour of the temptation, which shall come upon the whole world to try them that dwell upon the earth.
¹¹ Behold, I come quickly: hold fast that which thou hast, that no man take thy crown.
¹² He that shall overcome, I will make him a pillar in the temple of my God; and he shall go out no more; and I will write upon him the name of my God, and the name of the city of my God, the New Jerusalem, which cometh down out of heaven from my God, and my new name.
¹³ He that hath an ear, let him hear what the Spirit saith to the churches. (Apoc 3:1–13)

The Babylonian Exile lasted from 587 BC until the Persian King Cyrus ended the exile in 538 BC—approximately 49 years. However, the exile officially ended with the return of Prince Zerubbabel (of the messianic ancestry of King David) and Joshua the High Priest and the rebuilding of the Second Temple from 521–516 BC under the leadership of Esdras and Nehemias. From the destruction of the temple in 587 until the rebuilding of the temple in 516 was 70 or 71 years. They shall again "dwell upon the land" (v. 10). This restoration was a bittersweet time for the Jews. They were grateful to return home and reestablish the temple, but they recalled the former glory of what had been before. They also had to deal with the Samaritans who persecuted them as they attempted to rebuild Jerusalem—"a synagogue of Satan" who say they are Jews but are not, but lie" (v. 8). Christ speaks of the "key of David" (v. 7) as a return of a Davidic prince to Jerusalem. He has "opened the door, which no one can shut" (v. 8) as a reference to the Davidic kingdom in Isaias 22. Now, "no one can take their crown" (v. 11). To those that overcome, Christ will "make him a pillar in the temple...in the New Jerusalem" (v. 12), a reference to the rebuilt temple in the rebuilt Jerusalem.

7th Message to the Church of Laodicea as 7th Epoch of Christ and Rejection by Jerusalem

¹⁴ And to the angel of the church of Laodicea, write: These things saith the Amen, the faithful and true witness, who is the beginning of the creation of God:
¹⁵ I know thy works, that thou art neither cold, nor hot. I would thou wert cold, or hot.
¹⁶ But because thou art lukewarm, and neither cold, nor hot, I will begin to vomit thee out of my mouth.
¹⁷ Because thou sayest: I am rich, and made wealthy, and have need of nothing: and knowest not, that thou art wretched, and miserable, and poor, and blind, and naked.

¹⁸ I counsel thee to buy of me gold fire tried, that thou mayest be made rich; and mayest be clothed in white garments, and that the shame of thy nakedness may not appear; and anoint thy eyes with eyesalve, that thou mayest see.

¹⁹ Such as I love, I rebuke and chastise. Be zealous therefore, and do penance.

²⁰ Behold, I stand at the gate, and knock. If any man shall hear my voice, and open to me the door, I will come in to him, and will sup with him, and he with me.

²¹ To him that shall overcome, I will give to sit with me in my throne: as I also have overcome and am set down with my Father in his throne.

²² He that hath an ear, let him hear what the Spirit saith to the churches.

After the return from exile, the Jews fought off the Greeks during the Maccabean revolt, made an alliance with the Romans, and generally became complacent under Roman rule. Christ accuses them of being "neither cold nor hot and so he vomits them out of His mouth" (vv. 15-16). The Jews at the birth of Christ, because of their alliance with King Herod and Rome, had become rich. Jerusalem and its temple had become a wonder of the world. But the Jewish leaders were "wretched, and miserable, and poor, and blind, and naked" (v. 17). Christ challenges them to anoint their eyes (v. 18) because He often accuses them of being blind. They don't recognize their Messiah. Jesus was crucified and buried outside the walls of Jerusalem, and now He "stands at the gate and knocks" (v. 20). He invites them to His eucharistic sacrifice: "I will come into him and will sup with him and he with me" (v. 20). He has risen and ascended to sit on the right hand of God the Father. To those who overcome, "I will give to sit with me on my throne...set down with my Father in his throne" (v. 21).

So far, Jesus Christ in His Apocalypse has chosen the language of the seven epochs between Adam and Christ to speak to His church. This is certainly a preterist interpretation. However, there is another historicist interpretation of these seven messages to seven churches. Perhaps these messages refer to the thread of Church history from Christ to the Antichrist.

7 CHURCHES AS CHURCH HISTORY (HOLZHAUSER)

Various Christian commentators in the early church looked at the messages of the Apocalypse and tried to apply them to their times. Both Augustine and Jerome cataloged certain seers who claimed that the world would end 200, 300, 500, 666, or even 1,000 years after Christ. Augustine noted how the expectations of early seers were never met: "It is not for us to know the time and the hour which the Father has placed in his power."[68] After the collapse of the Western Roman Empire in the late 400's, few Christians interpreted the Apocalypse as ongoing in Church history.

The Protestant Reformers restored the historical interpretation of the Apocalypse. Martin Luther and the early Lutherans dogmatically identified the Antichrist with the pope and sought to connect their rebellion against the Catholic Church with the tribulation and end times. The heretical doctrinal documents of the Lutheran sect state that:

> The Pope is the real Antichrist who has raised himself over and set himself against Christ.[69]

> Therefore, just as little as we can worship the devil himself as Lord and God, we can endure his apostle the Pope, or Antichrist, in his rule as head or lord.[70]

> All Christians ... ought to desert and execrate the Pope with his members, or adherents, as the kingdom of Antichrist, just as Christ has commanded, 'Beware of false prophets.'[71]

---

[68] Augustine, Epistle 80 *ad Hesychium.*
[69] *Lutheran Smalcald Articles,* Part II, Art. IV, par. 10.
[70] *Lutheran Book of Concord,* Article X, par. 20.
[71] *Lutheran Book of Concord,* Article X. par. 22.

The apostate Archbishop Thomas Cranmer (d. 1556), who served as the puppet archbishop for King Henry VIII's freshly created Church of England, also identified the pope as the Antichrist:

> Whereof it followeth Rome to be the seat of Antichrist, and the Pope to be very Antichrist himself. I could prove the same by many other scriptures, old writers, and strong reasons.[72]

The French Reformer John Calvin (d. 1564) taught the same error:

> Though it be admitted that Rome was once the mother of all Churches, yet from the time when it began to be the seat of Antichrist it has ceased to be what it was before. Some persons think us too severe and censorious when we call the Roman Pontiff Antichrist.[73]

The Presbyterian *Westminster Confession of Faith* (1647) also affirms the pope as the Antichrist and Man of Sin:

> There is no other head of the Church but the Lord Jesus Christ. Nor can the pope of Rome, in any sense, be head thereof, but is that Antichrist, the man of sin, and son of perdition, that exalteth himself, in the church, against Christ and all that is called God.[74]

Cardinal Robert Bellarmine (d. 1621) shows how the testimony of Sacred Scripture repeatedly disproves the claims of Protestants in his *De Pontifice Romano*.[75] He demonstrates that the real Antichrist will be Jewish (not

---

[72] Thomas Cranmer, *Opera,* Vol. 1, pp. 6-7.
[73] John Calvin, *Institutes of the Christian Religion,* Vol. 3, p. 149.
[74] *Westminster Confession of Faith,* Art. 25.6,
[75] Robert Bellarmine, *De Romano Pontifice,* lib. III, cap. 18-24.

Italian), will reign for three and half years (not centuries), and will exist just before the return of Christ. We will examine all these facts in detail in the chapters to come.

But Luther and Calvin's historicist interpretations were also matched by the Catholic mystic Bartholomew Holzhauser (d. 1658). Holzhauser was a Catholic priest born in Laugna, Germany. Unlike Luther or Calvin, he claimed to interpret the book of the Apocalypse not according to personal study.

Bartholomew Holzhauser (1613-1658)

He claimed to be a visionary whose mystical insight interpreted the pages of the Apocalypse. Holzhauser taught that the seven messages to the seven churches were in fact a historical timeline of events unfolding from AD 33 to the end of time. Each of the seven messages and seven churches applied to the seven ages of the Church of Jesus Christ over time. Here are the seven Holzhauser Epochs:

1. *First Epoch.* Holzhauser names the first epoch as the *status seminationis*, or "state of seedtime." It is the time period from the preaching of our Lord Jesus Christ and His apostles to the martyrdom of Saint

Peter and Saint Paul under Nero in AD 67 and AD 68.

2. *Second Epoch.* Holzhauser names this period the *status irrigationis*, or "state of irrigation." It is the period from the death of Saint Peter to the conversion of the Roman Emperor Constantine (AD 68–337).

3. *Third Epoch.* This age is the *status illuminationis*, or "state of illumination," and it traces the time of imperial Christianity from Emperor Constantine to Emperor Charlemagne (AD 337–800).

4. *Fourth Epoch.* This is the *status pacificus*, or "state of peace," and it is the era from Emperor Charlemagne to Martin Luther, Emperor Charles V, and Pope Leo X (AD 800–1517). The decadence of the papacy, the fracturing of the empire, and the arrival of Protestantism bring an end to the era of peace.

5. *Fifth Epoch.* Holzhauser identifies the fifth epoch as the *status afflictionis*, or "state of affliction." The arrival of Martin Luther (1517), the Sack of Rome (1527), and the subsequent dissolution of European Christendom begins the affliction. The fifth message to the church of Sardis speaks to this post-Lutheran epoch: "being alive, thou art dead" (v. 1), "strengthen the things that remain" (v. 2), "observe and do penance" (v. 3), and "thou hast a few" (v. 4). As we saw above, it corresponds to the Babylonian exile of the Jews.

6. *Sixth Epoch.* This is a still-future *status consolationis*, or "state of consolation." It corresponds to the Old Testament sixth epoch of the return of the Jews after exile, the rebuilding of the temple, the return of the Davidic prince Zerubbabel, and the installation of High Priest Joshua. In Holzhauser's vision, this sixth epoch will be signaled by the end of the exile for the Catholic Church. Like Jerusalem, the Church will be rebuilt. This will include the

arrival of the great monarch (like Prince Zerubbabel) and the holy pope (like High Priest Joshua). This age of consolation will last until the birth of the Antichrist.

7. *Seventh Epoch.* This final age is the *status desolationis*, or "state of desolation," and begins with the birth of the Antichrist and lasts until the end of the world. This is the age of the Great Apostasy, when all the nations abandon and deny Jesus Christ. Christ accuses this age of being "lukewarm," and He "vomits" these Christians from His mouth. Lukewarm Christians will be rejected by Christ, and the Antichrist will begin his cruel persecutions to test the Church.

As you can see, Holzhauser associates each of the seven epochs of the Church to the seven church messages and to each of the seven Old Testament epochs:

Message	Church Message	OT Epoch	Holzhauser Epoch	Holzhauser Dates	Status
First	Ephesus	Adam	Apostolic	AD 33–100	Seedtime
Second	Smyrna	Patriarchs	Apostles–Constantine	100–337	Irrigation
Third	Pergamos	Moses	Constantine–Charlemagne	337–800	Illumination
Fourth	Thyatira	Kings	Charlemagne–Reformation	800-1517	Peace
Fifth	Sardis	Babylonian Exile	Reformation–Restoration	1517–?	Affliction
Sixth	Philadelphia	Restoration from Exile	Restoration	Future	Consolation
Seventh	Laodicea	Christ	Antichrist–2nd Coming	Future	Desolation

The Seven Seals (Apocalypse 4)

After the seven messages to the seven churches, God invites Saint John to enter heaven and watch the narrative from above.

John Enters Heavenly Throne Room (Apoc 4:1–3)
[1] After these things I looked, and behold a door was opened in heaven, and the first voice which I heard, as it were, of a trumpet speaking with me, said: Come up hither, and I will shew thee the things which must be done hereafter.
[2] And immediately I was in the Spirit: and behold there was a throne set in heaven, and upon the throne one sitting.
[3] And he that sat, was to the sight like the jasper and the sardius stone; and there was a rainbow round about the throne, in sight like unto an emerald.

Three jewels are mentioned as jasper (clear), sardius (red), and emerald (green). A rainbow is around the throne. The prophet Ezechiel also saw a rainbow around the throne of God (Eze 1:28).

The 24 Presbyters around the Throne (Apoc 4:4–6)
[4] And round about the throne were four and twenty seats; and upon the seats, four and twenty presbyters sitting, clothed in white garments, and on their heads were crowns of gold.
[5] And from the throne proceeded lightnings, and voices, and thunders; and there were seven lamps burning before the throne, which are the seven spirits of God.
[6] And in the sight of the throne was, as it were, a sea of glass like to crystal; and in the midst of the throne, and

round about the throne, were four living creatures, full of eyes before and behind.

The throne of God is surrounded by twenty-four seats for the twenty-four presbyters, or elders. These correspond to the twenty-four grandsons of High Priest Aaron, which became the twenty-four divisions of the Old Testament priesthood (1 Para[76] 25). This reveals that the New Covenant presbyters are priestly. They wear vestments and crowns like priests. The number twenty-four also refers to the twelve tribes of Israel joined with the twelve apostles of Christ.

The seven lamps symbolize the menorah that was in the Old Testament temple, and the seven spirits of God— the Holy Spirit. For those still concerned that "seven spirits" may refer to seven persons of the Holy Spirit or teach a heretical idea of the Holy Spirit, recall that the seven lamps of the Old Testament menorah were seven lamps incorporated as joined into one:

The Sevenfold Menorah in the Temple

In Roman Catholicism, High Mass includes six candles lit on the altar; a seventh candle is lit for a Pontifical High Mass, when the bishop celebrates High Mass in its fullness

---

[76] I use the Septuagint and Vulgate names and abbreviations. 1 Paralipomenon is 1 Chronicles. Paralipomenon means "Things Left Out." Note also that 1 and 2 Samuel are 1 and 2 Kings, and 1 and 2 Kings are 3 and 4 Kings in the Greek Septuagint and Latin Vulgate.

to correspond to these "seven lamps" in heaven.[77] The sea of glass corresponds to the bronze sea at the Old Testament temple (Ex 30:17–21) and to the baptistry font in New Covenant churches. The water is the portal by which people enter God's presence. The four living creatures are the celestial constellations and the four creatures of God's chariot:

Four Chariot Creatures (Apoc 4:7)

And the first living creature was like a lion: and the second living creature like a calf: and the third living creature, having the face, as it were, of a man: and the fourth living creature was like an eagle flying.

Saint John sees the same four creatures seen by the prophet Ezechiel. Ezechiel sees the rotating throne of God with four cherubim corresponding to the lion, the bull, the man, and the eagle (Eze 1:10). Saint Irenaeus interprets Christ surrounded by the "quadriform Gospel," with Mark as the lion, Luke as the bull, Matthew as the man, and John as the eagle.[78] This allegorical reading is true, but the original vision involves Saint John seeing the four seasonal star constellations of the zodiac. Perhaps the four animals being "full of eyes" refers to them covered in stars. Before moving forward, we are not endorsing the new-age zodiac or astrology. Many of the Church Fathers condemned using the twelve zodiacs determining human actions.[79] These are

---

77 "At a pontifical high Mass, celebrated by the ordinary, seven candles are lighted. The seventh candle should be somewhat higher than the others, and should be placed at the middle of the altar in line with the other six. For this reason, the altar crucifix is moved forward a little. In Requiem Masses, and at other liturgical services. e.g., Vespers, the seventh candle is not used. If the bishop celebrates outside his diocese. or if he be the administrator, auxiliary, or coadjutor, the seventh candle is not lighted." From Augustin Joseph Schulte, "Altar Candles," in *The Catholic Encyclopedia* Vol. 1. New York: Robert Appleton Company, 1907.

78 Irenaeus, *Against Heresies,* lib 3, cap. 11, 8. Jerome and Gregory the Great follow the same reading.

79 Using the twelve zodiacs to predict the future or human behavior was condemned by Tertullian, Hippolytus, Athanasius, Augustine, and John

superstitious and sinful practices. However, all human cultures recognized twelve constellations in the sky through which the sun and moon traveled during the course of the twelve-month year. These twelve constellations marked the months and harvest times. The Greek word *zodiakos* means "little animals" and is a diminutive for *zoon*, meaning "animal." In fact, the Greek word *zoon* is the same Greek word used by Saint John for the four creatures. The Prague Astronomical Clock, installed in AD 1410, reveals the time and the automated walking of the twelve apostles, but it also features the twelve astronomical zodiacs fitted with the twelve months and annual harvest cycles:

Astronomical Clock of Prague, AD 1410

Four of the twelve animals of the *zodiakos* are seen by John as framing the four corners of the altar of God. The lion is the constellation Leo. The bull is the constellation Taurus. The man is the constellation Aquarius. The eagle is the constellation Scorpio.[80]

Chrysostom. Saint Basil the Great wrote: "The Babylonians read in the planets that which will happen to us. By these very simple words 'let them be for signs,' they understand neither the variations of the weather nor the change of seasons; they only see in them, at the will of their imagination, the distribution of human destinies. What do they say in reality? When the planets cross in the signs of the zodiac, certain figures formed by their meeting give birth to certain destinies, and others produce different destinies" (*Hexameron,* 6:5).

[80] Greek zodiac has this constellation as the scorpion, but it has been also identified as an eagle.

1) **Taurus (Bull as Luke) in Spring**
2) Gemini
3) Cancer
4) **Leo (Lion as Mark) in Summer**
5) Virgo
6) Libra
7) **Scorpio (Eagle as John) in Autumn**
8) Sagittarius
9) Capricorn
10) **Aquarius (Man Water Carrier as Matthew) in Winter**
11) Pisces
12) Aries

The four cherubim animals around the throne of God are the constellations associated with the four seasons. The bull, lion, eagle, and man are positioned in the sky as every third animal constellation in the annual cycle of the sun. Ezechiel sees these four animals as rotating like a wheel. These four animals are the four spokes of the twelve constellations if you think of the cycle of twelve as a complete and annual circle. Within this celestial space, the Lamb comes forward to receive the book:

4 Creatures chant Holy, Holy, Holy (Apoc 4:8–11)
[8] And the four living creatures had each of them six wings; and round about and within they are full of eyes. And they rested not day and night, saying: Holy, holy, holy, Lord God Almighty, who was, and who is, and who is to come.
[9] And when those living creatures gave glory, and honour, and benediction to him that sitteth on the throne, who liveth for ever and ever.
[10] The four and twenty presbyters fell down before him that sitteth on the throne, and adored him that liveth for ever and ever, and cast their crowns before the throne, saying:
[11] Thou art worthy, O Lord our God, to receive glory, and honour, and power: because thou hast created all

things; and for thy will they were and have been created.

These creatures have "six wings," as seen by the prophet Isaias: "Two wings covered the face, two wings covered the feet, and with two wings he flew" (Isa 6:1–2). Notably, four creatures with six wings each brings us to twenty-four wings, the number of the twenty-four elders also surrounding the throne of God—one wing per elder. They chant the Trisagion: "Holy, holy, holy, Lord God Almighty, who was, and who is, and who is to come," which is chanted in every Christian liturgy from east to west. The four heavenly animals initiate the praise, and then the twenty-four elders join in the worship and fall down before the throne and worship God, casting down their crowns. God is enthroned above the stars.

The Lamb and His Scroll (Apocalypse 5)

Now that John is in the throne room of God, he has seen the Father enthroned and the sevenfold Holy Spirit. Where is the Son of God? He appears again, this time as the Lamb of God.

Who Is Worthy to Open the 7 Seals? (Apoc 5:1–4)

¹ And I saw in the right hand of him that sat on the throne, a book written within and without, sealed with seven seals.

² And I saw a strong angel, proclaiming with a loud voice: Who is worthy to open the book, and to loose the seals thereof?

³ And no man was able, neither in heaven, nor on earth, nor under the earth, to open the book, nor to look on it.

⁴ And I wept much, because no man was found worthy to open the book, nor to see it.

John sees a book or scroll. The Greek word he uses is *biblion*, from which we get the word "Bible." Yet *biblion* just means "parchment" or "paper." It likely derives from the location Byblos, the Phoenician port from which Egyptian papyrus was exported to Greece. It is written "on front and back"—a reference to how the Ten Commandments of Moses were written on tablets, front and back (Ex 32:15). Also, Ezechiel received a covenantal scroll written on front and back—that is, "within and without" (Eze 2:9). In the case of Moses and Ezechiel, God is giving covenantal documents to the prophets. John sees the same thing here, but this seven-sealed document is the New Covenant.

John did not see a bound book or codex. Rather, he saw a scroll rolled up and sealed on its edge with seven seals. In antiquity, classified documents were sealed with imperial seals. Only those with rightful authority could break the seal and read the contents. An angel laments, "Who is worthy to open the book?" No one in heaven, nor on earth nor under the earth (in hell) is worthy. Oddly, John weeps as if he doesn't know the answer.

The Lamb is Worthy to Open (Apoc 5:5–6)
[5] And one of the presbyters said to me: Weep not; behold the lion of the tribe of Juda, the root of David, hath prevailed to open the book, and to loose the seven seals thereof.
[6] And I saw: and behold in the midst of the throne and of the four living creatures, and in the midst of the presbyters, a Lamb standing as it were slain, having seven horns and seven eyes: which are the seven Spirits of God, sent forth into all the earth.

One of the elders says to weep not and to look for the "Lion of the tribe Juda . . . to open the book." The elder tells us to expect a lion, but that is not what we see. In the midst of the four animals and twenty-four presbyters appears not a lion but a lamb. As Saint John the Baptist announced at the baptism of Jesus, "Behold the Lamb of God, behold him who taketh away the sin of the world" (Jn 1:29). Jesus is the Lamb that was slain (crucified) yet still stands (resurrected). He has seven horns (holy strength) and seven eyes that are the seven spirits (Holy Spirit). Notably, the Antichrist will have seven heads and ten horns.

The Lamb Takes the Scroll (Apoc 5:7–8)
[7] And he came and took the book out of the right hand of him that sat on the throne.
[8] And when he had opened the book, the four living creatures, and the four and twenty presbyters fell down before the Lamb, having every one of them harps, and golden vials full of incense, which are the prayers of saints.

The Lamb of God stands before the throne of God the Father and takes the scroll from the "right hand" of God the Father. This corresponds to chapter 1, in which Jesus receives the Apocalypse *from* God the Father. This is an intra-Trinitarian gift from the Father to the Son. This gift from God the Father to God the Son was foretold by the prophet Daniel:

> **Daniel Sees Son of Man on the Clouds (Dan 7:13–14)**
> I beheld therefore in the vision of the night, and lo, one like the Son of Man came with the clouds of heaven, and he came even to the Ancient of days: and they presented him before him. And he gave him power, and glory, and a kingdom: and all peoples, tribes and tongues shall serve him: his power is an everlasting power that shall not be taken away: and his kingdom that shall not be destroyed.

The Son of Man is the incarnate Son of God. The Ancient of days is God the Father. Jesus comes on the clouds of heaven (His ascension) and stands before the Father. The Father gives imperial power in the form of an international kingdom. The scroll with the seven seals is the testament or deed to this kingdom consisting of "all peoples, tribes, and tongues."

Our Lord Jesus Christ as Lamb opens the book, and the four animals and twenty-four presbyters worship again with harps and golden bowls full of incense. The Greek word for "harp" is *kithara*, which was a triangular, *seven*-stringed harp or lyre. It comes into Latin as *cithara* and then into Spanish as *guitarra*—but the modern guitar is by no means the same instrument described in the Apocalypse. The incense is offered in golden *phialas*, which comes into English as "phials" or "vials." Going back as far as the Greek poet, these are broad, shallow bowls used for incense or offering sacrifices. The offered incense is the prayers of the saints. This reveals that the twenty-four presbyters in heaven present the prayers of those on earth to the Lamb, Jesus Christ, in a form of sub-mediation.[81]

The Lamb Redeems All Nations (Apoc 5:9–10)

[9] And they sung a new canticle, saying: Thou art worthy, O Lord, to take the book, and to open the seals thereof; because thou wast slain, and hast redeemed us to God, in thy blood, out of every tribe, and tongue, and people, and nation.

[10] And hast made us to our God a kingdom and priests, and we shall reign on the earth.

The presentation of the New Testament to Christ is accompanied by a New Canticle. Here we are told the reason why Jesus Christ can open the sealed New Testament: "because thou was slain and has redeemed us to God in thy blood." The redemptive blood reference conforms to the only time Jesus Christ says, "New Testament" in the Gospels: "For this is my blood of the New Testament, which shall be shed for many unto remission of sins" (Mt 26:28).

Lamb is Worthy to Open the Scroll (Apoc 5:11–14)

[11] And I beheld, and I heard the voice of many angels round about the throne, and the living creatures, and the presbyters; and the number of them was thousands of thousands,

[12] Saying with a loud voice: The Lamb that was slain is worthy to receive power, and divinity, and wisdom, and strength, and honor, and glory, and benediction.

[13] And every creature, which is in heaven, and on the earth, and under the earth, and such as are in the sea, and all that are in them: I heard all saying: To him that

---

[81] The human presbyters in heaven present prayers to Jesus the Lamb. This proves the Catholic tradition that our prayers on earth are *submediated* and presented to Christ as the one Mediator between God and men. The saints in heaven do have a role to play in the flow of prayers to Christ.

sitteth on the throne, and to the Lamb, benediction, and honor, and glory, and power, for ever and ever. [14] And the four living creatures said: Amen. And the four and twenty presbyters fell down on their faces, and adored him that liveth for ever and ever.

The unlocking of the seals unlocks the entry of "thousands and thousands." The kingdom of Jesus Christ is not just Israel. It is as international and universal as "every tribe, and tongue, and people, and nation." This universal community is the one holy, catholic, and apostolic church—the kingdom of God.

The Four Horsemen (Apocalypse 6)

While praise is happening in heaven, on earth, and under the earth, Jesus Christ breaks the first four seals, and then each of the four horsemen appears, the first on a white horse, the second on a red horse, the third on a black horse, and the fourth on a pale horse. In order, the four horsemen are conquest (white horse), international war (red horse), famine and starvation (black horse), and Death (pale horse), who kills with the sword, famine, and beasts.

Saint John seeing the horses is related to the "wind chariots" in Zecharias 6:

Four Horsemen as Wind Chariots (Zech 6:2–5)
[2] In the first chariot were red horses, and in the second chariot black horses.
[3] And in the third chariot white horses, and in the fourth chariot grisled horses, and strong ones.
[4] And I answered, and said to the angel that spoke in me: What are these, my lord?
[5] And the angel answered, and said to me: These are the four winds of the heaven, which go forth to stand before the Lord of all the earth.

The four kinds of colored horses correspond to the "four winds of heaven . . . to stand before the Lord." In antiquity, chariots were used in war but also to patrol regions. But here in the Apocalypse, the horses are saddled and mounted by a lone rider. They are out for speed and battle.

First Seal Opened and White Horse (Apoc 6:1–2)
[1] And I saw that the Lamb had opened one of the seven seals, and I heard one of the four living creatures, as it were the voice of thunder, saying: Come, and see.
[2] And I saw: and behold a white horse, and he that sat on him had a bow, and there was a crown given him, and he went forth conquering that he might conquer.

The rider of the white horse appears to be our Lord Jesus Christ. Later in Apocalypse 19:11–16, we definitely see Jesus Christ riding in on a white horse. If we follow the historicist interpretation of the seven seals, then the beginning is always with Jesus Christ. So having a crown and conquering the world describes what Jesus Christ did beginning in AD 33 through to the end of time.

Jewish readers would remember the white-horse rider from the battle of the Maccabees:

> Then Maccabeus himself, first taking his arms, exhorted the rest to expose themselves together with him, to the danger, and to succour their brethren. And when they were going forth together with a willing mind, there *appeared at Jerusalem a horseman going before them in white clothing*, with golden armor, shaking a spear" (2 Mac 11:7–8, emphasis added).

The white horseman leading the Maccabean warriors is the Son of God. The prophet Habacuc also describes God as going into war with a bow and "glittering spear" (Hab 3:9–11). And "conquering (*nikon*) that he might conquer"[82] refers to Christ in Apocalypse 3:21. In both places, we see the Greek word *nikon*—which means "one making victory or conquering." The running shoe brand Nike is the same word: "victory."

Second Seal Opened and Red Horse (Apoc 6:3–4)

³ And when he had opened the second seal, I heard the second living creature, saying: Come, and see.
⁴ And there went out another horse that was red: and to him that sat thereon, it was given that he should take peace from the earth, and that they should kill one another, and a great sword was given to him.

---

[82] νικων και ινα νικηση.

The second horse is red, and his rider takes away peace from the earth. This leads to international bloodshed. He has a great sword. The taking away of peace may be a reference to Saint Paul's doctrine of the *katechon*—that which withholds the mystery of iniquity (2 Thess 2:6–8).

Third Seal Opened and Black Horse (Apoc 6:5–6)

[5] And when he had opened the third seal, I heard the third living creature saying: Come, and see. And behold a black horse, and he that sat on him had a pair of scales in his hand.

[6] And I heard as it were a voice in the midst of the four living creatures, saying: A quart of wheat for a denarius, and three quarts of barley for a denarius, and see thou hurt not the wine and the oil.

The third horse is black, and the rider bears no weapon. He carries a pair of scales. One of the four creatures says, "A quart of wheat for a denarius, and three quarts of barley for a denarius," and these high prices signal economic collapse. This is a tenfold increase of the price of food. A denarius is a day's salary for a laborer. Imagine working an entire day for a quart of wheat—barely enough to eat. And yet "hurt not the wine and the oil"—these are items of luxury and wealth. Does this mean that the poor will suffer while the rich shall prosper? It might be that wine and oil refer to the matter of the sacraments, but that is incorrect because wheat also belongs to the matter of the sacraments. The meaning is not clear now, but it will be at the end.

Fourth Seal Opened and Pale Horse (Apoc 6:7–8)

[7] And when he had opened the fourth seal, I heard the voice of the fourth living creature, saying: Come, and see.

[8] And behold a pale horse, and he that sat upon him, his name was Death, and Hell followed him. And power was given to him over the four parts of the

earth, to kill with sword, with famine, and with death, and with the beasts of the earth.

The fourth horse is pale—a color of lifelessness. The rider is named Death, and he leads an army called Hell (*Hades* in Greek). He brings four scourges on earth to kill with sword, famine, death, and beasts of the earth. This is word for word what we find centuries before in the prophet Ezechiel: "For thus saith the Lord: Although I shall send in upon Jerusalem my four grievous judgments, the sword, and the famine, and the mischievous beasts, and the pestilence." (Eze 14:21) The four curses come from God upon Jerusalem as judgment for sin, just as we see Jesus Christ releasing the riders as He breaks each seal. This red rider may be the Antichrist and his army—known later as Gog and Magog, which we shall discuss later. Moreover, red is the color of blood, Satan, and the Beast in chapter 13. The identification with the Antichrist seems correct because the next seal reveals countless glorious martyrs killed under the future reign of the Antichrist.

Fifth Seal Opened and the Martyrs (Apoc 6:9–11)

⁹ And when he had opened the fifth seal, I saw under the altar the souls of them that were slain for the word of God, and for the testimony which they held.
¹⁰ And they cried with a loud voice, saying: How long, O Lord (holy and true) dost thou not judge and revenge our blood on them that dwell on the earth?
¹¹ And white robes were given to every one of them one; and it was said to them, that they should rest for a little time, till their fellow servants, and their brethren, who are to be slain, even as they, should be filled up.

The fifth seal reveals the Christian souls appearing "under the altar." They were slain for the Logos of God and for their "testimony," which in Greek is μαρτυρίαν, or *martyrian*. Souls are under the altar because the blood of the animal sacrifices in the Old Testament were poured out at the foot of the altar and Leviticus 17:11 says, "the soul of the flesh is in the blood."

The martyred souls join the Lamb of God perfectly at the heavenly altar of sacrifice. In her earliest days, the Catholic Church built her eucharistic altars on top of the tombs of the martyrs. The belief is that the sacrifice of the martyr echoes the sacrifice of Christ. Christ as Lamb is *upon* the altar, and the martyred saints are *under* the altar. Up until the Second Vatican Council (1962–1965), all Catholic altars contained a cavity that contained the relics (remains) of at least one saint. Saint Ambrose specifically mentions the importance of installing the relics of a saint in a church's altar.[83]

The martyrs ask the Lord how much longer until He will judge and revenge their blood. As sacrificial victims, these martyrs cry out just as "the blood of Abel cried out" to God in Genesis 4:10. No answer is given, but the Apocalypse will reveal how Christ avenges their deaths. Each martyr receives a white robe, a sign of baptism, and is told they should rest for a "little time" until the full number of the saints is "filled up." This "little time" is three and a half years, as we shall see when we learn about the Antichrist's rule upon the earth.

We now prepare for the sixth seal and the dissolution of creation. God created the world in six days and rested on the seventh day. The breaking of the sixth seal triggers the dissolution of creation. Christ as Logos created creation perfectly. The number six is especially evil, and the sixth seal shows the undoing of creation. This is the rule of the Antichrist who is Anti-Logos. As Jesus removes His power,

---

[83] One ancient example is the consecration of the Basilica Romana by Saint Ambrose with relics of Saint Peter and Saint Paul. See *Vita Ambros.*, by Paulinus, c. xxxiii. The ritual for consecrating altars in the early Gelasian Sacramentary is from of funeral liturgy, because the rite includes the entombing the saints' remains inside the altar. See also Hassett, Maurice. "History of the Christian Altar." *The Catholic Encyclopedia.* Vol. 1. New York: Robert Appleton Company, 1907.

creation begins to collapse and dissolve. The rule of Christ gives way to the rule of the Antichrist.

Sixth Seal: Creation Falls Apart (Apoc 6:12–17)

[12] And I saw, when he had opened the sixth seal, and behold there was a great earthquake, and the sun became black as sackcloth of hair: and the whole moon became as blood:

[13] And the stars from heaven fell upon the earth, as the fig tree casteth its green figs when it is shaken by a great wind:

[14] And the heaven departed as a book folded up: and every mountain, and the islands were moved out of their places.

[15] And the kings of the earth, and the princes, and tribunes, and the rich, and the strong, and every bondman, and every freeman, hid themselves in the dens and in the rocks of mountains:

[16] And they say to the mountains and the rocks: Fall upon us, and hide us from the face of him that sitteth upon the throne and from the wrath of the Lamb:

[17] For the great day of their wrath is come, and who shall be able to stand?

This stage after the sixth seal begins with a great earthquake. After this earthquake, the hierarchy of creation falls apart in order. The order of the sevenfold dissolution is as follows:

1) Great earthquake
2) Sun turns black
3) Moon turns to blood
4) Stars fall
5) Heaven folds up
6) Mountains and islands move
7) Humans hide themselves inside mountains and rocks

The mention of humans calling for the mountains to fall down to hide them comes from the prophet Osee (Hosea), who describes the punishment of God when He comes against the "sin of Israel" (Hos 10:7–8) Why do humans hide? They are afraid of Jesus Christ. "Hide us from the face of him that sitteth upon the throne and from the wrath of the Lamb" (Apoc 6:16). Many people wrongly believe God in the Old Testament was wrathful and He became suddenly peacefully tolerant in the New Testament. Not so. The wrath of the Lamb is terrifying.

Sign of the Cross on the Forehead (Apocalypse 7)

The Antichrist's tribulation as the dissolution of creation reveals the full number of saints as the true Israel. We already saw four horsemen associated with the four winds. Now again we see four wind angels standing at the four corners of the earth. Are these the four creatures? Perhaps so. They withhold the wind, a sign of the Holy Ghost.

God Signs Faithful on the Forehead (Apoc 7:1–4)

[1] After these things, I saw four angels standing on the four corners of the earth, holding the four winds of the earth, that they should not blow upon the earth, nor upon the sea, nor on any tree.

[2] And I saw another angel ascending from the rising of the sun, having the sign of the living God; and he cried with a loud voice to the four angels, to whom it was given to hurt the earth and the sea,

[3] Saying: Hurt not the earth, nor the sea, nor the trees, till we sign the servants of our God in their foreheads.

[4] And I heard the number of them that were signed, a hundred forty-four thousand were signed, of every tribe of the children of Israel.

Another angel, not one of the four wind angels, ascends from the rising sun. Who is this angel? It is Jesus Christ. He is one that ascended, and He comes from the rising of the sun. This refers to what Jesus taught when He said: "For as lightning cometh out of the east, and appeareth even into the west: so shall the coming of the Son of Man be" (Mt 24:27). God also taught the Jews that He always comes from the east where the sun rises.[84] Malachias calls the Messiah the "Sun of justice" (Mal 4:2). This is why the door of the

---

[84] For God's coming from the rising of the sun, see Isaias 41, 46:11 and Ezechiel 43:1–3.

temple in Jerusalem was to the east—so that God, with the sunrise, could daily enter it from the east. Zecharias, John the Baptist's father, specifically called Jesus Christ the sunrise who has visited us (Lk 1:78).

Should we be concerned that Christ is called an angel? Is this Christological heresy? Christ does not belong to angelic nature. He is the Second Person of the Trinity and fully God. Through the incarnation in the immaculate womb of Mary, He became fully man by assuming a full human nature—body, blood, soul, and will.

The mystery is solved when we understand the word "angel" in Hebrew and Greek. In Hebrew, the word for "angel" is מלאך, or *malak*, and all it means is "messenger." Likewise in Greek, the word *angelos* literally means "messenger." What we usually call angels are in fact the "ministering spirits" before God, such as Michael, Gabriel, and Raphael. They are each called *angelos* because they are messengers between God and men. Also, John the Baptist was an *angelos* of God by being a messenger of God.[85] But John the Baptist was a human and not like one of the ministering spirits before God. And Christ is also the messenger of God by being the Logos and priestly Mediator of the New Testament.

The Greek Church Fathers (for example, Saint Athanasius) are convinced that the angel messenger of the Lord is the pre-incarnate Christ.[86] They posit that the angel of the Lord is categorically different from lower angelic beings (as in the epistle to the Hebrews) and use this

---

[85] Mark 1:2: "As it is written in Isaias the prophet: Behold I send my *angel* before thy face, who shall prepare the way before thee."

[86] For more references to the Angel/Messenger of the Lord as the pre-incarnate Christ see also: Justin Martyr, *Dialogue with Trypho*, 58–61, 76, 86, 116, 126–128; Irenaeus, *Against Heresies*, 3.6.1–5, *Fragments*, 53; Tertullian, *Against Praxeas*, 16, *De Carne*, 14, *Against Marcion* 2.27, 3.9; Novatian, *De Trinitate*, 18, 19, 31; *Apostolic Constitutions*, 5.3.20; Clement of Alexandria, *The Instructor*, 1.7; Eusebius, *The Proof of the Gospel*, 1.5, 4.10, 5.10, *Church History*, 1.2.7–8, *Preparation for the Gospel*, VII. 5, 14–15; Origen, *Contra Celsus*, 5.53, 8.27; Methodious, *Symposium*, 3.4; Melito, *New Fragments*, 15; Ambrose, *Exposition of the Christian Faith*, 1.13.83; Athanasius, *Against the Arians*, 3.25.12–14; Gregory of Nyssa, *Against Eunomius*, 11.3.

distinction to refute Arian heretics who deny the divinity of Christ. We find the identity of the angel of the Lord with the pre-incarnate Christ also in the early Latin fathers, such as Saint Justin Martyr, Tertullian, Saint Hilary of Poitiers, and Saint Ambrose.

In Latin, the word is translated from Greek as *angelus*, or "angel" or "angelic being." In Greek, it's not a problem. But in the Latin West, there was a worry that identifying Christ as the angel of the Lord would lead to Arianism since "angel" in Latin implies a lower created being. (Jehovah's Witnesses make this very mistake.)

By the era of Saint Augustine in the 400's, the Latin Church is reading "angel of the Lord" as merely a chief angelic being or generic theophany of God, not as the pre-incarnate Christ. However, Saint Ambrose believed the angel of the Lord was the pre-incarnate Christ. Augustine does, however, grant that sometimes "angel of the Lord" is a reference to the pre-incarnate Christ, such as at Isaias 9:6 in the Septuagint, where Christ is called "Prince of Peace" and "Angel of Great Counsel."[87]

We can see in the opening books of the Bible that the angel messenger of the Lord is divine and speaks as God and is recognized as God:

- *In Genesis 16:7–14.* The angel messenger of the Lord speaks as God in the first person, and in verse 13 Hagar identifies "the LORD that spoke to her" as "Thou God sees me."
- *In Genesis 22:11–15.* The angel messenger of the Lord appears to Abraham and refers to God in the first person.
- *In Genesis 31:11–13.* The angel messenger of God says, "I am the God of Bethel."

---

[87] The Greek for Angels of the Great Counsel is μεγάλης βουλῆς ἄγγελος.

- *In Exodus 3:2–4.* The angel messenger of the Lord appears to Moses in a flame in verse 2, and God speaks to Moses from the flame in verse 4.

According to Saint Athanasius and Saint Hilary of Poitiers, in all these cases we have the Logos, or Second Person of the Trinity, acting as the divine Word or message to the people of God. If Christ is the Word of the Father, then we might expect Him to function in the Old Testament as the message or messenger of God.

Irenaeus of Lyons also identifies the angel messenger of the Lord with God the Son in Exodus 3:8: "And again, when the Son speaks to Moses, He says, I have come down to deliver this people."[88] Saint Hilary of Poitiers writes:

> To discriminate clearly between the Persons, He is called the Angel of God; He Who is God from God is also the Angel of God, but, that He may have the honor which is His due, He is entitled also Lord and God."[89]

Thomas Aquinas argues that the "Angel of Sacrifice" of the eucharistic liturgy of the Roman Canon is Christ Himself,[90] so there is no Christological heresy involved in seeing this angel of the sun as Jesus Christ. Moreover, he bears "the sign of the living God." This sign is a seal. The same Greek word used here for "seal" (*sphragis*) is also used for the seven seals on the scroll. But Jesus Christ doesn't apply this seal to books. He applies the seal of the living God to the foreheads of people. The Apostle Paul also uses the same Greek word for a seal having been already applied to Christians: "But the sure foundation of God standeth firm, having this seal: the Lord knoweth who are his; and let every one depart from iniquity who nameth the name of the

---

[88] Irenaeus, *Adversus haereses,* III, 6.
[89] *De Trinitate,* IV
[90] Thomas Aquinas, *Summa Theologiae* III q. 83, a. 4, ad 9.

Lord" (2 Tim 2:19). And again: "you were signed with the Holy Spirit of promise" (Eph 1:13).

What is this seal? It is the sign of the cross. We know this from the prophet Ezechiel. During the time of Ezechiel, God punished Jerusalem with death. Yet before the people were to be slain for their sins, God sent an angel into the streets to mark the foreheads of His righteous ones:

Ezechiel Sees the T Placed on Foreheads (Eze 9:4)
Go through the midst of the city, through the midst of Jerusalem: and mark *Tau* upon the foreheads of the men that sigh, and mourn for all the abominations that are committed in the midst thereof.

The letter tau in Greek is shaped like a *T*, and in ancient Hebrew it was also shaped like a *T*. So the seal of God is placed on the forehead as the sign of the cross. Tertullian noted that "the form of the cross which He predicted would be the sign on our foreheads in the true Catholic Jerusalem."[91] In his commentary on Ezechiel, Origen interprets the meaning of the mark:

The shape of the letter "Tau" presented a resemblance to the figure of the Cross and that therein was contained a prophecy of the sign which is made by Christians upon their foreheads, for all the faithful make this sign in commencing any undertaking and especially at the beginning of prayer or of reading Holy Scripture.[92]

Saint Hippolytus (d. 236) records the same sign on the forehead:

At every forward step and movement, at every going in and out, when we put on our clothes and shoes, when

---

[91] Tertullian, *Against Marcion*, 3, 22.
[92] Origen, *In Ezechiel* 3.

we bathe, when we sit at table, when we light the lamps, on couch, on seat, in all the ordinary actions of daily life, we trace upon the forehead the sign.[93]

In the North African church, Saint Cyprian, Bishop of Carthage (d. ca. 258), also describes the sign of the cross placed on the foreheads of Christians:

> This (the letter Tau) bears a resemblance to the figure of the cross; and this prophecy (Eze 9:4) is said to regard the sign made by Christians on the forehead, which all believers make whatsoever work they begin upon, and especially at the beginning of prayers, or of holy readings.[94]

Moreover, after the earliest Christians were baptized, the bishop laid hands on them, invoked the Holy Spirit into them, and then sealed them with chrism oil on the forehead with the sign of the cross. This is the sacrament of confirmation. As the seal is applied, we see the full number of Israel constituted:

12 Tribes (But Not Dan) in Heaven (Apoc 7: 5–8)

[5] Of the tribe of Juda, were twelve thousand signed: Of the tribe of Ruben, twelve thousand signed: Of the tribe of Gad, twelve thousand signed:
[6] Of the tribe of Aser, twelve thousand signed: Of the tribe of Nephthali, twelve thousand signed: Of the tribe of Manasses, twelve thousand signed:
[7] Of the tribe of Simeon, twelve thousand signed: Of the tribe of Levi, twelve thousand signed: Of the tribe of Issachar, twelve thousand signed:
[8] Of the tribe of Zabulon, twelve thousand signed: Of the tribe of Joseph, twelve thousand signed: Of the tribe of Benjamin, twelve thousand signed.

---

[93] Hippolytus, *De Corona* 3.
[94] Cyprian of Carthage, *Select. in Eze* c. ix.

Twelve thousand people from each of the twelve tribes of Israel are signed on the forehead. 12 times 12,000 yields 144,000 people. Heretics, such as the Jehovah's Witnesses, have interpreted this to mean that *only* 144,000 people will enter heaven. This is nonsense. The number 144,000 is one of perfection: 12 × 12 × 1,000. It signifies that Israel is now perfect.

In the Apocalypse, Judah is listed first because Jesus Christ was born of the tribe of Judah—King David's tribe. Missing from the Apocalypse list is the tribe of Dan. The reason, according to most early biblical commentators, is that the Antichrist will be born of the tribe of Dan. Dan was also Jacob's first baby born of a servant girl outside of formal wedlock. We will discuss this below in our section on the Antichrist. Manasses, the grandson of Jacob, is added to the list to replace Dan.

Great Multitude Baptized (Apoc 7:9–10)
⁹ After this I saw a great multitude, which no man could number, of all nations, and tribes, and peoples, and tongues, standing before the throne, and in sight of the Lamb, clothed with white robes, and palms in their hands:
¹⁰ And they cried with a loud voice, saying: Salvation to our God, who sitteth upon the throne, and to the Lamb.

After the 144,000 are sealed on their foreheads, John sees "a great multitude, which no man could number." This great number is the same as the 144,000, and this proves that the number is not literal but symbolic. They wear white baptismal robes and carry palms in their hands. Palms are a symbol of royal victory. Palms were also used symbolically by the Maccabees when they defeated the wicked king and rededicated the temple (1 Mac 13:51). This is why the Jews celebrated with palms when Christ entered Jerusalem on

Palm Sunday before His crucifixion. They cry out hosanna, which means salvation, to God the Father and to the Lamb, who is Jesus.

Who Are These Clothed in White? (Apoc 7:11–17)

[11] And all the angels stood round about the throne, and the presbyters, and the four living creatures; and they fell down before the throne upon their faces, and adored God,

[12] Saying: Amen. Benediction, and glory, and wisdom, and thanksgiving, honour, and power, and strength to our God for ever and ever. Amen.

[13] And one of the presbyters answered, and said to me: These that are clothed in white robes, who are they? and whence came they?

[14] And I said to him: My Lord, thou knowest. And he said to me: These are they who are come out of great tribulation, and have washed their robes, and have made them white in the blood of the Lamb.

[15] Therefore they are before the throne of God, and they serve him day and night in his temple: and he, that sitteth on the throne, shall dwell over them.

[16] They shall no more hunger nor thirst, neither shall the sun fall on them, nor any heat.

[17] For the Lamb, which is in the midst of the throne, shall rule them, and shall lead them to the fountains of the waters of life, and God shall wipe away all tears from their eyes.

Their robes are made white in the blood of Christ—a reference to baptism. This great multitude is the full number of the saints from the time of Jesus Christ and his first martyr Stephen the deacon, all the way up to the martyrs of the Great Tribulation (v. 14). This is the final Great Tribulation that Christ spoke of in Matthew 24:21. The first six seals also correspond to the events foretold by Christ in the so-called Little Apocalypse of Matthew 24:

Jesus Christ Describing the Great Tribulation (Mt 24:4–16)

⁴ And Jesus answering, said to them: Take heed that no man seduce you:

⁵ For many will come in my name saying, I am Christ: and they will seduce many.

⁶ And you shall hear of wars and rumours of wars. See that ye be not troubled. For these things must come to pass, but the end is not yet.

⁷ For nation shall rise against nation, and kingdom against kingdom; and there shall be pestilences, and famines, and earthquakes in places:

⁸ Now all these are the beginnings of sorrows.

⁹ Then shall they deliver you up to be afflicted, and shall put you to death: and you shall be hated by all nations for my name's sake.

¹⁰ And then shall many be scandalized: and shall betray one another: and shall hate one another.

¹¹ And many false prophets shall rise, and shall seduce many.

¹² And because iniquity hath abounded, the charity of many shall grow cold.

¹³ But he that shall persevere to the end, he shall be saved.

¹⁴ And this gospel of the kingdom, shall be preached in the whole world, for a testimony to all nations, and then shall the consummation come.

¹⁵ When therefore you shall see the abomination of desolation, which was spoken of by Daniel the prophet, standing in the holy place: he that readeth let him understand.

¹⁶ Then they that are in Judea, let them flee to the mountains.

Compare the description of Christ's foretelling of the Great Tribulation above with the action released by His first six seals so far:

Six Seals in Apocalypse 6 and 7	Christ's Tribulation in Mt 24
1st Seal: Christ conquers world with Gospel (6:2)	Gospel preached in whole world (14)
2nd Seal: Wars (6:3–4)	Wars and Rumors of Wars (6-7)
3rd Seal: Famines (6:5–6)	Famines (7)
4th Seal: "with sword, with famine, and with death, and with the beasts of the earth" (6:8)	Pestilences (7)
5th Seal: Martyrdom (6:9–11)	Martyrdom, betrayal, false prophets (9–11)
Fleeing to mountains (6:15–17)	Fleeing to mountains (16)
6th Seal: Earthquake & Baptisms (7)	Earthquakes (7)

The order of the events is not precise because the Apocalypse is not written to be read in sequential order. It repeats and reprises themes. It replays them again and again with different names, details, and symbols. The Apocalypse is telescoped and interlinked. The three final verses of this section describe the end of time after Christ has judged the world and restored all things. The references to wiping away tears and providing springs of water all derive from Isaias 49. The story could end here, but the vision will continue to swirl and retell the same events. Next, Christ will open the seventh seal, and this will remix and redescribe everything we have seen, but this time the seventh seal will trigger the seven trumpets.

The Seven Trumpets (Apocalypse 8)

The seven trumpets are the middle third of the twenty-one prophetic events. The first was the seven churches with seven messages. The second was the seven seals. Now the seventh seal triggers the seven trumpets. This section features all the well-known features of the Apocalypse: the two witnesses, the dragon, the sea beast Antichrist, the land beast False Prophet, the mark of the beast and 666, and the royal Woman who births Christ. This section of seven trumpets is where most people camp out because the visions are vivid and capture our imaginations.

The Seventh Seal Opened: Silence (Apoc 8:1–2)

[1] And when he had opened the seventh seal, there was silence in heaven, as it were for half an hour.

[2] And I saw seven angels standing in the presence of God; and there were given to them seven trumpets.

The eighth chapter of the Apocalypse contains the first four of the seven trumpets. When the Lamb of God, who is Jesus, breaks open the seventh seal, there is total silence in heaven for half an hour. Why is there silence for half an hour (thirty minutes)? We have established already that all numbers in the Apocalypse are symbolic. Several scholars have suggested that the Old Testament temple had an "intermission" of about a half hour when the incense was prepared in silence and that the Apocalypse is referencing this moment.[95] The significance more likely refers to the use of "hour" by Saint John in the rest of the book. Elsewhere, he speaks of ten kings receiving power for one hour after

---

[95] The thesis that the half-hour silence is actually an "intermission for incense" is suggested by Terry Milton, *Biblical Apocalyptics: A Study of the Most Notable Revelations of God and of Christ in the Canonical Scriptures* (New York: Eaton and Mains, 1898), pp. 343f; Alfred Edersheim, *The Temple: Its Ministry and Services as They Were at the Time of Jesus Christ* (Grand Rapids: William B. Eerdmans, 1980), pp. 167f; and thirdly by David Chilton, *The Days of Vengeance An Exposition of the Book of Revelation* (Horn Lake, MS: Dominion, 2006, pp. 329–330.

the beast who is Antichrist: "And the ten horns which thou sawest, are ten kings, who have not yet received a kingdom, but shall receive power as kings one hour after the beast" (Apoc 17:12). This hour is a short time, but the tribulation is often referred to as "half a week" or "three and a half years." The half of seven, half a week, and half an hour refer to this time of tribulation when the Antichrist persecutes the earth. Satan is released, and heaven falls silent for half a time.

The silence leads to seven angels assembling with their trumpets. We have seen seven angels previously. Christ, through John, sent seven messages to each of the seven angels (likely the seven human bishops of each of the seven churches). But there are also seven angels that stand before God. Saint John reaffirms the text of Tobit 12:15: "I am the angel Raphael, one of the seven who stand before the Lord." The seven angels are the created ministers of the sevenfold Holy Spirit.

In the Old Testament, trumpets were used to announce destruction (as in the fall of Jericho), to announce a new king, and to call people to worship on feast days (Num 10:1–10). These seven angels accomplish all three: they announce the destruction of the evil and the Antichrist, they announce Christ as the new King, and they call the Church to worship the Lamb.

An Angel Casts a Burning Censer on Earth (Apoc 8:3–6)

³ And another angel came, and stood before the altar, having a golden censer; and there was given to him much incense, that he should offer of the prayers of all saints upon the golden altar, which is before the throne of God.

⁴ And the smoke of the incense of the prayers of the saints ascended up before God from the hand of the angel.

⁵ And the angel took the censer, and filled it with the fire of the altar, and cast it on the earth, and there were thunders and voices and lightnings, and a great earthquake.

⁶ And the seven angels, who had the seven trumpets, prepared themselves to sound the trumpet.

Another angel, not one of the seven, appears and stands before the altar holding a golden censer. He is given "much incense," which he offers upon the golden altar. The incense, we are shown, is the prayer of all the saints. This passage reveals that angels (and humans) offer the "prayers of all the saints" to God. Jesus Christ is the Mediator between God and man, but angels and humans in heaven participate by offering these prayers to God the Father through Christ. The cloud of prayers rises before God.

Next, this angel performs an act of liturgical wrath. After the incense ascends before God, he fills the censer with fire from the altar (holy fire) and "casts it on the earth, and there were thunders and voices and lightnings." This same thing happened to Moses and the people "on the third day" in the book of Exodus:

Moses on the Mount with Thunder, Lightning, Cloud, Fire, and Smoke (Ex 19:16, 18)

¹⁶ And now the *third day* was come, and the morning appeared: and *behold thunders began to be heard, and lightning to flash, and a very thick cloud to cover the mount, and the noise of the trumpet* sounded exceeding loud, and the people that was in the camp, feared. . . .

¹⁸ And all mount Sinai was on a smoke: because the Lord was come *down upon it in fire, and the smoke arose* from it as out of a furnace: and all the mount was terrible.

Fire, smoke, cloud, thunders, lightning flashes. It's all there when God gives the Old Covenant to Israel. And it is here again when Christ opens the New Covenant to the Church.

This action produces "a great earthquake," an event we have already covered. The reoccurrence of this great earthquake again confirms that the Apocalypse is not a strictly chronological account of the end times. It is circular and interlinked. The earthquake begins the sequence of seven trumpets:

First Trumpet: Hail Fire Blood (Apoc 8:7)

And the first angel sounded the trumpet, and there followed hail and fire, mingled with blood, and it was cast on the earth, and the third part of the earth was burnt up, and the third part of the trees was burnt up, and all green grass was burnt up.

The first angel's trumpet leads to hail and fire mingled with blood. This is cast down upon the earth, and a third of the earth, trees, and grass burn up. The number here is three. The *threefold* curse of hail, fire, and blood causes a *one-third* destruction of *three things*: earth, trees, and grass. The green trees signify the righteous man: "And he shall be like a tree which is planted near the running waters, which shall bring forth its fruit, in due season. And his leaf shall not fall off: and all whatsoever he shall do shall prosper" (Ps 1:3). Men appearing as trees is also the first thing the blind man sees when Christ heals him: "And looking up, he said: I see men as it were trees, walking" (Mk 8:24). One-third of the angels fell from grace. And the scorching of a third here also likely refers to apostasy from Christ—the righteous becoming wicked.

Second Trumpet: Mountain Cast into the Sea (Apoc 8:8–9)

⁸ And the second angel sounded the trumpet: and as it were a great mountain, burning with fire, was cast into the sea, and the third part of the sea became blood:

⁹ And the third part of those creatures died, which had life in the sea, and the third part of the ships was destroyed.

The second angel blows his trumpet, and a burning mountain is cast into the sea, leading to a threefold catastrophe: a third of the sea becomes blood, a third of all water creatures die, and a third of the ships are sunk. The first trumpet angel destroys the land. The second angel destroys the sea. The burning mountain is the holy mountain of Moses that we discussed above. However, it is also wicked Jerusalem. The prophet Jeremias addresses idolatrous Babylon as a burned and destroying mountain:

Jeremias calls Jerusalem the Destroying Burnt Mountain (Jer 51:25–26)
²⁵Behold I come against thee, thou destroying mountain, saith the Lord, which corruptest the whole earth: and I will stretch out my hand upon thee, and will roll thee down from the rocks, and will make thee a burnt mountain.
²⁶And they shall not take of thee a stone for the corner, nor a stone for foundations, but thou shalt be destroyed forever, saith the Lord.

Jesus calls Jerusalem as "This Mountain" (Mt 21:21)
And Jesus answering, said to them: Amen, I say to you, if you shall have faith, and stagger not, not only this of the fig tree shall you do, but also if you shall say to this mountain, 'Take up and cast thyself into the sea,' it shall be done.

Jesus says this to His apostles after He enters Jerusalem. He is not talking about Christians praying and uprooting the Ural Mountains or the Rocky Mountains. Jesus Christ is giving an apocalyptic lesson about Jerusalem as the apostate mountain now identified as the wicked burnt mountain of Babylon thrown into the sea (Jer 51:42). In the Apocalypse, Jesus Christ shows us that this cursed and burning mountain (Jerusalem united to Babylone) is in fact cast into the sea. The sea, as we shall see in future chapters is a symbol of the nations. This is why the Antichrist is called the beast from the sea. Christ our Lord is telling His twelve apostles to have faith and say to this mountain Jerusalem: "Take up and cast thyself into the sea."

Third Trumpet: Fall of Lucifer (Apoc 8:10–11)
[10] And the third angel sounded the trumpet, and a great star fell from heaven, burning as it were a torch, and it fell on the third part of the rivers, and upon the fountains of waters:
[11] And the name of the star is called Wormwood. And the third part of the waters became wormwood; and many men died of the waters, because they were made bitter.

The third angel blows the third trumpet, and it triggers a great star falling from heaven, burning as a torch. The image of the "falling star" goes back to the prophet Isaias, who describes the fall of Babylon in terms of the fall of Satan as a falling star. But this fall of the king of Babylon is worded as the fall of Satan from heaven. Here is the passage from Isaias:

Isaias Foretells Fall of Lucifer (Isa 14:12–16, 22)
[12] How art thou fallen from heaven, O *Lucifer*, who didst rise in the morning? how art thou fallen to the earth, that didst wound the nations?
[13] And thou saidst in thy heart: I will ascend into heaven, I will exalt my throne above the stars of God, I will sit in the *mountain* of the covenant, in the sides of the north.[96]

---

[96] The north is associated with the dwelling of Satan. For this reason, the Gospel lessons are read on the north side of the altar during the traditional Latin Mass.

¹⁴ I will ascend above the height of the *clouds*, I will be like the most High.
¹⁵ But yet thou shalt be brought down to hell, into the depth of the pit.
¹⁶ They that shall see thee, shall turn toward thee, and behold thee. Is this the man that troubled the earth, that shook kingdoms,
²² And I will rise up against them, saith the Lord of hosts: and I will destroy the name of *Babylon*, and the remains, and the bud, and the offspring, saith the Lord.

The morning star is the first visible planet of the morning: Venus. In Hebrew, the Jews referred to the planet Venus as the morning star *Heylel*. The Greek Septuagint version of the Bible translates the Hebrew *Heylel* into Greek as *Heosphoros*, or "Dawnbearer."[97] The Romans referred to the planet in Latin as *Luciferus*, meaning "light-bearer," and it was depicted in art as a man carrying a torch—hence the reference to the star as a torch in Apocalypse 8:10. Apart from the sun or moon, the planet Venus is the brightest celestial body in the sky, and it appears before the sun every morning. Isaias the prophet uses the struggle between the sun and morning star as the battle between the enormous light of the sun (God) and the brightest lesser light that is overcome by the sun (Satan). The ancient middle eastern solar myth portrays the morning star as a lesser demigod who jumps ahead during the night and attempts to shine before the highest god (symbolized by the sun) has a chance to rise. This lesser light attempts to dethrone the highest god. But as the sun breaks above the horizon, his light overcomes the lesser light of the morning star, which disappears to the human eye. This morning battle reveals how the haughty morning star fails to reach the highest point in the sky before being outshone by the rising sun.

---

[97] See the Septuagint text Isaias 14:12: πῶς ἐξέπεσεν ἐκ τοῦ οὐρανοῦ ὁ ἑωσφόρος ὁ πρωὶ ἀνατέλλων συνετρίβη εἰς τὴν γῆν ὁ ἀποστέλλων πρὸς πάντα τὰ ἔθνη.

Every ancient person was aware of this heavenly phenomenon.[98]

The prophet Isaias applies this solar myth to the king of Babylon, but also to its original reference as the fall of Satan, who tried to outshine God through his pride. Satan was the brightest star, but he attempted to beat God at being the light-bearer (*Lucifer*). The New Testament reinterprets the solar myth and sees Jesus Christ as the true morning star and light-bearer. Christ says in Apoc 22:16: "I Jesus have sent my angel, to testify to you these things in the churches. I am the root and stock of David, the bright and morning star." Christ, like the morning star, rose from the dead *before sunlight* on Sunday morning. He is the Light of the World but does not compete with God. Rather, he illuminates all men (Jn 1:9) to be partakers of the divine nature (2 Pet 1:4). This is why the deacon stands before the paschal candle in the ancient Roman Rite and chants in the *Exultet* on the day before Easter. At the end of the prayer, he addresses Jesus Christ as Lucifer. Lucifer is the morning star, and Christ says He is for us the morning star (light-bearer) by rising from the dead before sunlight. Toward the end of the Easter *Exultet* the deacon chants:

Latin Text of Easter Exultet:	English text of Easter Exultet:
Flammas eius lúcifer matutínus invéniat:	May the Morning **Daystar** find its flame:
ille, inquam, lúcifer, qui nescit occásum.	That **Daystar** which knoweth no setting:
qui, regréssus ab ínferis,	Who returning from the grave,
humáno géneri serénus illúxit.	has shed serene light on the human race.

Catholics should have no scruples in naming Christ as the morning star or *lúcifer matutínus*. Jesus Christ, not Satan, is the true light-bearer ("Light from Light") for the human race. It is theologically incorrect to say that Satan is a "light-bearer" or *luciferus* after his fall from heaven.

---

[98] See Hermann Gunkel, "Isa 14:12–14 (pp. 89ff.)" *Creation and Chaos in the Primeval Era and the Eschaton. A Religio-historical Study of Genesis 1 and Revelation 12.* Contributor Heinrich Zimmern, foreword by Peter Machinist, translated by K. William Whitney Jr. Grand Rapids, Michigan: Wm. B. Eerdmans, 2006.

At the third trumpet, Satan is cast down to the earth and the sea. Later, we will find this warning in Apocalypse 12:12: "Woe to the earth, and to the sea, because the devil is come down unto you, having great wrath." Satan's sin is described by Isaias as self-deification: "I will exalt my throne above the stars of God, I will sit in the mountain of the covenant, in the sides of the north" (Isa 14:13). Satanism is not a "belief in Satan" but the false pursuit to deify oneself. This is the sin of the king of Babylon—he made himself into a god. And this will be the supreme sin of the Antichrist—he will claim to be God and enthrone himself as such in Jerusalem.

The fallen star who is Satan will fall upon the third part of the rivers and the fountains of water. The waters will become bitter and people will die. The star that falls upon the drinking water of mankind is not just named *Lucifer*, but also wormwood. The original Greek word for "wormwood" used by Saint John is *apsinthos*. It comes into English as "absinthe," which is best known as the bitter hallucinogenic substance consumed by Ernest Hemingway, James Joyce, Pablo Picasso, Vincent van Gogh, Oscar Wilde, Marcel Proust, Aleister Crowley, Edgar Allan Poe, and Lord Byron. It makes the earth's water bitter and deadly. The prophet Jeremias explains how God will punish Jerusalem with this bitter wormwood (absinthe): "Therefore thus saith the Lord of hosts to the prophets: Behold I will feed them with wormwood, and will give them gall to drink: for from the prophets of Jerusalem corruption has gone forth into all the land" (Jer 23:15). The prophet Amos also features wormwood in judgment: "You that turn judgment into wormwood, and forsake justice in the land" (Amos 5:7).

Fourth Trumpet: One-Third of the Sun, Moon, Stars Smitten (Apoc 8:12–13)

[12] And the fourth angel sounded the trumpet, and the third part of the sun was smitten, and the third part of the moon, and the third part of the stars, so that the

third part of them was darkened, and the day did not shine for a third part of it, and the night in like manner. ¹³ And I beheld, and heard the voice of one eagle flying through the midst of heaven, saying with a loud voice: Woe, woe, woe to the inhabitants of the earth: by reason of the rest of the voices of the three angels, who are yet to sound the trumpet.

The first three angels and their trumpets trigger death on earth, in the salt seas, and then in the freshwater sources. The fourth trumpet angel triggers destruction upon the heavens. One-third of the sun, one-third of the moon, and one-third of the stars are darkened. They don't shine for a third of the day and night. This conforms to the dissolving of creation as the Logos removes His influence and the Antichrist arises.

After the four trumpets, we have an interlude with the eagle flying in the midst of heaven, saying, "Woe, woe, woe to the inhabitants of the earth: by reason of the rest of the voices of the three angels, who are yet to sound the trumpet." Just as the four creatures say, "Holy, holy, holy," in heaven, now we have "woe, woe, woe" to those on earth. These three woes correspond exactly to the fifth, sixth, and seventh trumpets.

Locust Demons from Hell (Apocalypse 9)

The fifth trumpet (corresponding with the first woe) revisits the fallen star. The fallen star is Satan, who is also wormwood (absinthe). He goes to the abyss. The apostle Paul teaches that the word "abyss" in Greek refers to the place where Christ's soul descended after his death, and it is the place of the dead (Rom 10:7).

Fifth Trumpet: Locust Demons from Hell (Apoc 9:1–2)

[1] And the fifth angel sounded the trumpet, and I saw a star fall from heaven upon the earth, and there was given to him the key of that shaft to the abyss.[99]
[2] And he opened the shaft to the abyss: and the smoke of the pit arose, as the smoke of a great furnace; and the sun and the air were darkened with the smoke of the pit.

When the abyss is opened, there will be darkness and smoke. And then come forth the locusts:

Demon Locusts Emerge (Apoc 9:3–6)

[3] And from the smoke of the pit there came out locusts upon the earth. And power was given to them, as the scorpions of the earth have power:
[4] And it was commanded them that they should not hurt the grass of the earth, nor any green thing, nor any tree: but only the men who have not the sign of God on their foreheads.
[5] And it was given unto them that they should not kill them; but that they should torment them five months: and their torment was as the torment of a scorpion when he striketh a man.

---

[99] The Douay-Rheims translation here is unfortunately bad and breaks with the Greek and Latin. I have fixed it to be "key of that shaft to the abyss."

⁶ And in those days men shall seek death, and shall not find it: and they shall desire to die, and death shall fly from them.

The locusts come from the smoke, and their power is like that of scorpions. Jesus Christ taught that demons are serpents and scorpions. When His disciples returned to Him, they said "The devils also are subject to us in thy name. And he said to them: I saw Satan like lightning falling from heaven. Behold, I have given you power to tread upon serpents and scorpions" (Lk 10:17–20). These scorpion locusts come from hell, and so they are certainly demons—wicked angels who fell with Satan. Here we learn that "green things and trees" signify the baptized disciples of Jesus Christ. They are opposed to those "who do not have the sign of God on their foreheads." He showed previously that the seal of God on the forehead is the sacrament of baptism. The demons torment them for five months. The number is symbolic. Ancient farmers knew that locusts attacked their crops for five months—from May to September. If the locusts did not destroy the crops during those five months, then the crop would come to harvest in the autumn.

Demon Locusts Described (Apoc 9:7–10)

⁷ And the shapes of the locusts were like unto horses prepared unto battle: and on their heads were, as it were, crowns like gold: and their faces were as the faces of men.

⁸ And they had hair as the hair of women; and their teeth were as lions:

⁹ And they had breastplates as breastplates of iron, and the noise of their wings was as the noise of chariots and many horses running to battle.

¹⁰ And they had tails like to scorpions, and there were stings in their tails; and their power was to hurt men five months.

These locusts are not actually locusts. They are allegorically described as horses prepared for battle. Since all demons attempt to self-deify themselves, they wear crowns of gold. They have faces like human men but hair like women. They are transsexualized, as in the blasphemous image of Baphomet. Their teeth are like a lion's, ready to devour. They wear breastplates of iron, and they have wings making the noise of chariots and horses of war. And they have a king over them:

The Angel of the Abyss (Apoc 9:11–12)
[11] And they had over them a king, the angel of the abyss; whose name in Hebrew is Abaddon, and in Greek Apollyon; in Latin Exterminans,
[12] One woe is past, and behold there come yet two woes more hereafter.

The king of the locusts is this angel of the abyss, who is Satan. His other names are supplied in Hebrew as Abaddon, and in Greek as Apollyon, and in Latin as Exterminans. The final Latin name, Exterminans (one who exterminates), is an interpolation found in the Latin Vulgate. The fact that Saint John gives both Hebrew and Greek reveals that his Christian audience consisted of both Jewish and Gentile converts. Abaddon in Hebrew means "destruction": "Hell (Sheol) is naked before him, and there is no covering for destruction (Abaddon)" (Job 26:6). Apollyon in Greek means "destroyer." Satan destroys and exterminates. As Jesus Christ said: "The thief comes only to steal, and to kill, and to destroy" (John 10:10).

Sixth Trumpet: Demon Horses (Apoc 9:13–14)
[13] And the sixth angel sounded the trumpet: and I heard a voice from the four horns of the golden altar, which is before the eyes of God,

¹⁴ Saying to the sixth angel, who had the trumpet: Loose the four angels, who are bound in the great river Euphrates.

The sixth angel's trumpet triggers a voice from the four corners/horns of the golden altar in heaven, before the eyes of God. We are encouraged that, even in the midst of Satan and his locust demons, God still sees. The voice instructs the release of four angels bound at the River Euphrates. When we read Isaias 14:13 regarding the fall of Satan, we also read that he takes his abode "in the sides of the north." The Euphrates River was the natural northern boundary of King Solomon between the Holy Land and the pagan kings of the north. The sixth epoch of the Old Testament is the return of the Jews from exile across the Euphrates, and this reference occurs at the sixth trumpet.

One-Third Killed (Apoc 9:15–18)
¹⁵ And the four angels were loosed, who were prepared for an hour, and a day, and a month, and a year: for to kill the third part of men.
¹⁶ And the number of the army of horsemen was twenty thousand times ten thousand. And I heard the number of them.
¹⁷ And thus I saw the horses in the vision: and they that sat on them, had breastplates of fire and of hyacinth and of brimstone, and the heads of the horses were as the heads of lions: and from their mouths proceeded fire, and smoke, and brimstone.
¹⁸ And by these three plagues was slain the third part of men, by the fire and by the smoke and by the brimstone, which issued out of their mouths.

One-third of men are killed by an enormous army characterized as horses, but these horses, like the locusts, are demonic. They wear breastplates of fire, hyacinth, and brimstone. The heads of the horses are as the heads of lions.

Like Satan, from their mouths proceed fire, smoke, and brimstone. These beings are demons in the image of Satan, doing his bidding.

The Rest of Men Do Not Repent (Apoc 9:19–21)

[19] For the power of the horses is in their mouths, and in their tails. For, their tails are like to serpents, and have heads: and with them they hurt.

[20] And the rest of the men, who were not slain by these plagues, did not do penance from the works of their hands, that they should not adore devils, and idols of gold, and silver, and brass, and stone, and wood, which neither can see, nor hear, nor walk:

[21] Neither did they penance from their murders, nor from their sorceries, nor from their fornication, nor from their thefts.

The horses have power in their mouths, which are lies. They have serpentine tails like Satan, their master. The remaining two-thirds of men who survive these demonic armies did not repent of their adoration of devils and idols, neither did they repent of their murder, sorceries, fornication, or thefts. These people are entirely given to sinful wickedness.

The Mighty Messenger (Apocalypse 10)

Just as the sixth seal prepared for the seventh seal, triggering the seven trumpets, so now the sixth trumpet signals an interlude featuring the Mighty Angel or Mighty Messenger, Jesus Christ. We previously explained how the early Eastern Church and even the Western Church (prior to the normalization of Latin) were comfortable calling Jesus Christ the *angelos*, meaning "messenger."[100] However, when *angelos* comes into Latin (and English), it refers strictly to the created ministering spirits of God. As explained before, when we refer to Christ as messenger in this way, we are not denigrating His consubstantial divinity with the Father or denigrating him as a created angel.[101] Saint John reveals that the Mighty Messenger after the sixth trumpet is a reappearance of Christ:

Mighty Messenger Clothed in the Cloud, His Face as the Sun (Apoc 10:1–3)

¹ And I saw another Mighty Angel [Greek: *angelos*] come down from heaven, clothed with a cloud, and a rainbow was on his head, and his face was as the sun, and his feet as pillars of fire.

² And he had in his hand a little book open: and he set his right foot upon the sea, and his left foot upon the earth.

³ And he cried with a loud voice as when a lion roareth. And when he had cried, seven thunders uttered their voices.

Seven details about the Mighty Messenger strongly suggest that He is Jesus Christ. First, the Mighty Messenger "comes

---

100 The Greek word for "Christ's Gospel" is *euaganelion*, which means "good message."

101 See the section above on Apocalypse chapter 7 for clarification on *angelos* in the New Testament and Septuagint Old Testament in the Eastern and Western traditions.

down" from heaven and is clothed in a cloud. This cloud is the Shekinah glory cloud that surrounds God in the Old Testament and fills His temple. That same divine glory cloud also surrounds Christ, who is God:

Jesus "With the Clouds" in the New Testament

And as he was yet speaking, behold a bright *cloud* overshadowed them. And lo, a voice out of the *cloud*, saying: This is my beloved Son, in whom I am well pleased: hear ye him. (Mt 17:5, emphasis added)

And then shall appear the sign of the Son of Man in heaven: and then shall all tribes of the earth mourn: and they shall see the Son of Man *coming in the clouds* of heaven with much power and majesty. (Mt 24:30, emphasis added)

Jesus saith to him: Thou hast said it. Nevertheless I say to you, hereafter you shall see the Son of Man sitting on the right hand of the power of God, and *coming in the clouds* of heaven.[102] (Mt 26:64, emphasis added)

Only the Son of God who is the Son of Man "clothes Himself with the cloud" and "makes the clouds thy chariot" (Ps 103:3). The second detail is that the rainbow is on His head. The rainbow is the sign of the covenant with Noah, when God said to Noah, "I will set my bow in the clouds, and it shall be the sign of a covenant between me, and between the earth" (Gen 9:13). The rainbow is a bow for shooting arrows. This bow points not down to humans but up to God. It foreshadows that the heavenly Son of God will suffer and die for men. The fourth chapter of the

---

[102] The coming of the Messianic Son of Man on the clouds was foretold in Daniel 7:13: "I beheld therefore in the vision of the night, and lo, one like the Son of Man came with the clouds of heaven, and he came even to the Ancient of days: and they presented him before him."

Apocalypse shows the rainbow around the throne of God. It is a sign of divine power and mercy.

The third detail is that the face of the Mighty Messenger is like the sun. Saint John already described the face of Jesus for us in chapter 1: "His face was as the sun shineth in his power" (Apoc 1:16). During the transfiguration, Jesus Christ is surrounded by a cloud and turns white, but Matthew also describes His face: "And he was transfigured before them. And *His face did shine as the sun*, and his garments became white as snow" (Mt 17:2). When Saint John looks at the Mighty Messenger, he is seeing the transfigured Jesus Christ.

Fourth, John looks at the Mighty Messenger and sees "his feet as pillars of fire." We know this is already a description of Jesus Christ in the Apocalypse: "his feet like unto fine brass, as in a burning furnace" (Apoc 1:15). King Solomon's Canticle describes the Bridegroom's legs as "pillars" (Cant 5:15). King Solomon also "set up the two pillars in the porch of the temple" (3 Kings 7:21).

The fifth detail about this Mighty Messenger is that he has a little book in His hand. This is another sign that the Mighty Messenger is Jesus Christ. Before Moses died, he described how he once saw God: "The Lord came from Sinai . . . in his right hand a fiery law" (Deut 33:2). This little book is the scroll that the Lamb already opened by breaking the seven seals! That's why John says "a little book open." This book is the New Covenant in His blood. He sets his burning right foot on the sea and his burning left foot on the land. The sea and land signify the Gentile nations (sea) and the Jews (holy land). This Mighty Messenger is enormous with the feet on earth and His head in the rainbow of God's celestial throne. With the New Testament in His hand, He is the Mediator between heaven and earth.

The sixth detail suggesting that the Mighty Messenger is Christ is that he "cried with a loud voice as when a lion roareth. And when he had cried, seven thunders uttered their voices." This description refers to the seven seals, where the Lamb of God is said to also be the lion of Judah (Apoc 5:5). God's voice is often associated with thunder (Ps 17:14, 28:3, 76:19, 103:7 LXX).[103] An seventh detail relates to the Greek word used here by John to describe the Mighty Angel: *Ischyros Angelos*. The Church has traditionally associated Christ with the Greek word *Ischyros* in her ancient liturgical Trisagion ("Thrice Holy") chant:

Ἅγιος ὁ Θεός, Ἅγιος ἰσχυρός, Ἅγιος ἀθάνατος, ἐλέησον ἡμᾶς.
Hagios ho Theos, Hagios ischyros, Hagios athanatos, eleison hemas.

Translation:
Holy God, Holy Mighty One, Holy immortal one, have mercy on us.

In the Eastern Church, this Trisagion is chanted to Christ in the Divine Liturgy before the prokeimenon and the epistle reading. In the Roman Church, this Trisagion is chanted to Christ in both Greek and Latin on Good Friday. This ancient refrain is also found in the East Syrian, West Syrian, Armenian, and Coptic Orthodox liturgies.[104] Christ is certainly the *Ischyros*, or "Mighty One," and this liturgical tradition is one of the oldest in the Church and is universally present in the East and West.

The Messenger Swears Oath (Apoc 10:4–7)

⁴ And when the seven thunders had uttered their voices, I was about to write: and I heard a voice from heaven saying to me: Seal up the things which the seven thunders have spoken; and write them not.
⁵ And the Messenger, whom I saw standing upon the sea and upon the earth, lifted up his hand to heaven,
⁶ And he swore by him that liveth for ever and ever, who created heaven, and the things which are therein;

---

103 This book uses the Septuagint/Vulgate numbering of the Psalms.
104 Hugh Henry, "Agios O Theos," *The Catholic Encyclopedia*. Vol. 1. New York: Robert Appleton Company, 1907.

and the earth, and the things which are in it; and the sea, and the things which are therein: That time shall be no longer.

[7] But in the days of the voice of the seventh angel, when he shall begin to sound the trumpet, the mystery of God shall be finished, as he hath declared by his servants the prophets.

The seven thunders said something, and Saint John was about to write them down. This reveals that John is writing *during the vision*. But a voice says to him: "Seal up the things which the seven thunders have spoken; and write them not." So we will never know, at least in this life, what the seven thunders said. God wanted Saint John to hear this message, but not us.

Then the Messenger raises His hand to heaven and makes a covenantal oath "that the time shall be no longer." Raising one's hand is a sign of being an honest witness in court. The voice of the seventh angel says, "when he sounds his trumpet, the mystery of God shall be finished." So between the sixth and seventh trumpet, we find the Mighty Messenger standing between heaven and earth, with the open book in His hand, and making an oath.

The Messenger Feeds Scroll to John (Apoc 10:8–11)

[8] And I heard a voice from heaven again speaking to me, and saying: Go, and take the book that is open, from the hand of the Messenger who standeth upon the sea, and upon the earth.

[9] And I went to the Messenger, saying unto him, that he should give me the book. And he said to me: Take the book, and eat it up: and it shall make thy belly bitter, but in thy mouth it shall be sweet as honey.

[10] And I took the book from the hand of the Messenger, and ate it up: and it was in my mouth, sweet as honey: and when I had eaten it, my belly was bitter.

[11] And he said to me: Thou must prophesy again to many nations, and peoples, and tongues, and kings.

Saint John is next instructed to approach the Messenger and take the open book. The Messenger instructs John to eat the book, which is as sweet as honey in the mouth but bitter in his belly. Catholics will quickly recognize the words "Take, eat" as the words of Christ at the institution of the Eucharist. The Eucharist is the "New Covenant in my blood," and as such, it is the oath (Latin: *sacramentum*) of the New Covenant. In Christ, the Word is made flesh. The New Covenant is not actually an inanimate book, but the flesh and blood of Christ. Recall also that this vision happens on the Lord's Day— Sunday.

The Prophet Ezechiel once ate God's covenantal scroll as well:

The Prophet Ezechiel Also Ate a Scroll (Eze 3:1–3)
[1] And he said to me: Son of Man, eat all that thou shalt find: eat this book, and go speak to the children of Israel.
[2] And I opened my mouth, and he caused me to eat that book:[105]
[3] And he said to me: Son of Man, thy belly shall eat, and thy bowels shall be filled with this book, which I give thee. And I did eat it: and it was sweet as honey in my mouth.

The taste of honey goes back to Exodus, where the heavenly bread called manna also tasted like honey (Ex 16:31). Christ is the heavenly Bread of Life. Receiving Christ in Holy Communion is sweet to the tongue. But by this reception, we become bearers of the passion of Christ. We carry His cross. And this is the bitterness. The conclusion to this chapter is mysterious. The Messenger

---

[105] God places the book in Ezechiel's mouth. This reveals that this covenantal and sacramental meal was received by communion on the tongue and not in the hand.

says to John personally, "Thou must prophesy again to many nations, and peoples, and tongues, and kings." This likely means that Saint John should pick up the pen again and begin writing, since he was just told previously *not* to record the words of the seven thunders. This is also a reference to John being the last living apostle. The other apostles have all met their deaths in martyrdom, and John alone remains. This important prophetic role of Saint John was foretold by Jesus Christ to Saint Peter:

Jesus Explains That John Will be the Last Living Apostle (Jn 21:21–24)

[21] Him therefore when Peter had seen, he saith to Jesus: Lord, and what shall this man [Saint John] do?

[22] Jesus saith to him: So I will have him [Saint John] to remain till I come, what is it to thee? follow thou me.

[23] This saying therefore went abroad among the brethren, that that disciple [Saint John] should not die. And Jesus did not say to him: He should not die; but, So I will have him to remain till I come, what is it to thee?

[24] This is that disciple who giveth testimony of these things, and hath written these things; and we know that his testimony is true.

So John was destined to be the last apostle, and the Messenger's instructions for John to remain to the end and "eat the open book" seem to dovetail with Christ's explanation of John somehow remaining.

The Two Witnesses (Apocalypse 11)

We now begin to approach the detailed descriptions of the Antichrist and his evil reign. Between the sixth and seventh trumpets, several important events happen: We have the Mighty Messenger who makes an oath upon sea and land. John as the final apostle eats the open book. The Messenger tells John to make ready to prophesy. Now we get the details on the Antichrist and the end of days. The reign of Antichrist will be three and a half years and will be marked by the coming of the two witnesses of Apocalypse chapter 11.

John Measures the Temple (Apoc 11:1–3)
[1] And there was given me a reed like unto a rod: and it was said to me: Arise, and measure the temple of God, and the altar and them that adore therein.
[2] But the court, which is without the temple, cast out, and measure it not: because it is given unto the Gentiles, and the holy city they shall tread under foot two and forty months:
[3] And I will give unto my two witnesses, and they shall prophesy a thousand two hundred sixty days, clothed in sackcloth.

Saint John receives a reed shaped like a rod to measure the temple of God, the altar, and those that adore God there. John's command to measure the temple seems to indicate that the temple is still standing at the time of the vision.[106] The prophet Ezechiel prophesied this when he saw a dazzling man measure the ideal temple, which is actually the one true Church of the New Covenant (Eze 40-43). The reed is used for measuring, but it is also a rod, which is a sign of authority—particularly the authority of a priest or a king. John can measure the Church accurately because he is an apostle. He measures the worship area of the temple and

---

106 This detail in chapter 11 is one reason why we might believe that the vision was given before the destruction of the temple in AD 70.

those inside (the Church), but he is specifically instructed *not* to measure the courtyard because it is given over to the Gentiles, "and the holy city they shall tread under foot two and forty months." In fact, John is to "cast out" the courtyard, and the same word is used as the one for casting out demons by exorcism. The idea here is that the heavenly Jerusalem is where the Church will be safe, measured, and governed. The earthly Jerusalem will be tread underfoot for forty-two months, which is exactly three and a half years—the total reign of the Antichrist.

Jerusalem shall be persecuted for forty-two months, which is 3.5 years (42 months ÷ 12 months = 3.5 years). Then shall come the two witnesses for 1,260 days, which is 3.5 years (1,260 days ÷ 365 = 3.5 years). The three-and-a-half-year duration is half that of a perfect seven. It also goes back to the prophecy of Daniel, who identifies persecution as "a time, times, and half a time" in Daniel 7:25 and Daniel 12:7. We find the phrase once more in Apocalypse 12:14. It is certain, then, that the tribulation of the Antichrist will last three and half years.

PRETERIST MOMENT: DESTRUCTION OF JERUSALEM IN AD 66–70

The book of the Apocalypse can be interpreted as past events (preterist), future events (futurist), or the flow of history from Christ to the Antichrist (historicist). We are treating all three as true, valid, and interconnected. The preterist-futurist interpretation (my own view) asserts that the three and a half years from AD 66–70 and the destruction of Jerusalem is a micro-apocalypse mirroring the final Great Tribulation under the Antichrist in the last three and half years before the return of Christ.

Our Lord Jesus Christ telescoped the Jerusalem tribulation of AD 70 with the final tribulation in his Apocalypse sermon in Matthew 24. Several "terrors and great signs" (Lk 21:11) preceded the judgment and fiery destruction of Jerusalem. The Jewish Talmud records four signs occurring "forty years before the Temple was destroyed, the lot never came into the right hand, the red wool no longer became white, the western light would not burn, and the gates of the temple opened of themselves."[107] All four of these signs revealed that God had rejected the temple and the Levitical priesthood in favor of the one true priest (Jesus Christ) and His new temple (the Catholic Church).

The first sign was that the "lot never came into the right hand." This is a reference to the Jewish high priest casting lots (one white and one black) on the Day of Atonement (always in autumn) to choose which goat would be sacrificed to the Lord and which would be sent into the wilderness as the scapegoat.[108] There are two goats and two lots. Each goat has a fifty-fifty chance—like flipping a coin—of being offered to God or sent into the desert. However, beginning around AD 30, the black lot appeared in the right hand of the priest every year for forty years until

---

[107] Talmud, *Yoma* 39 b.
[108] The ceremony of the scapegoat is described at Leviticus 16:7–10.

the temple was destroyed by the Romans. This is equivalent to flipping *heads* on a coin forty times in a row. If you enter into a probability calculator an equation for a fifty-fifty-chance lot with two outcomes (white or black) for a sequence of forty times (forty years) with the *same repeated result* (black always wins), the probability is 0.000000000091 percent. This is virtually impossible, and it reveals that God was trying to teach something to the high priests of Jerusalem. What is the message? The Jewish priesthood had become the rejected goat. Christ alone is the acceptable priest and sacrifice.

The second sign was that the red wool never became white again. On this Day of the Atonement, the high priest cast the black and white lots to choose the goats. For the goat to be taken into the desert, he performed the following rite: "And putting both hands upon the goat's head, let him confess all the iniquities of the children of Israel, and all their offences and sins: and praying that they may light on his head, he shall turn him out by a man ready for it, into the desert" (Lev 16:21). After the high priest symbolically placed all the sins of Israel on the head of the scapegoat, he would tie a red woolen cord to the horns of the goat. Next, the high priest would tie a corresponding second red woolen cord to the gate of the temple. Then they would send the scapegoat with the red cord on its horns out into the desert to die. By a miracle, when the scapegoat reached the desert, the red woolen cord on the gates of the temple would turn white. This was seen as a mystical fulfillment of the prophecy of Isaias:

> If your sins be as scarlet, they shall be made as white as snow: and if they be red as crimson, they shall be white as wool. (Isa 1:18)

> The Rabbis taught that formerly the ribbon of crimson wool used to be tied to the outside door of the (temple's) porch, so that everyone could see. When it

became white, all were rejoiced. When it did not become white, all became out of spirits and ashamed.[109]

Beginning around AD 30, this miracle ceased to occur for forty years until the temple was completely destroyed. Even the Talmud records that the red woolen cord never became white after AD 30. This symbolizes that God the Father only forgives sin through Jesus Christ.

The third sign was that the western lamp would no longer burn. The door to the temple was to the east so that the sun could rise into the temple every day. This was a symbol of God entering into his sanctuary, so the holy of holies was at the westernmost end of the temple. Also, nearest to the holy of holies was the western lamp or menorah. The seven-branched menorah is a symbol of the sevenfold Holy Spirit. The priests knew that this menorah was miraculous and should never be allowed to run out of lamp oil. It was an eternal flame. But beginning around AD 40, the menorah would go out every night.[110] In fact, all the lamps in the temple would go out. This was a sign of God that His presence was leaving them.

The fourth and final sign of AD 30 signaling the impending doom of the temple in AD 70 was that the massive gates of the temple opened by themselves. The Rabbinical Talmud records how these heavy gates opened forty years before the destruction of the temple and that the priests knew it symbolized the destruction of the temple:

> The doors of the Hekal (holy place of the temple) opened of their own accord, until Rabbi Johanan Ben Zakkai rebuked them, saying "Oh Hekal, Hekal, why do you alarm us? I know full well that you are destined to be destroyed, for Zechariah Ben Iddo has already prophesied concerning you (citing Zech 11:1): Open

---
[109] Talmud, *Rosh Hashanah* 31 b.
[110] Talmud, *Yoma* 39.

thy doors O Lebanon, that the fire may devour thy cedars."[111]

The doors were made of cedar and overlaid with brass. The Rabbi realizes that "Open thy doors" signals that these massive cedar will be burned with fire—which did in fact happen in AD 70.

---

[111] Talmud, *Yoma* 39.

Signs and Wonders in AD 66

A second round of "terrors and great signs" (Lk 21:11) occurred three and a half years before the destruction of Jerusalem and the temple. The Jewish historian Josephus was an eyewitness of these events. In his history *The Jewish War*, Josephus describes eight miraculous signs in Jerusalem leading up to the destruction of Jerusalem.

The first warning sign: "Thus there was a star resembling a sword, which stood over the city, and a comet, that continued a whole year."[112] The second warning sign happened at Passover in the Spring of AD 66 at around three in the morning:

> When the people were come in great crowds to the feast of unleavened bread, on the eighth day of the month Nisan, and at the ninth hour of the night, so great a light shone round the altar and the holy house, that it appeared to be bright day time; which lasted for half an hour. This light seemed to be a good sign to the unskillful, but was so interpreted by the sacred scribes, as to portend those events that followed immediately upon it.[113]

The third warning happened again at Passover in AD 66: "At the same festival also, a heifer, as she was led by the high priest to be sacrificed, brought forth a lamb in the midst of the temple."[114] The fourth warning happened when

> the eastern gate of the inner temple, which was of brass, and vastly heavy, and had been with difficulty shut by twenty men, and rested upon a basis armed with iron, and had bolts fastened very deep into the firm floor, which was there made of one entire stone,

---

112 Josephus, *Jewish War*, lib.VI, 5, 3.
113 Ibid.
114 Ibid.

was seen to be opened of its own accord about the sixth hour of the night.[115]

Here, again, the Jewish men of learning interpreted this prodigy as God abandoning the temple and allowing the Romans to desolate it. Josephus explains, "But the men of learning understood it, that the security of their holy house was dissolved of its own accord, and that the gate was opened for the advantage of their enemies. So these publicly declared that the signal foreshowed the desolation that was coming upon them."[116]

The fifth warning happened after the feast was over. Josephus reports, "before the setting of the sun, chariots and troops of soldiers in their armor were seen running about among the clouds, and surrounding of cities."[117] Not long after this omen, the sixth warning happened in conjunction with the feast of Pentecost in AD 66:

> Moreover, at that feast which we call Pentecost, as the priests were going by night into the inner court of the temple, as their custom was, to perform their sacred ministrations, they said that, in the first place, they felt a quaking, and heard a great noise, and after that they heard a sound as of a great multitude, saying, "Let us remove hence."[118]

These last two signs reveal that the armies of heaven and a "great multitude" are leaving the temple behind. So far in the Apocalypse we have already seen armies of angels and a "great multitude."

The seventh warning, according to Josephus, was the appearance of a prophet named Jesus ben Ananus, who, for seven and a half years before the destruction of Jerusalem,

---

[115] Ibid.
[116] Ibid.
[117] Ibid.
[118] Ibid.

146

shouted "Woe, woe to Jerusalem" every day and especially on Jewish feast days:

> But, what is still more terrible, there was one Jesus, the son of Ananus, a plebeian and a husbandman, who, four years before the war began, and at a time when the city was in very great peace and prosperity, came to that feast whereon it is our custom for every one to make tabernacles to God in the temple, began on a sudden to cry aloud, "A voice from the east, a voice from the west, a voice from the four winds, a voice against Jerusalem and the holy house, a voice against the bridegrooms and the brides, and a voice against this whole people!" This was his cry, as he went about by day and by night, in all the lanes of the city. The Jews scourged him and he remained quiet. During the final siege of Jerusalem in AD 70 he shouted: "Woe, woe to the city again, and to the people, and to the holy house!" And just as he added at the last, "Woe, woe to myself also!" there came a stone out of one of the engines, and smote him, and killed him immediately; and as he was uttering the very same presages he gave up the ghost.[119]

The eighth warning was a prophecy and its misunderstanding. A Jewish prophecy was found in their scriptures that promised that there would come from their country a king to rule the entire world. This could be any Messianic prophecy; Josephus does not tell us which. But the Jewish scribes were wrong because they already killed their Messianic king, Jesus Christ, and he had already sent his apostle Peter to Rome to assume pastoral leadership of the kingdom of the Romans—and all kingdoms. Josephus says these Jewish scribes were deceived because, in fact, the Roman Emperor Vespasian had come to rule over them ruthlessly as Emperor in Judea. Josephus laments that, even

---

[119] Ibid.

with all these warnings, the Jewish priests and scribes did not repent. All this reveals that Jerusalem had indeed become spiritually Sodom and Egypt—rejected by God in favor of Jesus Christ. Just as Jerusalem was the spiritual capital of the world in the first century, so it will again become the spiritual capital of the world under the Antichrist with a rebuilt temple. God will send warning signs and prophets to warn her and convert her. But the Antichrist will persecute them. Chiefly, the prophetic witness will come by means of the two witnesses.

ENOCH AND ELIAS

Saint John then describes the two witnesses preaching for 1,260 days and wearing sackcloth in penance. John does not name these two witnesses, but tradition identifies them as Henoch and Elias, also known as Enoch and Elijah. Irenaeus of Lyons (d. AD 202) confirms that both men "have been translated and remain until the consummation."[120] The teaching that Enoch and Elias would return at the end of time was already accepted by Christians in the second century. These are the only two men in human history who have not died.

Scripture Explains that Enoch Never Died
And all the days of Enoch were three hundred and sixty-five years. And he walked with God, and was seen no more: because God took him. (Gen 5:23–24)

No man was born upon earth like Enoch: for he also was taken up from the earth. (Ecclus 49:16)

Enoch pleased God, and was translated into paradise, that he may give repentance to the nations. (Ecclus 44:16)

Unlike the pre-Flood patriarchs who lived for many centuries, Enoch lived until the perfect solar age of 365 years, and then God took him. He did not die. Enoch becomes the centerpiece of Jewish prophecy and apocalyptic literature since his life and death are hidden. The book of Enoch was found among the Dead Sea Scrolls and even quoted by Saint Jude in the New Testament: "Now of these Enoch also, the seventh from Adam, prophesied, saying: Behold, the Lord cometh with thousands of his saints." (Jude 1:4) Saint Peter includes the narrative of the book of Enoch in both of his epistles.[121]

---

120 Irenaeus, *Adversus haereses,* lib. 5, 5.
121 The judgment of the Watchers and the giants is referenced in 1 Peter 3:19–20 and 2 Peter 2:4–5.

Like Enoch, Elias was also assumed into heaven by God without human death. "And as they went on, walking and talking together, behold a fiery chariot, and fiery horses parted them both asunder: and Elias went up by a whirlwind into heaven" (2 Kings 2:23–24). Since it is divinely "appointed unto men once to die" (Heb 9:27), it is required that Enoch and Elias die. And these two prophets shall return in the last days to preach against the Antichrist and then die as martyrs under him.

The belief that Enoch and Elias shall return again at the end of time is prophesied in the book of Ecclesiasticus, one of the seven books removed by Martin Luther from the Old Testament. Ecclesiasticus (also called Sirach) references a future return for both Enoch and Elias.

It is true that John the Baptist was in the spirit and power of Elias. But he was not actually Elias. The prophecy, therefore, remains: "Behold I will send you Elias the prophet, before the coming of the great and dreadful day of the Lord" (Mal 4:5). The great and terrible day was not the baptism of Christ in the Jordan River, but it will be the final Day of Judgment. Christ confirmed this: "But he answering, said to them: Elias indeed shall come, and restore all things" (Mt 17:11). Christ is referring to the Old Testament prophecy that Elias will restore the twelve tribes of Israel as prophesied also in Ecclesiasticus:

Elias Will Restore Tribes of Jacob (Ecclus 48:4, 9–10)
[4] Thus was Elias magnified in his wondrous works. And who can glory like to thee? . . .
[9] Who wast taken up in a whirlwind of fire, in a chariot of fiery horses.
[10] Who art registered in the judgments of times to appease the wrath of the Lord, to reconcile the heart of the father to the son, and to restore the tribes of Jacob. [122]

---

[122] Ecclesiasticus, also called Sirach, is one of the seven books removed from the Old Testament by Protestants. Catholic and Orthodox Christians accept Ecclesiasticus as canonical. It should not be confused with Ecclesiastes.

Tradition is that Enoch shall come to preach to the Gentiles (he predated Abraham and the Israelite tribes), but that Elias will come to preach to the Jewish people and "restore the tribes of Jacob" (v. 10). This teaching of the return of Enoch and Elias before the Antichrist is affirmed by Saint Irenaeus,[123] Saint Hippolytus,[124] Origen, Lactantius,[125] Saint Hilary, Saint Augustine,[126] Saint Jerome,[127] Saint Gregory the Great,[128] Saint John Damascene,[129] Saint Thomas Aquinas,[130] and other esteemed biblical commentators.[131] Saint Arethas, an Arab Christian commentator who died as a martyr in AD 523, testified that the belief that Enoch and Elias would return to face the Antichrist is without a doubt believed by the entire Church of the sixth century.[132]

Two Witnesses Murdered by Beast (Apoc 11:4–7)

[4] These are the two olive trees, and the two candlesticks, that stand before the Lord of the earth.

[5] And if any man will hurt them, fire shall come out of their mouths, and shall devour their enemies. And if any man will hurt them, in this manner must he be slain.

[6] These have power to shut heaven, that it rain not in the days of their prophecy: and they have power over waters to turn them into blood, and to strike the earth with all plagues as often as they will.

---

[123] Irenaeus, *Adversus haereses, lib.* 5, 5.

[124] Hippolytus, *On Christ and Antichrist,* 43.

[125] Lactantius, *In cap. ult. Malachiae.*

[126] Augustine, *Tract 4 in Joannem* and also at *Genes. Ad litteram* lib. 9, cap. 6, *De civitate Dei,* lib. 20, cap. 29.

[127] Jerome, *Epistle to Pammachius against John of Jerusalem.*

[128] Gregory the Great, Moralium, lib. 21, 36 et lib. 9, 4

[129] John of Damascus, *De Fide Orthodoxa,* lib. 4, cap. 26-28.

[130] Thomas Aquinas, *Summa theologiae* III, q. 49, a. 5.

[131] For a full list, see Robert Bellarmine's *De Pontifice Romano,* lib. 3, cap. 6.

[132] Robert Bellarmine's *De Pontifice Romano,* lib. 3, cap. 6.

⁷ And when they shall have finished their testimony, the beast, that ascendeth out of the abyss, shall make war against them, and shall overcome them, and kill them.

The two prophets are called the two olive trees and two lampstands that stand before the Lord of the earth. Prophet Zechariah also saw two olive trees: "And two olive trees over it: one upon the right side of the lamp, and the other upon the left side thereof" (Zech 4:3). Later God reveals that "These are two sons of oil who stand before the Lord of the whole earth" (Zech 4:14). The two witnesses are Joshua (the high priest) and Zerubbabel (the king of Jerusalem). You might remember that this event corresponds to Holzhauser's sixth epoch, which will be the era of Catholic restoration with the holy pope and the great monarch. It's amazing that the sixth trumpet corresponds so well with the sixth message to the sixth church. This once again confirms that the seven church messages, seven seals, and seven trumpets are interlinked remixes of the sequences of seven. It seems that Enoch would correspond to the royal king and Elias to the holy pope. Enoch's royalty is revealed by his cosmic powers—having lived three hundred sixty-five years—and identity with the sun. Elias offered sacrifice and battled the idolatrous priests of Baal.

These two witnesses project fire from their mouths to devour their enemies. This recalls the fire from heaven that consumed Sodom and Gomorrah. Likewise, Moses condemned the uprising of Core, and "a fire coming out from the Lord, destroyed the two hundred and fifty men" (Num 16:35). In the same manner, Elias challenged the pagan priests of Baal and fire fell down from heaven and consumed only his sacrifice. Saint John likely recalled how he and his brother once made a similar request to Christ: "And when his disciples James and *John* had seen this, they said: Lord, wilt thou that we command fire to come down from heaven, and consume them?" (Lk 9:54, emphasis added).

These two witnesses also have power to shut heaven and prevent the rains for three and a half years. Jesus Christ confirmed this was a power of Elias: "In truth I say to you, there were many widows in the days of Elias in Israel, when heaven was shut up *three years and six months*, when there was a great famine throughout all the earth" (Lk 4:25, emphasis added). The two witnesses will also turn water into blood and strike the earth with plagues—a clear reference to the power of Moses against Pharaoh and Egypt with the ten plagues. The powers are clearly those of Moses and Elias. Not surprisingly, both prophets appeared with Christ at his transfiguration, where Saint John was also present.

After the two witnesses finish their testimony, the beast who is the Antichrist will ascend out of the abyss and make war against them and kill them. This is the first mention of the beast in the Apocalypse, and the Greek is the neuter word *therion*. It is the word not merely for an animal but for a wild beast, and it is related to the Greek word *thera*, meaning "hunting."[133] The origin of the beast Antichrist will be described by John in the next chapter. The murder of the two witnesses by the wild beast reveals their true identity as witnesses, since Saint John uses the Greek word *martyrian* for their prophetic testimony.

Two Witnesses Rise Again (Apoc 11:8–12)

⁸ And their bodies shall lie in the streets of the great city, which is called spiritually, Sodom and Egypt, where their Lord also was crucified.

⁹ And they of the tribes, and peoples, and tongues, and nations, shall see their bodies for three days and a half: and they shall not suffer their bodies to be laid in sepulchres.

¹⁰ And they that dwell upon the earth shall rejoice over them, and make merry: and shall send gifts one to

---

133 The Syrian Peshitta version of the New Testament translates this word as "toothed beast" to signify it as a carnivore.

another, because these two prophets tormented them that dwelt upon the earth.

[11] And after three days and a half, the spirit of life from God entered into them. And they stood upon their feet, and great fear fell upon them that saw them.

[12] And they heard a great voice from heaven, saying to them: Come up hither. And they went up to heaven in a cloud: and their enemies saw them.

The bodies of Enoch and Elias will lie in the streets of Jerusalem for three and a half days—half a week. The great city in the Apocalypse is not Rome as many (especially Lutherans) suppose. The great city is the spiritual capital of planet earth: Jerusalem. It is the great city "where their Lord was also crucified." Since the high priest, temple priests, Sanhedrin, and people shouted "crucify him" and rejected Christ as Messiah, this once-great city is now called Sodom and Egypt. The spiritual leadership of Jerusalem has imported the infidelity of Sodom (unnatural sex) and the spiritual death of Egypt (idolatry). The death of the witnesses in Jerusalem indicates either that they spent their entire three and a half years within Jerusalem or that their prophetic mission culminated in their arrival at Jerusalem. Either way, the beast Antichrist was there and slayed them in Jerusalem.

Their bodies will not be buried for three and a half days—a broken seven. Oddly, all the tribes, peoples, tongues, and nations shall see their bodies lying in the streets. In the first century, it would have seemed impossible for all the nations of the world to see the two dead witnesses, but television makes this easily possible today. All the people of the world will rejoice over their deaths and send gifts to one another. The beast, it would seem, will not allow their bodies to be properly buried because their dead carcasses are a sign of victory over God and His two prophets. But after three and a half days, "the spirit of life from God entered into them, and they stood

154

upon their feet" (v. 11). The Antichrist makes a show of them, but they rise again like our Lord Jesus Christ. This will cause a panic because great fear will fill the earth. John hears a voice from heaven say, "Come up hither," and the two resurrected witnesses go up to heaven in a cloud, just as Jesus Christ did. John adds, "and their enemies saw them" (v. 12). This is a humiliation of the beast and a warning to mankind. Then we hear again of the "great earthquake":

Earthquake Destroys a Tenth of City (Apoc 11:13–14)

[13] And at that hour there was made a great earthquake, and the tenth part of the city fell: and there were slain in the earthquake names of men seven thousand: and the rest were cast into a fear, and gave glory to the God of heaven.

[14] The second woe is past: and behold the third woe will come quickly.

The "great earthquake" repeats in the Apocalypse. When Christ was resurrected, "there was a great earthquake" (Mt 28:2). Here the great earthquake accompanies the resurrection of Enoch and Elias. Notably, a great earthquake happened also between the sixth and seventh seals (Apoc 6:12). Here again we have the great earthquake between the sixth and seventh trumpets. A tenth of Jerusalem falls. This may be a reference to the priestly order of Jerusalem since they were entitled to a "tenth," or tithe, of everything the Jews produced. Moreover, seven thousand people are killed in this earthquake. God once told Prophet Elias (who has just died and resurrected) that God still had seven thousand Israelites faithful to Him who would not bend the knee to the idol Baal (3 Kings 19:18). Now, however, it is seven thousand wicked Israelites who are killed. The rest of the city "gave glory to the God of heaven." This indicates a conversion to God. This turn of events shows how the Jews in the Great Tribulation turn to

Christ and foil the plans of the Antichrist. The Antichrist beast attempted to end the lives and humiliate the witnesses in death, but it has backfired. Ultimately, the war of the Antichrist will end up totally destroying the city of earthly Jerusalem. People are turning to God. This sixth-trumpet cycle that includes the two witnesses is the second woe. John now says, "behold the third woe," and this leads to the seventh trumpet.

Seventh Trumpet: The Ark Revealed (Apoc 11:15–18)

[15] And the seventh angel sounded the trumpet: and there were great voices in heaven, saying: The kingdom of this world is become our Lord's and his Christ's, and he shall reign for ever and ever. Amen.

[16] And the four and twenty presbyters, who sit on their seats in the sight of God, fell on their faces and adored God, saying:

[17] We give thee thanks, O Lord God Almighty, who art, and who wast, and who art to come: because thou hast taken to thee thy great power, and thou hast reigned.

[18] And the nations were angry, and thy wrath is come, and the time of the dead, that they should be judged, and that thou shouldest render reward to thy servants the prophets and the saints, and to them that fear thy name, little and great, and shouldest destroy them who have corrupted the earth.

The seventh trumpet signals the victory of God over the Antichrist. Just as Israel blew trumpets and summoned an earthquake that sent the walls of Jericho tumbling down, seven trumpets sound, and the earthly Jerusalem falls after a great earthquake. It may very well be that the "great earthquake" in Jerusalem at the resurrection of Jesus Christ is the apocalyptic great earthquake of the Apocalypse. The victory of Christ was eternally established by His glorious resurrection on Paschal Sunday. This is why the voices in heaven proclaim in verse 15, "the kingdom of this world is become our Lord's and his Christ." This refers to the prophet Daniel who saw the Ancient of days (God the Father) give the kingdom of this world to the Son of Man (God the Son). The transfer is complete.

Christ on the cross was already King of the Jews, but by His glorious resurrection, he also receives all the kingdoms of the world, chief of which is the Roman Empire that cooperated in killing Him on a Roman cross. Christ is born under a Roman census. He is condemned by the Roman Pontius Pilate. He dies on a Roman cross. His chief apostle, Peter, rules and dies in Rome. The book of Acts follows the transition from Jerusalem to Rome. Saint Paul goes to Rome after Jesus commands him to go there and also dies as a martyr in Rome. The Roman Empire was given to Christ by the Father.[134] The seventh trumpet announces that the kingdom of Christ will not be strictly Jewish or based in Jerusalem. Jerusalem is now spiritually Sodom and Egypt. The limit of God's kingdom is not Jewish; it is universal, catholic.

With the transferal of the kingdom of the world to Christ, the twenty-four presbyters fall on their faces and worship God. Their hymn of praise is full of gratitude:

Heaven Performs Eucharist (Apoc 11:17–19)

[17] We give thee thanks (Greek: *eucharistoumen*), O Lord God Almighty, who art, and who wast, and who art to come: because thou hast taken to thee thy great power, and thou hast reigned.
[18] And the nations were angry, and thy wrath is come, and the time of the dead, that they should be judged, and that thou shouldest render reward to thy servants the prophets and the saints, and to them that fear thy name, little and great, and shouldest destroy them who have corrupted the earth.

---

[134] For a full account of the transferal of Rome to Christ, see Taylor R. Marshall, *The Eternal City: Rome and the Origins of Catholic Christianity* (Dallas: Saint John Press, 2012).

¹⁹ And the temple of God was opened in heaven: and the ark of his testament was seen in his temple, and there were lightnings, and voices, and an earthquake, and great hail.

The twenty-four presbyters offer thanks, and the Greek is literally *eucharistoumen*, or "we offer Eucharist." Christ has received power and reigns from the right hand of the Father. The presbyters thank Him because He is about to reward the prophets and saints and also destroy those that corrupted the earth.

Up until now, it seemed that the temple in heaven was closed. This temple is the paradise of Eden, from which Adam and Eve were excluded. Now it is open. The death and resurrection of Christ have opened the temple of heaven to the children of Adam and Eve, and suddenly the ark of the testament (ark of the covenant) is seen again inside the temple. The ark had not been inside the temple since the prophet Jeremias removed the ark from the temple in about 587 BC. The temple in which Christ walked was an empty shell. The ark of the covenant was not in there. It was an empty tabernacle. But Jeremias had told the Jews that the ark of the testament would appear once again when God would gather His people and show mercy. Here is the full account of how Jeremias hid away the ark of the testament before the Babylonians destroyed Jerusalem and its temple:

Jeremias Hides the Ark Secretly (2 Mac 2:4–8)

⁴ It was also contained in the same writing, how the prophet, being warned by God, commanded that the tabernacle and the ark should accompany him, till he came forth to the mountain where Moses went up, and saw the inheritance of God.

⁵ And when Jeremias came thither he found a hollow cave: and he carried in thither the tabernacle, and the ark, and the altar of incense, and so stopped the door.

⁶Then some of them that followed him, came up to mark the place: but they could not find it.

⁷And when Jeremias perceived it, he blamed them, saying: The place shall be unknown, till God gather together the congregation of the people, and receive them to mercy.

⁸And then the Lord will shew these things, and the majesty of the Lord shall appear, and there shall be a cloud as it was also shewed to Moses, and he shewed it when Solomon prayed that the place might be sanctified to the great God.

Jeremias teaches that the ark will be hidden away for centuries, but eventually it will be revealed again, and there shall be a cloud. Saint John now sees that moment. The temple is open and the ark is already inside! But what is the ark? Or, rather, *who* is the ark?

The Dragon against the Woman (Apocalypse 12)

Jeremias prophesied that the ark of the testament would be shown again when God gathered His people. Saint John sees that ark in the temple in heaven and then immediately states, "And a great sign appeared in heaven: A woman clothed with the sun" (Apoc 12:1). The ark of the covenant foreshadowed something much more than a gold-plated wooden receptacle. The ark of the covenant foreshadowed the Woman who would contain the Messiah promised in Genesis 3:15. The ark was wood plated in gold. The Woman is a mother clothed with the sun.

It was Saint John and him alone who took care of the mother of Jesus Christ. Hanging from the wood of the cross, Jesus took a moment to make this special arrangement:

Mary as "Woman" or New Eve (Jn 19:26–28)

²⁶ When Jesus therefore had seen his mother and the disciple standing whom he loved, he saith to his mother: *Woman*, behold thy son.

²⁷ After that, he saith to the disciple: Behold thy mother. And from that hour, the disciple took her to his own.

²⁸ Afterwards, Jesus knowing that all things were now accomplished, that the scripture might be fulfilled, said: I thirst.

Jesus calls her *Woman*. She is the New Eve, and in the Apocalypse, her title is also Woman. Jesus tells his mother, Mary, "Behold thy son [John]," and to Saint John, "Behold thy mother [Mary]." From that hour, Saint John took Mary as his own mother. But the next verse is so important. "Afterwards, Jesus knowing that all things were now accomplished." This transferal of His mother as Woman to Saint John signaled "all things were now accomplished."

The Blessed Virgin Mary fulfilled an essential role in the incarnation and birth of Christ. She was the instrument of His first miracle. She stood at the cross. But her transference to John as his mother, and by extension her motherhood to the entire Church, makes it so that "all things were now accomplished."

New Eve Appears as the New Ark (Apoc 12:1–2)
[1] And a great sign appeared in heaven: A woman clothed with the sun, and the moon under her feet, and on her head a crown of twelve stars:
[2] And being with child, she cried travailing in birth, and was in pain to be delivered.

Eve was the first woman. Now we have a special Woman who is more than Eve. She is pregnant, but not with Cain or Abel. She is pregnant with Jesus Christ. She is clothed with the sun. This is usually a description of God. But this is not God. This woman shares in the glory of God. The moon is under her feet. For the Jews, but also for the Greeks, the moon was the upper limit of the changeable world. The sun and the stars were in the upper heavens. The upper heavens were fixed, and the sun and stars traveled in predictable orbits. But the moon waxes and wanes. It belongs to the lower heavens. It changes like the changeable world down on earth. Life also waxes and wanes. This woman stands above that. Moreover, the Jewish calendar was a lunar calendar. She also stands above the liturgical calendar of Jewish feasts. She wears a crown of twelve stars. She is a cosmic queen. The Great Messenger wore the rainbow as a crown. She wears twelve stars. The number twelve evokes the twelve tribes and the twelve apostles.

The most important detail is that she is "with child." Her glory derives from her relationship to her Divine Son, Jesus Christ. Saint John introduces this mother as "a great sign." The reference is to Isaias 7:14: "Therefore the Lord himself shall give you *a sign*. Behold a virgin shall conceive, and bear a son, and his name shall be called Emmanuel." This is the great sign. The Blessed Virgin Mary is pregnant with a son, who is Emmanuel, meaning "God with us." The prophet Jeremias also gives us a sign of the future New Covenant: "for the Lord hath created a new thing upon the earth: A Woman shall compass a Man" (Jer 31:22).

The Catholic Church holds that the Blessed Virgin Mary gave birth to Jesus Christ without pain. We might ask how this can be when Saint John specifically writes that she "was in pain to be delivered." At least twenty of the Doctors of the Church explicitly affirm that the birth of Christ was painless and miraculously left Mary's physical virginity intact. They hold this as a matter of dogma based on Isaias 66:7: "before her pain came, she was delivered of a man child." This prophecy refers to Christ. The Church Fathers refer to two other verses as affirming the painless birth of Mary and her physical virginity in birthing Christ:

The Gate of the Lord is Shut (Eze 44:1–3)
And he brought me back to the way of the gate of the outward sanctuary, which looked towards the east: and it was shut. And the Lord said to me: This gate shall be shut, it shall not be opened, and no man shall pass through it: because the Lord the God of Israel hath entered in by it, and it shall be shut for the prince.

The Enclosed Garden is Sealed (Canticles 4:12)
A garden enclosed is my sister, my spouse; a spring shut up, a fountain sealed.

This second passage shows that the womb of Mary is shut and closed even though God comes in and out. The Church Fathers interpreted this to mean that the womb of the Virgin Mary is "shut" and "sealed" by God, not to be "opened" in natural childbirth. Saint Gregory of Nyssa wrote

Of Him then His mother's burden was light, the birth immaculate, *the delivery without pain,* the nativity without defilement, neither beginning from wanton desire, nor brought to pass with sorrow. For as she who by her guilt engrafted death into our nature, was condemned to bring forth in trouble, it was fitting that she who brought life into the world should accomplish her delivery with joy.[135]

Saint Augustine wrote: "In conceiving thou wast all pure, in giving birth thou wast without pain."[136] The teaching that the Blessed Virgin Mary gave birth to Christ without pain and retained her physical integrity was affirmed at the Lateran Council (AD 649), which condemns anyone who denies it:

> If anyone does not in accord with the Holy Fathers acknowledge the holy and ever virgin and immaculate Mary was really and truly the Mother of God, inasmuch as she, in the fullness of time, and without seed, conceived by the Holy Spirit, God in the Word Himself, who before all time was born of God the Father, and *without loss of integrity brought Him forth, and after His birth preserved her virginity inviolate, let him be anathema.* (emphasis added)

The Council of Toledo XVI (AD 693) taught the same. And the Roman Catechism teaches:

> To Eve it was said: "In pain you shall bring forth children" (Gen. 3:16). Mary was exempt from this law, for preserving her virginal integrity inviolate, she brought forth Jesus the Son of God, *without experiencing, as we have already said, any sense of pain.*[137]

---

[135] Gregory of Nyssa, *Homily on the Nativity,* AD ca. 388, emphasis added.
[136] Augustine, *Sermon on Nativity.*
[137] Roman Catechism of 1566, "The Creed" Article III, emphasis added.

The travail and the pain of the woman in birth refers to her mission as mother of the Head (Christ) and mother of His body (His Church). The Blessed Virgin Mary bears twice. First, she gives birth to Christ in Bethlehem without pain as the New Eve. But as Eve she also stands next to the tree of life (the cross) and watches the "fruit of her womb" be immolated for the sins of mankind. Christ on the cross states, "Behold your mother," and this is the birth of the Church. The Church is united with Christ and receives God as Father and Mary as mother. And it is at the foot of the cross that she, with deep pain and agony, gives birth to the Church as mother of the faithful.

Red Dragon with 7 Heads & 10 Horns (Apoc 12:3–4)
³ And there was seen another sign in heaven: and behold a great red dragon, having seven heads, and ten horns: and on his head seven diadems:
⁴ And his tail drew the third part of the stars of heaven, and cast them to the earth: and the dragon stood before the woman who was ready to be delivered; that, when she should be delivered, he might devour her son.

Mary's role as the New Eve would not be complete without conflict with the serpent. "Another sign in heaven" is the great red dragon, having seven heads and ten horns with seven diadems (crowns). This is Satan, and he appears as depicted in the seventh chapter of Daniel. The fourth beast of Daniel's vision had ten horns. The difficulty is the seven heads, since none of Daniel's beasts had seven heads. The problem is solved when we count all four of Daniel's beasts. The lion beast (Babylon) had one head, the bear beast (Persia) had one head, the leopard beast (Greeks) had *four* heads, and the final terrible beast (Rome) had one head. The four heads of the leopard with the singular heads of the three other beasts bring us to seven heads. These four pagan nations were the four nations that ruled over the Jews between the fall of Jerusalem and the birth of Jesus. These four successive kingdoms were personally animated by Satan. According to Daniel, the Ancient of days (God the Father) will give all these kingdoms and more to the Son of Man (Jesus Christ). But Satan is not going to allow this without a fight. Chapter 12 depicts this fight.

One-third of the stars (angels) are cast down to earth because Satan led them in rebellion against God. The dragon stands before the Woman waiting to eat her baby. The chief mission of Satan is to find the Woman and eat her Divine Child. This mission was attempted when Satan inspired King Herod to slaughter innocent baby boys. But the Father would not allow it.

The Messianic Man Child with Iron Rod (Apoc 12:5)
And she brought forth a man child, who was to rule all nations with an iron rod: and her son was taken up to God, and to his throne.

The Blessed Virgin Mary gives birth to a man child. Some commentators say that the woman here is not personally the singular Mary, but the entirety of the faithful of Israel. Allegorically this is true, but the rest of the personages in this chapter are all real singular persons: Jesus the man child, Satan the red dragon, and Michael the archangel. Why wouldn't the mother also be a historical and real person— that is, the actual mother of Jesus?

Jesus rules with a rod of iron. Psalm 2 indicates that the Messianic king rules with a rod of iron:

Son of God Rules with an Iron Rod (Ps 2:7–11)
[7] The Lord hath said to me: Thou art my son, this day have I begotten thee.
[8] Ask of me, and I will give thee the Gentiles for thy inheritance, and the utmost parts of the earth for thy possession.
[9] Thou shalt rule them with a rod of iron, and shalt break them in pieces like a potter's vessel.

¹⁰ And now, O ye kings, understand: receive instruction, you that judge the earth.

¹¹ Serve ye the Lord with fear: and rejoice unto him with trembling.

The true Messiah and Son of God does not carry a symbolic scepter made of gold or silver. No, he carries an iron rod used for actual war. He breaks the nations into pieces like pottery. Daniel also associates the fourth and final kingdom (Rome) as being of iron. Christ is born, dies, and is resurrected under the fourth kingdom of Rome. In a great reversal, His scepter is also iron. "Her son was taken up to God, and to his throne" (Apoc 13:15). The life of Christ is fast-forwarded to His ascension into heaven to God the Father. But God does not forget His mother Mary.

The Woman Flees to the Wilderness (Apoc 12:6)
And the woman fled into the wilderness, where she had a place prepared by God, that there they should feed her a thousand two hundred sixty days.

The woman flees to the wilderness, where she had a place prepared by God for 1,260 days (three and a half years). Here the Church is protected, likely for its obedience to Christ: "When you shall see the abomination of desolation, standing where it ought not: he that readeth let him understand: then let them that are in Judea, flee unto the mountains" (Mk 13:14). Elias the prophet also sought safe refuge in the wilderness for three and a half years, where he was fed by ravens (3 Kings 17). So also "they should feed her" (Mother Church) during this tribulation of three and a half years.

Michael Expels Satan from Heaven (Apoc 12:7–9)
⁷ And there was a great battle in heaven, Michael and his angels fought with the dragon, and the dragon fought and his angels:

⁸ And they prevailed not, neither was their place found any more in heaven.

⁹ And that great dragon was cast out, that old serpent, who is called the devil and Satan, who seduceth the whole world; and he was cast unto the earth, and his angels were thrown down with him.

This great battle in heaven is not millennia after the birth and ascension of Jesus Christ. We know that the fall of Satan from heaven happened *before* the creation of Adam and Eve. The great battle between Satan and Michael happened before creation, and Saint Augustine states that God separating the darkness from the light was the removal of Satan and the demons from heaven.[138] The archangel Michael is mentioned in the Old Testament only by the prophet Daniel, who calls him the great prince.[139] His name in Hebrew means "Who is like God?" or "He who is like God," and it refers to the tradition that when Satan attempted to self-deify himself over the one true God, one angel responded, "Who is like God?" This rhetorical question alone defeated Satan, and Michael now wears that question as his princely name.

Saint Jude the Apostle writes of another conflict between Michael and Satan: "When Michael the archangel, disputing with the devil, contended about the body of Moses, he durst not bring against him the judgment of railing speech, but said: The Lord command thee" (Jude 1:9). So Michael is the chief angel assigned to counter the ploys of Satan. Michael is the general under Christ the King. Satan and his wicked angels fight against Michael and his holy angels. Their place is no longer found in heaven and they are expelled.

If there was any doubt over who the red dragon is, now we are told explicitly: "And that great dragon was cast out,

---

[138] Saint Augustine addresses this very question in his *De civitate Dei,* lib. 11, cap. 9.

[139] Daniel 12:1.

that old serpent, who is called the devil and Satan, who seduceth the whole world; and he was cast unto the earth, and his angels were thrown down with him" (Apoc 12:9). Here he has four names and titles: great dragon, old serpent, devil, and Satan. Some wrongly assert that the serpent in Genesis is not called the devil anywhere in the Bible and ascribe that to a later interpretation. Not so. God specifically reveals here that the old serpent is Satan. They are cast to the earth and become reptilian. Serpents and snakes live close to the earth and within the holes and caverns of the earth. Satan and his demons are like this. They are on the earth but also descend below the earth into hell and then back up again to find their prey. They are cold-blooded predators who rely on the warmth of the sun to move. Satan deceives the whole world. No nation is immune to his venom. Without Jesus Christ, every human person is subject to the reign of the old serpent.

There is a tradition in Catholic mysticism regarding the meaning and chronology of this vision in chapter 12. Perhaps the chronology is accurate. A human mother appears in heaven. She is shown to give birth. Satan and a third of the angels rebel. Michael the archangel removes them. But how does the narrative work if Christ was born of the Virgin Mary just over two thousand years ago and Satan fell so long before that? An answer is found in the mystical writing of Maria Agreda (d. 1665). She describes the creation of all the angels:

Maria Agreda on the Battle of Michael against Satan
In the first instant they were all created and endowed with graces and gifts, coming into existence as most beautiful and perfect creatures. Then followed a short pause, during which the will of the Creator was propounded and intimated, and the law and command was given to them, to acknowledge Him as their Maker and supreme Lord, and to fulfill the end for which they

have been created. During this pause, instant or interval, Saint Michael and his angels fought that great battle with the dragon and his followers, which is described by the apostle Saint John in the twelfth chapter of the Apocalypse. The good angels, persevering in grace, merited eternal happiness and the disobedient ones, rebelling against God, merited the punishment, which they now suffer.[140]

During this pause, it was revealed to all the angelic minds that the Logos who is the Son of God would become incarnate by a human mother and assume a human nature that ranks *below* that of the angelic nature. So they were given the vision that we see in the twelfth chapter of the Apocalypse: "A woman clothed with the sun, and the moon under her feet, and on her head a crown of twelve stars: and she was with child" (Apoc 12:1-2).

The angels were told to accept that God would humble Himself to a low estate and then the angels were asked to serve Him as an inferior servant. Satan and a third of the angels found this irrational and demeaning to the Godhead. And so they shouted, *"Non serviam"* ("I will not serve"), and the battle in heaven began with Michael responding, *"Mi cha El?"* ("Who is like God?") Maria Agreda explains what she perceived mystically:

Maria Agreda on Why Satan Fell

This sign or vision of the Queen of heaven and of the Mother of the incarnate Word was made known and manifest to all the angels, good and bad. The good ones at the sign of it broke forth in admiration and in canticles of praise and from that time on began to defend the honor of the God incarnate and of his holy Mother, being armed with ardent zeal and with the invincible shield of that vision. The dragon and his allies on the contrary conceived implacable hatred and

---

140 Maria Agreda, *The Mystical City of God,* Book 1, chapter 3.

fury against Christ and his most holy Mother. Then happened all that which is described in the twelfth chapter of the Apocalypse, which I will explain, as far as it has been given me.[141]

So, as it were, God revealed to the primordial angels an image or icon of the future incarnation of the Son of God in the immaculate womb of the Blessed Virgin Mary. Those who praised God remained holy angels in league with Michael. Those who were enraged by the humility of God became serpentine demons in league with Satan. Maria Agreda then explains how Satan turned all his efforts toward finding the Woman and destroying her. This is why Satan focused first on Eve and not on Adam.

Victory by the Blood of the Lamb (Apoc 12:10–12)

[10] And I heard a loud voice in heaven, saying: Now is come salvation, and strength, and the kingdom of our God, and the power of his Christ: because the accuser of our brethren is cast forth, who accused them before our God day and night.

[11] And they overcame him by the blood of the Lamb, and by the word of the testimony, and they loved not their lives unto death.

[12] Therefore rejoice, O heavens, and you that dwell therein. Woe to the earth, and to the sea, because the devil is come down unto you, having great wrath, knowing that he hath but a short time.

The victory of Michael over Satan leads to a loud voice of praise announcing the salvation and kingdom of God and His Christ. Satan receives successive defeats: first, his casting forth from heaven, when heaven rejoices with his expulsion; second, his punishment in the garden of Eden; third, his defeat when Christ survives the knives of King Herod; and fourth, the death and resurrection when Christ

---

[141] Ibid.

as New Adam defeats death and rises to new life. The Blood of the Lamb defeats Satan. As Christ says to His disciples in the Gospel of Luke:

Jesus Saw Satan Fall from Heaven (Lk 10:17–20)

[17] And the seventy-two returned with joy, saying: Lord, the devils also are subject to us in thy name.

[18] And he said to them: I saw Satan like lightning falling from heaven.

[19] Behold, I have given you power to tread upon serpents and scorpions, and upon all the power of the enemy: and nothing shall hurt you.

Satan is bound for this time period but will be released one last time for his attempt to establish the Antichrist and deceive humanity one last time. He will have only "a short time." (v. 12) and will, as we shall see, be utterly defeated once and for all and removed from the earth entirely.

The Dragon Persecutes the Woman (Apoc 12:13–16)

[13] And when the dragon saw that he was cast unto the earth, he persecuted the woman, who brought forth the man child:

[14] And there were given to the woman two wings of a great eagle, that she might fly into the desert unto her place, where she is nourished for a time and times, and half a time, from the face of the serpent.

[15] And the serpent cast out of his mouth after the woman, water as it were a river; that he might cause her to be carried away by the river.

[16] And the earth helped the woman, and the earth opened her mouth, and swallowed up the river, which the dragon cast out of his mouth.

When Satan arrives on earth, he immediately seeks to persecute the Woman: "He casts out of his mouth after the woman, water as it were a river; that he might cause her to be carried away by the river" (v. 15). The river reminds us of the Garden of Eden. How did Satan deceive the Woman Eve? With the deceptive words of his mouth. He carried her away from God and sold her down the river.

Now the Woman, who is New Eve, receives the two wings of a great eagle. Christ gave Mary to Saint John the Apostle, and John is signified as the eagle.[142] Saint John already sees himself as the protective eagle over the Mother of Christ. But John also knew that being upon the eagle's wings was a sign of God caring for Israel in the wilderness:

> You have seen what I have done to the Egyptians, *how I have carried you upon the wings of eagles*, and have taken you to myself. If therefore you will hear my voice, and keep my covenant, you shall be my peculiar possession above all people: for all the earth is mine." (Ex 19:4–5, emphasis added)

The Psalms also repeatedly describe God's care and protection as wings.

The Woman is given wings to fly above the water flowing from Satan's mouth. She is unstained, or immaculate, when it comes to the deception of Satan. The words of Satan bring death. She is lifted up from this reign of Satan. (Catholic tradition documented in the fifth century holds that the Blessed Virgin Mary as the New Eve was exempt from original sin, and after she fell asleep at the end of her life, she secretly was assumed into heaven. The apostles then found her tomb empty. Christ, the Son of David, had brought the ark of the new covenant into His heavenly temple.) She stands above the moon. She is clothed in the sun. The stars are on her head. She is raised on eagle's wings. She is raised body and soul into the glory of the Savior's heaven.

---

[142] Matthew is the man. Mark is the lion. Luke is the ox. John is the eagle.

She is nourished for a time, times, and a half—once again, a three-and-a-half, a broken seven. Our preterist-futurist interpretation must make mention of the historical account of Eusebius, who says that as the Roman armies came to siege Jerusalem, the Judean Christians fled the region to hide in the wilderness in obedience to Christ's instructions in Matthew 24.[143] During the years leading up to the Roman destruction of Jerusalem in AD 70, the early Christians in Jerusalem (those Hebrew Christians who likely received the epistle to the Hebrews) removed themselves from Jerusalem before the Romans sieged the walls of Jerusalem.

The earth helped the Woman by opening and swallowing Satan's river of lies. Satan's attack as a river recalls the Garden of Eden, but it also refers to the Pharaoh's decree to kill all baby boys of Israel and how Moses was floated down the Nile River. The name Moses means "drawn from the water." We also recall how Pharaoh followed the Israelites to the Red Sea and how the Red Sea opened to receive and protect Israel. And again, the Jordan River opened so that the Israelites could enter the Promised Land on dry land. The prophets Elias and Eliseus also crossed the Jordan River in a miraculous way (4 Kings 2).[144] The earth opening up recalls how the earth opened to swallow those leaders rebelling against Moses (Num 16). The wording of the Apocalypse here points back to all these Old Testament events whereby God intervenes to save His people and prophets.

Dragon Wars against Her Seed (Apoc 12:17–18)

[17] And the dragon was angry against the woman: and went to make war with the rest of her seed, who keep the commandments of God, and have the testimony of Jesus Christ.

---

[143] Eusebius, *Ecclesiastical History*, 3, 5.
[144] In the Greek and Latin, 1 and 2 Samuel and 1 and 2 Kings are fourfold as: 1-4 Kings.

¹⁸ And he stood upon the sand of the sea.

Once Satan has been thwarted, he becomes angry at the free Woman. He turns his wrath against "the rest of her seed." The mention of her seed here points back to God's promise in the Garden to place enmities between the serpent's seed and the Woman's seed. The Seed is Jesus Christ, but "the rest of her seed" are those who follow Jesus Christ. The "rest of her seed" are not justified by faith alone but must also "keep the commandments." The Woman is mother to the Messiah and to His followers. This means that Mary is the mother of the faithful and that the universal Catholic Church is rightly defined as "Holy Mother Church." In a similar fashion, the prophet Isaias finishes his eschatological prophecies by describing the Messianic New Jerusalem as a nursing mother of the faithful:

New Jerusalem as Nursing Mother (Isa 66:9–13)
⁹ Shall not I that make others to bring forth children, myself bring forth, saith the Lord? shall I, that give generation to others, be barren, saith the Lord thy God?
¹⁰ Rejoice with Jerusalem, and be glad with her, all you that love her: rejoice for joy with her, all you that mourn for her.
¹¹ That you may suck and be filled with the breasts of her consolations: that you may milk out, and flow with delights, from the abundance of her glory.
¹² For thus saith the Lord: Behold I will bring upon her as it were a river of peace, and as an overflowing torrent the glory of the Gentiles, which you shall suck; you shall be carried at the breasts, and upon the knees they shall caress you.
¹³ As one whom the mother caresseth, so will I comfort you, and you shall be comforted in Jerusalem.

The Heavenly Jerusalem, which will appear at the end of the Apocalypse, is a heavenly mother who brings forth children for God. She nurtures her children with her own milk. Instead of a river of Satan, a river of peace flows. Not only the Jews but also the Gentiles will be invited to find comfort in her maternal breasts and upon her lap.

The Woman in this chapter has two meanings. First, the Woman is the historical mother of the Messiah taken away to heaven: the Blessed Virgin Mary. Secondly, the Woman is symbolically the New Jerusalem and Holy Mother Church. She is the Church Triumphant over time. By being lifted to heaven, the Woman is totally removed from Satan's power. "The rest of her seed" is the Church Militant still here on earth. Satan focuses all his attention on them "who keep the commandments of God and have the testimony of Jesus Christ" (Apoc 12:17). Satan then stands on the sand of the sea—at the intersection of the sea and the land as he is now about to call forth the sea beast (the Antichrist) and the land beast (the False Prophet).

The Antichrist & His False Prophet
(Apocalypse 13)

Saint John the Apostle describes the Antichrist as the "beast of the sea." In the same chapter he also describes a second "beast of the land" and the requisite "mark of the beast." Chapter 13 is perhaps the most popular chapter of the Apocalypse because it reveals the sacrilegious trinity of Satan. The previous chapter described the red dragon, who is Satan. Satan then deputizes the sea beast to be his earthly king and the Antichrist: "And they adored the dragon, who gave power to the beast" (Apoc 13:4). This sea beast, who is the Antichrist, receives vivid descriptions. In order to appreciate every detail, let us examine line by line:

The Antichrist Described in Detail (Apoc 13:1–10)

[1] And I saw a beast coming up out of the sea, having seven heads and ten horns, and upon his horns ten diadems, and upon his heads names of blasphemy.

In Hebrew, "sea" refers to chaos and the nations. The seven heads are seven hills. Both Rome and Jerusalem have seven hills. The ten horns are ten kings with ten crowns.

[2] And the beast, which I saw, was like to a leopard, and his feet were as the feet of a bear, and his mouth as the mouth of a lion. And the dragon gave him his own strength, and great power.

The fourfold features refer to Daniel, who saw the progress of the pagan domination of Israel as a lion (Babylonians), a bear (Medo-Persians), a leopard (Greeks), and the final beast with ten horns (Romans).

[3] And I saw one of his heads as it were slain to death: and his death's wound was healed. And all the earth was in admiration after the beast.

The Antichrist receives a head injury from which he recovers. Verse 14 below says that the head wound was inflicted by a sword. This is a false death and resurrection and may be the reason that the Antichrist gains such a following.

> [4] And they adored the dragon, which gave power to the beast: and they adored the beast, saying: Who is like to the beast? and who shall be able to fight with him?

Adoration is focused on the dragon (Satan) and on the beast (the Antichrist).

> [5] And there was given to him a mouth speaking great things, and blasphemies: and power was given to him to do two and forty months.

The Antichrist speaks blasphemy and rules for forty-two months, which is three years and six months—the Great Tribulation.

> [6] And he opened his mouth unto blasphemies against God, to blaspheme his name, and his tabernacle, and them that dwell in heaven.

The Antichrist is not content to blaspheme only God and His name. He also blasphemes His tabernacle and His saints who dwell in heaven.

> [7] And it was given unto him to make war with the saints, and to overcome them. And power was given him over every tribe, and people, and tongue, and nation.

The Antichrist persecutes the followers of Christ (saints) and overcomes them (martyrs). He gains universal power over every nation on earth.

> [8] And all that dwell upon the earth adored him, whose names are not written in the book of life of the Lamb, which was slain from the beginning of the world.

Everyone on earth, whose name is not in the book of the Lamb, adores the Antichrist as God. This is the abomination of desolation.

> [9] If any man have an ear, let him hear.
> [10] He that shall lead into captivity, shall go into captivity: he that shall kill by the sword, must be killed by the sword. Here is the patience and the faith of the saints.

There will be a great reversal against the Antichrist, but it will require patience and faith.

So far, we have seen the origin of the Antichrist and his Great Tribulation. But Saint John then introduces the third person of the Satanic trinity. This is the land beast, who is the False Prophet. He is not a king like the Antichrist. He is a spiritual leader—one who functions as a priest and prophet for the sea beast Antichrist. These two beasts function as the two false witnesses: a false king and a false high priest—a false Enoch and false Elias. Some have suggested that the sea beast and land beast are one and the same person,[145] the former describing his royal dignity and the latter describing his magical arts. Yet this seems to go against the clear teaching that the dragon, the sea beast,

---

[145] Robert Bellarmine at *De Romano Pontifice* lib. 3, cap. 15.

and the land beast denote three distinct persons in Apocalypse 20:9–10.[146] Here is the advent of the land beast:

The Land Beast or False Prophet (Apoc 13:11–15)

[11] And I saw another beast coming up out of the earth, and he had two horns, like a lamb, and he spoke as a dragon.

This beast comes out of the earth or land. Often, "the land" refers to the Holy Land, and perhaps that is the intention here. The sea beast comes from the sea of nations, and the land beast comes from the Holy Land. This second beast has two horns like a lamb. Two verses before we saw the book of the Lamb, but this beast speaks as the dragon (Satan).

[12] And he executed all the power of the former beast in his sight; and he caused the earth, and them that dwell therein, to adore the first beast, whose wound to death was healed.

The False Prophet, who is the land beast, serves the Antichrist king, who is the sea beast. This False Prophet is a high priest who organizes and promotes the worship of the Antichrist, whose head wound is healed.

[13] And he did great signs, so that he made also fire to come down from heaven unto the earth in the sight of men.

The False Prophet performs false miracles and makes fire come down from heaven to earth. This is some sort of wizardry that mimics the power of Elias, who called down fire from heaven.

---

[146] "[A]nd the devil, who seduced them, was cast into the pool of fire and brimstone, where both the beast and the false prophet shall be tormented day and night for ever and ever" (Apocalypse 20:9–10).

179

¹⁴ And he seduced them that dwell on the earth, for the signs, which were given him to do in the sight of the beast, saying to them that dwell on the earth, that they should make the image of the beast, which had the wound by the sword, and lived.

The sorcery and false miracles will compel people to worship the Antichrist. We learn here that the Antichrist was healed from a sword wound. Also, an image of the Antichrist is constructed. The Greek word for image is *eikona,* or "icon." The fact that it is not "idol" is peculiar, especially considering the next verse.

¹⁵ And it was given him to give life to the image of the beast, and that the image of the beast should speak; and should cause, that whosoever will not adore the image of the beast, should be slain.

The False Prophet gives life to the icon of the Antichrist, and this icon speaks. Whoever will not adore this speaking icon of the Antichrist receives martyrdom.

The Satanic trinity of Satan, Antichrist, and False Prophet have constructed the speaking icon of the Antichrist. Finally, they institute the mark of the beast as a condition for buying and selling.

Mark of the Beast (Apoc 13:16–18)

¹⁶ And he shall make all, both little and great, rich and poor, freemen and bondmen, to have a character in their right hand, or on their foreheads.

Every human must now receive the mark of the beast. The Greek word for mark is χαραγμα, or *charagma*. It is an engraving or an etching. The Greek verb χαράσσω means "to engrave." Saint Paul in Acts 17 uses the word to refer to graven pagan idols found in Athens, Greece. The reference to having it on the right hand or on the forehead is likely a reference to Moses. Moses commands the Israelites to bind God's law "as a sign on thy hand, and between thy eyes" (Deut 6:8). Although Pharisees literally bound written laws on their foreheads and right hands with phylacteries, Jesus Christ condemned this as superstition. The real meaning is that God's law should be placed in our minds (faith) and upon our right hand (works). We must believe (head) and perform (hand) the laws of God. The Antichrist will mock the teaching of Moses by imposing wicked laws placed on the head and on the right hand.

> [17] And that no man might buy or sell, but he that hath the character, or the name of the beast, or the number of his name.

The consequence of not taking the engraving on our heads (faith) or right hands (actions) is that one is removed from the economy.

> [18] Here is wisdom. He that hath understanding, let him count the number of the beast. For it is the number of a man: and the number of him is six hundred sixty-six.

The last verse here invokes wisdom, who is Christ. The number of the Antichrist is 666. Seven is the perfect number of holiness. Six is one less. It is sacrilege. Land beasts and humans were created on the sixth day, and God rested on the seventh day. This removes the Sabbath of God and focuses on the land beast and humans.

MARK OF THE BEAST

Regarding the mark and number of the beast, there is much controversy. We have already seen how some have sought to identify 666 with the year AD 666. Lutherans favored the meaning as AD 666 in order to identify the number with the so-called creation of the Papacy by Saint Gregory the Great in AD 600. Others seek to reckon the number refers to the creation of Islam and the Quran, as the death of Mohammad occurred in AD 632. These dates have already been shown to be inaccurate, and Saint John explicitly informs us that 666 is not a date but a "number of a man." (Apoc 13:18).

The Greek for 666 reads XΞF, where the letter X (chi) means six hundred, the letter Ξ (xi) means sixty, and the letter F (digamma) means six. In Greek, the letters of the alphabet also serve as numbers, so that A (alpha) is the sound for a and also the number one. Likewise B (beta) is the sound for b and also the number two.

Ⴥ	= 1	I	= 10	P	= 100
B	= 2	K	= 20	C	= 200
Γ	= 3	Λ	= 30	T	= 300
Δ	= 4	M	= 40	Υ	= 400
Є	= 5	N	= 50	Φ	= 500
Ϛ,F	= 6	Ξ	= 60	X	= 600
Z	= 7	O	= 70	Ψ	= 700
H	= 8	Π	= 80	Ⲱ	= 800
Θ	= 9	Ϙ	= 90	ϡ	= 900

This means that the letters for any name in Greek can be added up. One noteworthy example is the Greek name for Jesus (IHSOYS or IHSOYC), which adds up to 888.

IHSOYS

$$(I)10 + (H)8 + (S)200 + (O)70 + (Y)400 + (S/C)200 = 888$$

The number eight is associated with the eighth day, one beyond seven, and thus eternity or infinity. The number six, however, is one short of seven and thereby man-centered and wicked. So, if Jesus is 888, then the Antichrist is 666.

Saint Irenaeus, writing in the late AD 100's, gives us the first written account of 666 as found described in the Apocalypse. First, he says that some manuscripts have 666 while others have 616. Scholarship backs this up because a number of manuscripts have been discovered that have 616 instead of 666. The Codex Ephraemi Rescriptus and an ancient Armenian version of the Apocalypse preserve versions showing 616 instead of 666. Irenaeus, however, claims that 616 must be a copyist error and that the sixty was mistakenly turned into a ten to render it as 616, not 666. He explains, "I am inclined to think that this occurred through the fault of the copyists, as is wont to happen, since numbers also are expressed by letters; so that the Greek letter which expresses the number sixty was easily expanded into the letter Iota of the Greeks."[147]

Irenaeus is saying that XΞF (666) was accidentally changed into XIF (616). But how does Ξ (60) accidentally become I (10)? It is likely because early Christians had already associated the mark of the beast with Emperor Nero Caesar. Hebrew, like Greek, also assigns numbers to letters. When we add up the letters for Neron Caesar, we arrive at 666, but if we omit the final *n* in Hebrew pronunciation to read "Nero Caesar," we get 616. Hebrew speaking Jews referred to Nero as "Neron" but Latin speakers called the emperor "Nero" (but with the genitive as "Neronis"). Different audiences would use a different pronunciation and a different lettering.

The variation of 666 and 616 in relation to Nero may relate to the legend of Nero Redivus—the belief that the Nero Caesar would return again in the future. The legend is found in the *Sibylline Oracles*, in which Nero is said to have

---

147 Irenaeus, *Adversus haereses,* lib. 5, cap. 30.

escaped to Persia, where he was building an enormous army to destroy Rome.[148]

The legend likely derives from the fact that there are a number of Nero imposters who appeared after the death of Nero. The first Nero pretender appeared in AD 69. He looked identical to the original Nero and sang and played the harp like Nero. A second Nero pretender appeared during the reign of Titus around AD 80. He also sang and played the harp but was exposed as an imposter. The Roman historian Suetonius recounts that there was a third Nero pretender who persuaded the Parthians that he was the real Nero: "Some person of obscure birth gave himself out for Nero, that name secured for him so favorable a reception from the Parthians, that he was very zealously supported, and it was with much difficulty that they were prevailed upon to give him up."[149] Saint Augustine relates that two centuries later, there are those who believe that Nero "lives in concealment in the vigor of that same age which he had reached when he was believed to have perished, and will live until he is revealed in his own time and restored to his kingdom."[150]

If the discrepancy between 666 and 616 does have to do with an identity with Nero Caesar, it is not stated as known to Irenaeus. In the same passage, Irenaeus confesses that he does not know the meaning of the number, and he rebukes those who claim to know it: "Moreover, another danger, by no means trifling, shall overtake those who falsely presume that they know the name of Antichrist."[151]

Irenaeus then does us the service of listing the various solutions created by Christians during his time, circa AD 150–200:

---

[148] *The Sibylline Oracles,* IV, 119–124; V.137–141; V.361–396.
[149] Suetonius, *De vita Caesarum,* Nero, 57.
[150] Augustine, *De civitate Dei,* lib. 20, 19.3
[151] Irenaeus, *Adversus haereses,* lib. 5, 30.

For the name *Euanthas* (ΕΥΑΝΘΑΣ) contains the required number, but I make no allegation regarding it. Then also *Lateinos* (ΛΑΤΕΙΝΟΣ) has the number six hundred and sixty-six; and it is a very probable solution, this being the name of the last kingdom [of the four seen by Daniel.] For the Latins are they who at present bear rule: I will not, however, make any boast over this coincidence. *Teitan* (ΤΕΙΤΑΝ), too the first syllable being written with the two Greek vowels ε and ι, among all the names which are found among us, is rather worthy of credit.[152]

Irenaeus, as the first Christian to address 666 in writing, does not mention Nero. Instead, he finds Teitan as the most likely name of the Antichrist, but he confesses that no one shall know the truth of this matter until the time comes:

So, neither has his name been declared, for the name of that which does not exist is not proclaimed. But when this Antichrist shall have devastated all things in this world, he will reign for three years and six months, and sit in the temple at Jerusalem; and then the Lord will come from heaven in the clouds, in the glory of the Father, sending this man and those who follow him into the lake of fire.[153]

Thus far, the demonic trinity of dragon, sea beast, and land beast have promulgated the icon of the beast and the mark of the beast in order to recruit an army of humans who are publicly against God. Readers of the Apocalypse must ask themselves: Would I worship the icon of the beast? Would I take the mark? Saint John, after observing so much evil and the final plot of Satan, looks up to heaven, and there he sees the Christ the Lamb assembling His own army for battle.

---

[152] Ibid.
[153] Ibid.

King Christ on Mount Sion (Apocalypse 14)

Saint John looks and sees Jesus Christ with the army of 144,000. These are the baptized warriors who took the sign of the cross upon their foreheads. They are the new twelve tribes of Israel: $1,000 \times 12 \times 12$:

Christ Appears on Mount Sion (Apoc 14:1–3)

[1] And I beheld, and lo a Lamb stood upon Mount Sion, and with him a hundred forty-four thousand, having his name, and the name of his Father, written on their foreheads.

[2] And I heard a voice from heaven, as the noise of many waters, and as the voice of great thunder; and the voice which I heard, was as the voice of harpers, harping on their harps.

[3] And they sung as it were a new canticle, before the throne, and before the four living creatures, and the presbyters; and no man could say the canticle, but those hundred forty-four thousand, who were purchased from the earth.

Previously, the Lamb (Christ) stood on the altar (Apoc 5:6), and the great multitude stood before the throne, within sight of the Lamb (Apoc 7:9). Now, the "Lamb stood upon Mount Sion, and with him a hundred forty-four thousand" (Apoc 14:1). Did they move and change location? No, the altar in heaven and heavenly throne room of God are the same place as the heavenly Mount Sion. All three places refer to the same place. This fulfills the prophecy of Psalm 2:6: "I am appointed king by him over Sion his holy mountain, preaching his commandment." Sacred Tradition also tells us that Christ celebrated the Last Supper in the "Blood of the New Testament" on earthly Mount Sion within the walls of earthly Jerusalem. Saint Paul in his epistle to the Hebrews[154] confirms the same associations:

Mount Sion vision in Hebrews 12:22–24:

[22] But you are come to *Mount Sion*, and to the *city of the living God*, the *heavenly Jerusalem*, and to the company of *many thousands of angels*,

[23] And to the *church of the firstborn*, who are written in the heavens, and to God the judge of all, and to the spirits of the just made perfect,

[24] And to *Jesus the mediator of the New Testament*, and to the sprinkling of blood which speaketh better than that of Abel. (emphasis added)

In the epistle to the Hebrews, Mount Sion is the (1) City of God, (2) the Heavenly Jerusalem, and (3) the Church of the Firstborn, which is occupied by many thousands of angels and Jesus, the Mediator of the New Testament. Hebrews' description of heaven is identical to what we see in Saint John's vision of heaven in the Apocalypse. The theologies of each text depicting a spiritual Mount Sion as the city of God and Heavenly Jerusalem are identical, but even the Greek diction appears to coincide with one another.[155] I would add that even Galatians by Saint Paul speaks of two women and two mountains. This is primitive apostolic theology that derives from the mountain theology of Jesus Christ. The vision reveals the Lamb standing on a heavenly mountain is superior to: (1) Satan, who comes from the

---

[154] I hold the position of Thomas Aquinas that Hebrews was authored by Saint Paul theologically but written and published by Saint Luke. For my full position and defense that Luke, Acts, and Hebrews are a group package delivered to Hebrew Christians in Jerusalem in the early AD 60's, see my book *The Catholic Perspective on Paul: Paul and the Origins of Catholic Christianity* (Saint John Press, 2010).

[155] The parallel is so close that some commentators think that one depends on the other. J. Stuart Russell argued that Hebrews chapter 12 was dependent on Apocalypse chapter 14. See J. Stuart Russell's *The Parousia: A Critical inquiry into the New Testament Doctrine of Our Lord's* Coming (Grand Rapids: Baker Book House, 1983).

lower abyss; (2) the sea beast who crawls from the lower sea; and (3) the land beast who emerges from the lower earth.

Jesus Christ sealed His great multitude with a seal on their foreheads through baptism. This great multitude has "his name and the name of his Father, written on their foreheads" (Apoc 14:1). The dragon (Satan), the sea beast (Antichrist), and the land beast (False Prophet) are likewise sealing their damned devotees on the forehead and hand in mockery of Christ's sacramental seal. Saint John receives another indication of sacramental baptism in the second verse: "And I heard a voice from heaven, as the noise of many waters, and as the voice of great thunder." Baptism is a simple sacrament that requires the proper formula spoken with the human voice: "NAME, I baptize you in the name of the Father and of the Son and of the Holy Spirit." The sealing on the forehead with the name of God recalls this sacramental voice and the "noise of many waters."

The assembly of baptized Christians on Mount Sion initiates worship with harps played by the twenty-four presbyters (Apoc 5:8), and they sing a "new canticle" before the throne and four living creatures. This new canticle is a secret. No man can sing this canticle except for those 144,000 "who were purchased from the earth." This is liturgy and it is exclusive. In the early Church, the unbaptized were not allowed to attend the Mass of the Faithful, which included the Sanctus, consecration of the Eucharist, and Communion. These faithful were purchased from the earth, and the word for "earth" is the same Greek word as the word "land" in "land beast." They are redeemed away from this false religion of false worship and false promises.

Warrior Virgin Priests (Apoc 14:4–5)
⁴ These are they who were not defiled with women: for they are virgins. These follow the Lamb whithersoever

he goeth. These were purchased from among men, the first fruits to God and to the Lamb:

⁵ And in their mouth there was found no lie; for they are without spot before the throne of God.

They are virgins: "These are they who were not defiled with women: for they are virgins. These follow the Lamb whithersoever he goeth. These were purchased from among men, the first fruits to God and to the Lamb" (v. 4). Does this mean that heaven is only for virgins? In the Old Testament, men were called to abstain from women, even their wives, for two reasons. First, it was a sign of penance and ceremonial purity. When Moses was preparing men for the manifestation of God upon the mountain he said, "Be ready against the third day, and come not near your wives. (Ex 19:15). Under the law of Moses, any seminal ejaculation (sinful or not) rendered the Israelite man unclean: "The man from whom the seed of copulation goes out shall wash all his body with water: and he shall be unclean until the evening" (Lev 15:16).[156] And the priests of the Old Testament were not allowed to have sex with their wives for a time during the term of their priestly ministry in the temple.

Secondly, Israelite soldiers were considered to be warrior-priests since war was a sacred vocation in Israel. God made commands and promises regarding waging war against His enemies. This is why the Levitical priests in the temple make a provision for King David and his warrior-priest companions to eat the holy bread of the presence in the temple *only after* David attested to his soldiers not having had sex with women:

David Attests to His Soldiers as Not Having Sex
⁴ And the priest answered David, saying: I have no common bread at hand, but only holy bread, if the young men be clean, especially from women?

---

[156] See also Deut 23:10–11.

⁵ And David answered the priest, and said to him: Truly, as to what concerneth women, we have refrained ourselves from yesterday and the day before, when we came out, and the vessels of the young men were holy. Now this way is defiled, but it shall also be sanctified this day in the vessels.

⁶ The priest therefore gave him hallowed bread: for there was no bread there, but only the loaves of proposition, which had been taken away from before the face of the Lord, that hot loaves might be set up (1 Kings 21:4–6).¹⁵⁷

The soldiers of Israel were expected to be chaste while fighting. This detail comes up in the story of David and Bathsheba. King David commits adultery and impregnates Bathsheba, who is married to the soldier Urias. To hide the fault, King David calls Urias away from the battlefields and tells him to go and spend the night in his house—with the presumption that Urias would have sex with his wife Bathsheba. The baby would then be passed off as having been conceived by Urias, covering up the adulterous conception. But Urias, a righteous man of God, refuses! Urias will not go to his home and sleep with his beautiful wife, Bathsheba, because he is acting as a warrior-priest. Urias explains why he will not sleep with her:

Urias Refuses Sex with His Wife While on Duty

¹⁰ And it was told David by some that said: Urias went not to his house. And David said to Urias: Didst thou not come from thy journey? why didst thou not go down to thy house?

¹¹ And Urias said to David: The ark of God and Israel and Juda dwell in tents, and my lord Joab and the servants of my lord abide upon the face of the earth: and shall I go into my house, to eat and to drink, and

---

¹⁵⁷ As explained above, the King James naming for this book is 1 Samuel. The Greek Septuagint and Latin Vulgate name it 1 Kings.

to sleep with my wife? By thy welfare and by the welfare of thy soul I will not do this thing (2 Kings 11:10–11).

Urias rightly understood that this was a holy war and that he was a warrior-priest fighting in the presence of the ark of the covenant. It would be unjust for him to sleep with his wife.[158] The Lamb of God and his great multitude of 144,000 are assembled for holy war against Satan and the Antichrist. They are warrior-priests, and thus they must be virgins. They must be like Urias, who sleeps outside the gate and won't go home to sleep with his wife while the ark of the covenant is in the battlefields. This is why Christian clergy are celibate. They are the warrior-priests. Saint Paul was celibate and wished that all men would be like him regarding celibacy (1 Cor 7:7). Our Lord Jesus Christ commended celibacy: "There are eunuchs who have made themselves eunuchs for the kingdom of heaven. He that can take, let him take it" (Mt 19:12).[159] Jeremias the prophet was also a virgin, as was Saint John the Apostle.

We will learn that this great multitude of 144,000 is the Bride of Christ, and this is another reason why virginity is so important. Saint Paul understood this long before Saint John received this vision when he said: "For I am jealous of you with the jealousy of God. For I have espoused you to one husband that I may present you as a chaste virgin to Christ" (2 Cor 11:2). This is emphasized in the next verse of the Apocalypse describing these 144,000 virgins: "These follow the Lamb whithersoever he goes." They have been "purchased" and are "the first fruits to God and to the Lamb" (v. 4). Firstfruits are the first portion of the harvest

---

[158] This response of Urias incriminates David even more. While his soldiers are fighting in the field with the ark of the covenant, King David is back in Jerusalem sleeping with a soldier's wife.

[159] And although Peter was married, he says, "Behold, we have left all things, and have followed thee. He said to them: Amen, I say to you, there is no man that hath left house, or parents, or brethren, or wife, or children, for the kingdom of God's sake." (Lk 18:28–29)

crop offered back to God in thanksgiving. But the collage of references to virginity, marriage, following Christ, and firstfruits evoke God's message to the virgin Jeremias regarding Jerusalem as God's virgin wife:

Jeremias Recalls Jerusalem as a Young Virgin Bride

[2] Go, and cry in the ears of *Jerusalem*, saying: Thus saith the Lord: I have remembered thee, pitying thy soul, pitying thy youth, and the love of *thy espousals*, when thou *followedst me* in the desert, in a land that is not sown.

[3] Israel is holy to the Lord, *the firstfruits* of his increase: all they that devour him offend: evils shall come upon them, saith the Lord (Jer 2:2-3, emphasis added).

One of the best arguments for the full divinity of Christ is His identity as Bridegroom. In the Old Testament, God and Jerusalem are depicted as husband and wife. Now in the New Testament, Christ (as God) and the Church (as New Jerusalem) are husband and wife. Therefore, Jesus Christ is God. The Lamb of God Jesus Christ is the Bridegroom to the Virgin Church, comprised of the 144,000 virgin warrior-priests. They have no lies in their mouths, and they are without blemish (v. 5). Now that Christ the Lamb has assembled his virgin "warrior-bride," he prepares to wage war against the dragon and his two beasts.

Christ and his army are in heaven. The order of seven events moving forward will be the action of three angels, then the appearance of Christ the Reaper, and then the action of three more angels:

1. Angel of Eternal Gospel (Apoc 14:6–7)
2. Angel of Fallen Is Babylon the Great (Apoc 14:8)
3. Angel of "If Anyone Adore the Beast" (Apoc 14:9–13)
4. Son of Man on a Cloud as Reaper (Apoc 14:14)

5. Angel from temple calls for Reaping (Apoc 14:15–16)
6. Angel from temple and Sharp Sickle (Apoc 14:17)
7. Angel from altar and the Fire (Apoc 14:18–20)

Let's examine the first three angels who make announcements:

First Three Angels (Apoc 14:6–7)
⁶ And I saw another angel flying through the midst of heaven, having the eternal gospel, to preach unto them that sit upon the earth, and over every nation, and tribe, and tongue, and people:
⁷ Saying with a loud voice: Fear the Lord, and give him honour, because the hour of his judgment is come; and adore ye him, that made heaven and earth, the sea, and the fountains of waters.

The first angel flies "in the midst of heaven" just like the eagle-angel in Apocalypse 8:3. He proclaims "the eternal gospel." The eternal gospel is first for the Jew and then for the Gentile. Saint John designates the Jews as those "that sit upon the [holy] land" since "earth" and "land" are the same word in Greek. He then mentions "every nation" as receiving the eternal gospel. Acceptance of the eternal gospel consists of three simple actions: fear the Lord, honor Him, and adore Him.

Fallen Is Babylon (Apoc 14:8)
⁸ And another angel followed, saying: That great Babylon is fallen, is fallen, which made all nations to drink of the wine of the wrath of her fornication.

The second angel proclaims that Babylon has fallen. But what city is Babylon? Most commentators will say that Babylon is either Rome or Jerusalem. The apostle Peter refers to Rome as Babylon (1 Pet 5:13). Yet John also identifies *earthly* Jerusalem as "the great city, which is called spiritually, Sodom and Egypt, where their Lord also was crucified" (Apoc 11:8). Saint John specifically identifies the "great city" as Jerusalem (Apoc 11:8) and elsewhere identifies it as Babylon (Apoc 16:19).

Is Babylon the city of Rome or Jerusalem? My proposal in this book is that the name Babylon refers to the invaded status of earthly Jerusalem. Babylon is Jerusalem fornicating with Rome. "We have no king but Caesar" is the rebellious shout of an adulterous wife fornicating with a foreign king (Jn 19:15). She murders her Husband on a Roman cross to caress the face of Caesar. The mystery of Babylon makes the nations "drink of the wine of the wrath of her fornication" (Apoc 14:8). Fornication takes two partners: Babylon is the adulterous union of Rome and Jerusalem that crucified the Son of Man outside the gates of Jerusalem on a Roman cross. As I will explain in future chapters, "the mystery of Babylon" is a whore (Jerusalem) *riding* the beast (Rome).

If Anyone Worships the Beast (Apoc 14:9–13)

[9] And the third angel followed them, saying with a loud voice: If any man shall adore the beast and his image, and receive his character in his forehead, or in his hand; [10] He also shall drink of the wine of the wrath of God, which is mingled with pure wine in the cup of his wrath, and shall be tormented with fire and brimstone in the sight of the holy angels, and in the sight of the Lamb.

[11] And the smoke of their torments shall ascend up for ever and ever: neither have they rest day nor night, who have adored the beast, and his image, and whoever receiveth the character of his name.

[12] Here is the patience of the saints, who keep the commandments of God, and the faith of Jesus.

[13] And I heard a voice from heaven, saying to me: Write: Blessed are the dead, who die in the Lord. From

henceforth now, saith the Spirit, that they may rest from their labours; for their works follow them.

The third angel preaches a warning against two actions: do not worship the beast and his image/icon, *and* do not receive his character on your forehead or hand. An interesting parallel emerges here between beast/forehead and image/hand. The beast is the head of the damned. The image is the work of his hand. Christ as God has sealed only the forehead of His people. The Antichrist beast seals on forehead *and on the hand.*

If one adores the beast or takes the mark of the beast, he will drink wine of the wrath of God "mingled with pure wine in the cup of his wrath" (v. 10). The Greek word here for "cup" is *poterion,* which is the same Greek word used for "chalice" by Christ at the Last Supper: "In like manner also the chalice, after he had supped, saying: This chalice is the New Testament in my blood: this do ye, as often as you shall drink, for the commemoration of me" (1 Cor 11:25). This is not the Eucharistic chalice of blessing. This is the chalice of wrath. Those that drink the chalice of wrath are "tormented with fire and brimstone in the sight of the holy angels, and in the sight of the Lamb."

Many popular Protestant preachers define the agony of hell as "the absence of God," but hell most certainly is not the absence of God. Saint John sees the torment of the damned "in the sight of the Lamb." God is everywhere: "If I ascend into heaven, thou art there. If I descend into hell, thou art present" (Ps 138:8 LXX). The torment is by fire and brimstone, which first appears in Scripture with the destruction of Sodom and Gomorrah with fire and brimstone (Gen 19:24). Moreover, the pouring out of fire and brimstone is associated with the cup of God: "He shall rain snares upon sinners: fire and brimstone and storms of winds shall be the portion of their cup" (Ps 10:7 LXX).

Protestant universalists, who teach that all human souls will be saved, have a problem with the next verse, which teaches everlasting torment of the damned: "the smoke of their torments shall ascend up for ever and ever" (Apoc 14:10). Saint John sees people in the lake of fire, which is the hell of the damned. It is not a hypothetical threat. It is not a temporary purification like purgatory. It is forever and ever. The Greek reads *eis aionas aionon (into eons of eons)*, which the Latin Vulgate translates as *in sæcula sæculorum*.

After mentioning the adoration of the beast and the reception of his mark, John says, "Here is the patience of the saints, who keep the commandments of God, and the faith of Jesus" (v. 11). Salvation requires endurance and justification comes from faith in Jesus and obedience to His commandments. John is commanded to write: "Blessed are the dead, who die in the Lord. From henceforth now, saith the Spirit, that they may rest from their labors; for their works follow them" (v. 13). The witness of Christians is their willingness to die for Jesus Christ. The Christian has rest in death, which is not the experience of the damned who "neither have they rest day nor night." The Holy Spirit speaks directly to John here. They are at rest. Their works follow them. These two verses teach against the Lutheran heresy of "justification by faith alone." Faith is required, but so are works and loving obedience to His commandments. The New Testament knows nothing of a gospel with the words "faith alone."

Jesus as Son of Man & Grand Reaper (Apoc 14:14–20)

[14] And I saw and behold a white cloud; and upon the cloud one sitting like to the Son of Man, having on his head a crown of gold, and in his hand a sharp sickle.
[15] And another angel came out from the temple crying with a loud voice to him that sat upon the cloud: Thrust in thy sickle, and reap, because the hour is come to reap: for the harvest of the earth is ripe.
[16] And he that sat on the cloud thrust his sickle into the earth, and the earth was reaped.

¹⁷ And another angel came out of the temple, which is in heaven, he also having a sharp sickle.

¹⁸ And another angel came out from the altar, who had power over fire; and he cried with a loud voice to him that had the sharp sickle, saying: Thrust in thy sharp sickle, and gather the clusters of the vineyard of the earth, because the grapes thereof are ripe.

¹⁹ And the angel thrust in his sharp sickle into the earth, and gathered the vineyard of the earth, and cast it into the great press of the wrath of God:

²⁰ And the press was trodden without the city, and blood came out of the press, up to the horses' bridles, for a thousand and six hundred furlongs.

We have seen three angels so far, and in verse 14, we behold the "white cloud" (always a sign of Christ) and the Son of Man sitting on that cloud. The cloud imagery of the messianic Son of Man is revealed in Daniel 7, as we covered previously. Jesus Christ quotes Daniel 7 during his trial before the Jewish high priest Caiaphas:

Jesus is Son of Man with Clouds (Mk 14:62–63)

⁶² And Jesus said to him: I am. And you shall see the *Son of Man sitting* on the right hand of the power of God and coming *with the clouds of heaven.*

⁶³ Then the high priest rending his garments, saith: What need we any further witnesses? (emphasis added)

When this perfidious high priest tore his garments, he defiled his high priesthood and committed a heinous blasphemy against God. I argue that the high priest deposed himself from the high priesthood by rending his garments based on the teaching of Leviticus:

Moses said to Aaron, and to Eleazar and Ithamar, his sons: Uncover not your heads, *and rend not your garments, lest perhaps you die, and indignation come upon all the congregation.* (Lev 10:6, emphasis added)

> The high priest, that is to say, the priest, is the greatest among his brethren, upon whose head the oil of unction hath been poured, and whose hands have been consecrated for the priesthood, and who hath been vested with the holy vestments, shall not uncover his head, *he shall not rend his garments.* (Lev 21:10, emphasis added)

Twice the high priest was told not to rend his garments. It is a sacerdotal sacrilege. By this act, the Levitical high priest voided his priesthood and passed it on to Jesus Christ, who served as the true High Priest, offering His own blood as the propitiation for the sins of the world.

The Son of Man here wears a crown of gold and has a sickle in His hand. This is not a super-angel. The crowned Son of Man upon a white cloud is Jesus Christ, who has ascended to the right hand of God the Father. Once he is introduced, Saint John shows three more angels who will direct the action of reaping upon earth.

Verse 15 introduces the second triad of angels: the fourth, fifth, and sixth angels. The fourth angel comes out of the temple and cries out to the Son of Man on the clouds (Jesus) with this instruction: "Thrust in thy sickle, and reap, because the hour is come to reap: for the harvest of the earth is ripe." Jesus then thrusts His sickle into the earth and reaps the earth. The fifth angel in the triad comes out of the temple in heaven, also having a sharp sickle. Then the sixth and final angel "who had power over the fire" cries out for the fifth angel with the sharp sickle to thrust the sickle and gather the clusters of the vineyard because the grapes are ripe. This can be confusing because the Son of Man has a sharp sickle and reaps the harvest of the earth. And then the sixth angel tells the fifth angel to reap again. The difference here is that the first reaping by Christ seems to be a grain harvest, while the second reaping by the fifth angel is a grape harvest. Bread first, wine second.

The sixth angel is the angel with power over fire. This is presumably the same "fire angel" who gathered fire into the censer of incense and cast it upon earth (Apoc 8:5). The fourth book of Esdras (listed as apocryphal in the Latin Vulgate) mentions the angel Uriel, whose name means "fire of God."[160] The apocryphal book of Enoch also lists the four archangels as Michael, Uriel, Raphael, and Gabriel.[161] In Ethiopian iconography, Saint Uriel is an angel carrying the chalice filled with the blood of Christ. An ancient tradition holds that the angel Uriel guided Elizabeth to protect her infant son, John the Baptist, during the massacre of the Holy Innocents by King Herod. Leonardo da Vinci also took interest in the angel Uriel. He painted the angel Uriel protecting John the Baptist and pointing his angelic finger to the Christ Child in this way in his painting *Virgin of the Rocks* (Louvre Edition).

At the Council of Rome in AD 745, Pope Zachary curbed an obsession with angel devotion by limiting the liturgical commemoration of angels by name to Michael, Gabriel, and Raphael. But in 1541, the Sicilian friar Antonio del Luca claimed that the archangel Uriel appeared to him in the ruins of the baths of Diocletian and asked for a church.[162] After making the request known to Pope Pius IV for a Roman church dedicated to the seven archangels, the

---

[160] 4 Esdras 4:1

[161] 1 Enoch 9.

[162] Friar Antonio del Luca, while serving as choirmaster in the cathedral of Palermo from 1513–1515, discovered an ancient icon of the seven angelic princes. Beyond the already recognized Michael, Gabriel, and Raphael, he added Uriel, Selaphiel, Jegudiel, and Barachiel. In the summer of 1541, he received an apparition in the ruined baths of Diocletian that seems to have included the angel Uriel and also seven martyred saints: Saturnino, Ciriaco, Largo, Smaragdo, Sisinnio, Trasone, and Pope Marcellus I. He dedicated his life to promoting devotion to the seven angelic princes; he even composed a liturgy for the Mass of the Seven Angels, which was never approved. He appealed to the mosaic in Saint Mark's cathedral in Venice that depicted Our Lady with seven angels. Although Pope Pius IV commissioned the church to be built, he left "seven" out of the title, and it was simply dedicated to "all angels and martyrs."

pope asked Michelangelo to design the church, which is the church of Santa Maria of All the Angels and Martyrs in the Baths of Diocletian (currently in the Termini area).[163] Despite there being some history devotionally of Uriel as a fire angel, it is not possible to confirm whether this angel "who had power over fire" is the angel named "Fire of God," or Uriel.

Next is the angel who "gathered the vineyard of the land." The vineyard is code for Israel living in the Promised Land. As Isaias prophesies, "For the vineyard of the Lord of hosts is the house of Israel" (Isa 5:7). He gathers the vineyard (Israel) of the Land and "cast it into the great press of the wrath of God" (Apoc 14:19). The focus here is Israel and the capital city of Jerusalem: "press was trodden without the city, and blood came out of the press, up to the horses' bridles, for a thousand and six hundred stadia" (v. 20). Jerusalem is filled with blood up to the mouth bridle of a horse and extends for 1,600 stadia. Many translations read "1,600 furlongs," but the Greek is *stadia* (plural of *stadium*). A Greek stadium was calculated as the length of six hundred human feet. Using the modern length of a foot as twelve inches, a Greek stadium would be two hundred standard yards long. However, the average human foot varied in length depending on local ethnicity. Scholars have concluded that the Greek stadium (based on textual descriptions of ancient monuments and distances) was about 172 yards, or 157 meters—which would be based on ancient human foot length equivalent to the modern length of 10.32 inches.

The number 1,600 is likely symbolic for $4 \times 4 \times 100 = 1{,}600$ stadia. But how big of a literal area is 1,600 stadia? How much blood would it take to be "up to the horses' bridles, for a thousand and six hundred stadia"? One thousand six hundred stadia calculates to about two hundred Roman miles or 184 American miles. A bridle in a

163 Notably, the number seven was left out of the Basilica's title, even though "seven angels" is a common reference in the Apocalypse.

horse's mouth is about five feet off the ground. Now imagine a lake of blood five feet high and extending out 184 miles in all directions. For reference, the distance from Jerusalem to Nazareth is only sixty-four American miles or 104 kilometers. This amount of blood would cover all the land promised by God to Abraham, King David, and King Solomon. This vineyard is the "house of Israel," and the wine (blood) of this vintage covers the entire Promised Land. We know this is the Promised Land because it is "outside of the city" of Jerusalem. God is not pleased with Israel. They are complicit with the beast and have taken his mark. They are engulfed in human blood.

Canticle of Victory (Apocalypse 15)

The fifteenth chapter of the Apocalypse is the shortest chapter, with only eight verses. It serves as a prologue to the seven angels pouring out seven vials or chalices. This is the second sign in heaven, the first having been the Woman clothed in the sun (Apoc 12:1).

The Final Seven Plagues (Apoc 15:1–4)

[1] And I saw another sign in heaven, great and wonderful: seven angels having the seven last plagues. For in them is filled up the wrath of God.

[2] And I saw as it were a sea of glass mingled with fire, and them that had overcome the beast, and his image, and the number of his name, standing on the sea of glass, having the harps of God:

[3] And singing the canticle of Moses, the servant of God, and the canticle of the Lamb, saying: Great and wonderful are thy works, O Lord God Almighty; just and true are thy ways, O King of ages.

[4] Who shall not fear thee, O Lord, and magnify thy name? For thou only art holy: for all nations shall come, and shall adore in thy sight, because thy judgments are manifest.

Satan and his two beasts have assembled an army, and the wrath of God is released. The chalice of wrath is followed by a break in the action before the seven angels pour out their seven vials (Greek: *phialas*). These seven angels have the "last plagues." Saint John sees a sea of glass mixed with fire. The battle with the beast has already commenced because we see the casualties: "and them that had overcome the beast, and his image, and the number of his name, standing on the sea of glass, having the harps of God" (v. 2). These martyrs refused the beast, his icon, and the number of his name. They are literally walking on water like Christ the King. They stand on the sea of glass. This sea is like a baptistry. It is the entry point into the heavenly Mount Sion, which is also the heavenly temple. They are given harps to play like the twenty-four priests.

The victory of the Christians is compared to the people of Israel crossing the Red Sea in victory. They sing the canticle of Moses (after crossing the Red Sea) and the canticle of the Lamb (after baptism). Saint Paul confirmed this association of Red Sea and baptism: "And all in Moses were baptized, in the cloud, and in the sea" (1 Cor 10:2). After their baptismal victory, they sing the new canticle of Moses and Jesus:

> Great and wonderful are thy works, O Lord God Almighty; just and true are thy ways, O King of ages. Who shall not fear thee, O Lord, and magnify thy name? For thou only art holy: for all nations shall come, and shall adore in thy sight, because thy judgments are manifest." (Apoc 15:3-4).

The nations shall come to Jesus Christ. God the Father has given all nations to Him. He is not just the King of the Jews. He is also the King of the Nations.

The Temple Opens and Angels Fly Out (Apoc 15:5–8)

⁵ And after these things I looked; and behold, the temple of the tabernacle of the testimony in heaven was opened:

⁶ And the seven angels came out of the temple, having the seven plagues, clothed with clean and white linen, and girt about the breasts with golden girdles.

⁷ And one of the four living creatures gave to the seven angels seven golden vials, full of the wrath of God, who liveth for ever and ever.

⁸ And the temple was filled with smoke from the majesty of God, and from his power; and no man was

able to enter into the temple, till the seven plagues of the seven angels were fulfilled.

The temple *in heaven* is opened. This is not the hollow building in Jerusalem. This is the court and sanctuary of God in heaven. Then, the seven angels process out from the temple. They are dressed like priests of the Old Testament wearing linen robes and golden girdles.

The Greek word for vials here is *phialas*, coming into English as "phials" or "vials." As mentioned above, ceremonial *phialas* were used by the Old Testament priests and by Greek idolaters (see Homer) as offertory dishes.[164] These seven priest-angels already have the seven plagues. But then one of the four cherubim creatures gives seven golden vials to the seven priest-angels. The order of events seems to indicate the seven priest-angels have the seven plagues *before* they receive the seven golden vials. And then the plagues are mixed with the wrath of God with the appearance of the seven golden vials. In the Old Testament, the high priest would have sacrificed the calf *outside* the temple, carried a golden vial containing blood *into* the temple, and then brought the blood back out to the altar, which was *outside*:

---

[164] *Phialas* are broad, shallow bowls used to offer sacrifices of incense, grain, wine, and animal blood. Some commentators such as David Chilton and Scott Hahn have suggested that these seven golden vials are really seven gold chalices and should be translated as "chalices" to indicate a "negative sacrament."[164] They argue for this translation, as the seven plagues are then "poured out," resembling the chalice of Christ's blood "poured out" for mankind. But this is a leap too far. In Apocalypse 5:8, we read "Each bore a harp, and they had golden *phialas* full of incense, the prayers of the saints." These are wide, shallow bowls that offer incense, grain, wine, or blood. They are *not* drinking cups. They are more like libation dishes. Jewish priests would use them to offer elements to God, much as a Catholic priest uses the gold paten (not chalice) to offer the Host to the Father.

How the OT High Priest Offered Blood (Lev 4:5–7)

⁵ He shall take also of the blood of the calf and carry it into the tabernacle of the testimony.

⁶ And having dipped his finger in the blood, he shall sprinkle with it seven times before the Lord, before the veil of the sanctuary.

⁷ And he shall put some of the same blood upon the horns of the altar of the sweet incense most acceptable to the Lord, which is in the tabernacle of the testimony. And he shall pour all the rest of the blood at the foot of the altar of holocaust in the entry of the tabernacle.

The high priests sprinkled the blood *seven* times, smeared the four corners of the altar with blood, and then poured out all the blood (from a golden vial) at the foot of the altar. Something like this is happening in heaven with these seven priest-angels. Christ is the sacrificial victim and High Priest who brings his blood into the holy of holies and sprinkles it before the Father seven times, ratifying the New Covenant. Now the seven priest-angels are taking something from within the temple and pouring it out as punishment.

After this, the heavenly temple is filled with smoke from the majesty and power of God, and no man can enter into the temple until the seven plagues are fulfilled. This seems to point back to Adam and Eve being blocked off from God's sanctuary (Paradise) until Jesus Christ made propitiation for the sins of the world. We are told that cherubim blocked the way back into Eden, and here one of the four cherubim gives the golden vials of wrath to the seven priest-angels. The temple is blocked off. This is why the veil of the temple ripped in half, from top to bottom, when Jesus Christ died on the cross for our sins. No man can enter the heavenly temple until Jesus offers His blood *within* the temple.

Seven Vials Poured Out (Apocalypse 16)

The red dragon, who is Satan, has appointed his Antichrist King (sea beast) and his False Prophet (land beast) and mandated Satanic worship (beast icon) and the reception of the beast sacrament (666) on the head or hand. He has persecuted the two witnesses and the Woman, and her children have fled into the desert. They are sealed with the name of the Trinity on their foreheads and have also crossed the Red Sea of baptism successfully by entering the heavenly Promised Land. Now is the time to pour out the wrath of God on His enemies and end the evil. Apocalypse Chapter 16 is a rapid-fire progression of seven vials of wrath—the final set of sevens of our twenty-one prophetic events.

First Angel Pours the First Plague (Apoc 16:1–2)
¹ And I heard a great voice out of the temple, saying to the seven angels: Go, and pour out the seven vials of the wrath of God upon the earth.

² And the *first* went, and poured out his vial upon the earth, and there fell a sore and grievous wound upon men, who had the character of the beast; and upon them that adored the image thereof. (emphasis added)

God *commands* the seven priest-angels to pour the wrath of God upon the earth. God is wrathful. He is just. The dragon and the beast are leading Israel and the world into formal rebellion. God promised seven plagues, and now He is fulfilling His holy word:

God Promised "Seven Plagues" in Leviticus
If you walk contrary to me, and will not hearken to me, I will bring *seven times more plagues* upon you for your sins. (Lev 26:21, emphasis added)

I will also go against you with opposite fury, and I will *chastise you with seven plagues for your sins.* (Lev 26:28, emphasis added)

The first angels pour out his plague upon the earth, producing skin sores on whoever received the mark of the beast or worshipped the beast's icon. This is divine irony. Men take the defiling stamp of Satan upon their forehead or hand, and God shows it for what it truly is—a leprous sore in their skin.

Second, Third, Fourth Angel Plagues (Apoc 16:3–9)

³ And the *second angel* poured out his vial upon the sea, and there came blood as it were of a dead man; and every living soul died in the sea.

⁴ And the *third* poured out his vial upon the rivers and the fountains of waters; and there was made blood.

⁵ And I heard the angel of the waters saying: Thou art just, O Lord, who art, and who wast, the Holy One, because thou hast judged these things:

⁶ For they have shed the blood of saints and prophets, and thou hast given them blood to drink; for they are worthy.

⁷ And I heard another, from the altar, saying: Yea, O Lord God Almighty, true and just are thy judgments.

⁸ And the *fourth angel* poured out his vial upon the sun, and it was given unto him to afflict men with heat and fire:

⁹ And men were scorched with great heat, and they blasphemed the name of God, who hath power over these plagues, neither did they penance to give him glory. (emphasis added)

The second angel pours out his golden vial upon the sea, and it turns into blood. The third angel (the "angel of the waters" according to verse 5)[165] pours out his golden vial upon the rivers and fountains, and they turn to blood. This third plague is judgment for murdering the "saints and prophets." Jesus Christ confirmed that this would happen:

Christ on Punishment on Jerusalem (Mt 23:35–37)

[35] That upon you may come *all the just blood* that hath been shed upon the earth, from the blood of Abel the just, even unto the blood of Zacharias the son of Barachias, whom you killed *between the temple and the altar.*

[36] Amen I say to you, all these things shall come upon this generation.

[37] *Jerusalem, Jerusalem, thou that killest the prophets,* and stonest them that are sent unto thee, how often would I have gathered together thy children, as the hen doth gather her chickens under her wings, and thou wouldest not? (emphasis added)

Who did this? "Jerusalem, Jerusalem!" Jesus Christ confirms for us that Jerusalem is the great city that has murdered the prophets and betrayed God *for centuries.* Jerusalem is spiritually Sodom, Egypt, and Babylon. Previously, the martyrs under the heavenly altar had cried out for justice. God vindicates them as a voice confirms: "True and just are thy judgments."

The fourth angel pours out his golden vial upon the sun, and it scorches men who respond by blaspheming God. You may have noticed already that the first four

---

[165] Traditionally, the angel of the waters is associated with the angel Raphael. The traditional Gospel lesson appointed for the Mass of Saint Raphael on October 24 is John 5:1–4 about the unnamed angel who periodically stirred the waters in the pool of Bethesda: "In these lay a great multitude of sick, of blind, of lame, of withered; waiting for the moving of the water. And an angel of the Lord descended at certain times into the pond; and the water was moved. And he that went down first into the pond after the motion of the water, was made whole, of whatsoever infirmity he lay under."

plagues' destinations match the destinations of the first four trumpets:

1st Trumpet: 1/3 of earth burned	1st Vial on earth yielding a sore
2nd Trumpet: 1/3 of sea becomes blood	2nd Vial on sea becoming blood
3rd Trumpet: 1/3 of rivers become undrinkable	3rd Vial on rivers becoming blood
4th Trumpet: 1/3 of sun, moon, stars go dark	4th Vial on sun becoming scorching hot

So far, the vials of plagues have been against the worshippers of the beast. Now God turns His wrath against the beast.

Fifth Angel Pours Days of Darkness (Apoc 16:10-11)
10 And the *fifth angel* poured out his vial upon the seat of the beast; and his kingdom became dark, and they gnawed their tongues for pain:
11 And they blasphemed the God of heaven, because of their pains and wounds, and did not penance for their works. (emphasis added)

The fifth angel pours out a plague on the "seat of the beast." This is the throne of the kingdom belonging to the Antichrist. Where is it located? According to Our Lord Jesus Christ, it is "Jerusalem, Jerusalem." Darkness fills the kingdom of Antichrist. The worshippers of the beast gnaw their tongues. As with the first plague, their response is to blaspheme God. They do not repent. This reminds us of Pharoah and Egypt receiving the plagues of bloody water, sores, and darkness, but never repenting. Several mystics have foreseen a coming three days of darkness coming at the end of the fifth epoch. This fifth vial signals this universal punishment of darkness, corresponding to the vision of Blessed Anna Maria Taigi (1769–1837):

Three Days of Darkness Described by Anna Maria Taigi

There shall come over the whole earth an intense darkness lasting three days and three nights. Nothing can be seen, and the air will be laden with pestilence which will claim mainly, but not only, the enemies of religion. It will be impossible to use any man-made lighting during this darkness, except blessed candles. He, who out of curiosity, opens his window to look out, or leaves his home, will fall dead on the spot. During these three days, people should remain in their homes, pray the Rosary and beg God for mercy. All the enemies of the Church, whether known or unknown, will perish over the whole earth during that universal darkness, with the exception of a few whom God will soon convert. The air shall be infected by demons who will appear under all sorts of hideous forms.[166]

Visionaries place the three days of darkness as the culminating event of the Minor Chastisement (also known as the Little Tribulation) between the fifth epoch of the Church and the sixth epoch of the Church. This structure will be analyzed toward the end of this book in the section providing a suggested timeline of future events.

Sixth Angel Pours His Vial on Euphrates River (Apoc 16:12–16)

[12] And the *sixth angel* poured out his vial upon that great river Euphrates; and dried up the water thereof, that a way might be prepared for the kings from the rising of the sun.

[13] And I saw from the mouth of the dragon, and from the mouth of the beast, and from the mouth of the false prophet, three unclean spirits like frogs.

[14] For they are the spirits of devils working signs, and they go forth unto the kings of the whole earth, to

---

166 Anna Maria Taigi, *Private Prophecies* (Rome, 1863).

gather them to battle against the great day of the Almighty God.

¹⁵ Behold, I come as a thief. Blessed is he that watcheth, and keepeth his garments, lest he walk naked, and they see his shame.

¹⁶ And he shall gather them together into a place, which in Hebrew is called Armageddon. (emphasis added)

The sixth angel pours out his vial on the Euphrates River. This action mirrors the sixth trumpet, when the four angels bound up the Euphrates River so that a vast army of horsemen with serpent tails could cross over and kill one-third of mankind. In fact, the word "Euphrates" only appears two times in the Apocalypse, here at 16:12 (sixth plague) and at 9:14 (sixth trumpet). The sixth trumpet triggers an army of demonic horsemen coming down from the north over the Euphrates. This sixth plague allows "kings from the rising sun" to cross over the Euphrates. It's worth noting that the message to the sixth church at the beginning of the Apocalypse corresponds to the age of the Israelites returning from Babylonian exile from beyond the Euphrates River. Two of Jeremias's prophecies speak of the Euphrates River as the symbol of the Jews going into exile and eventually returning to Jerusalem.¹⁶⁷

Suddenly the Satanic anti-Trinity appears—the dragon (Satan), the beast (the Antichrist), and the False Prophet. The land beast is directly labeled as the False Prophet. Three unclean spirits come forth from each of the three personages. Their spirits are frogs, evoking the second plague of frogs against Pharaoh by Moses (Ex 8:2–4). Saint John says the three frogs are the "spirits of devils working signs" (Apoc 16:14). The Satanic anti-Trinity breathes out deceptions. These three unclean frogs gather the kings of the earth to make battle against the great day of the Almighty God. How can they make war against God, who

---

¹⁶⁷ See Jeremias chapters 13 and 46.

is invisible and in heaven? They make war against God by attacking the servants of God still on earth.

Jesus Christ interrupts to remind us that "I come as a thief" (Apoc 16:15). Our Lord earlier in Apocalypse 3:3 said He comes as a thief. Saint Paul also taught "that the day of the Lord shall so come as a thief in the night" (1 Thess 5:2). Our Lord also previously told us, "I counsel thee to buy of me gold fire tried, that thou mayest be made rich; and mayest be clothed in white garments, and that the shame of thy nakedness may not appear" (Apoc 3:18). In Christian tradition, "being clothed" refers to the white baptismal garment given to the newly baptized after baptism.[168] We are commanded to keep it white until the great Day of Judgment.

The three frog spirits lead the kings of the earth into one place called *Armageddon* in Hebrew. *Armageddon* is two words in Hebrew. *Har* means "mountain." Megiddo is a town on the Plain of Jezreel in northern Israel. The problem is that Megiddo is geographically located on a flat plain, not a mountain. Even the prophet Zacharias calls it the "plain of Mageddon" when he prophesies:

Mageddon: Where Jews Will See God as "Pierced" (Zech 12:10–11)

[10] And I will pour out upon the house of David, and upon the inhabitants of Jerusalem, the spirit of grace, and of prayers: and they shall look upon me, whom they have pierced: and they shall mourn for him as one mourneth for an only son, and they shall grieve over him, as the manner is to grieve for the death of the firstborn.

[11] In that day there shall be a great lamentation in Jerusalem like the lamentation of Adadremmon in the plain of Mageddon.

---

[168] The Sunday after Easter is traditionally named *Dominica in albis depositis*, or "the Sunday of the laying aside of white robes." This is because the catechumens were baptized on Easter and wore their white baptismal robes for the entire week before taking them off on the Sunday after Easter.

This is a Messianic prophecy describing Jesus Christ as "pierced" and "an only son . . . to grieve for the death of the firstborn." The prophetic feature is that God says, "they shall look upon me whom they have pierced." The one being pierced is God the Firstborn. Mageddon is an ideal battlefield that runs about fifty-eight kilometers (thirty-six miles) long with an average width of twenty-four kilometers (fifteen miles). Does it have a mountain? The nearest mountain is Mount Carmel toward the Mediterranean Sea on the northwest side of the Plain of Mageddon. To the northeast is Mount Tabor, the traditional site of Christ's transfiguration. Mount Carmel is famously associated with the Prophet Elias, who challenged, defeated, and slayed the false prophets of Baal at Mount Carmel. Mount Carmel symbolizes the remnant church and the prophetic power of Elias—reoccurring themes in the Apocalypse. Very likely, Mount Carmel is the *har*, and the enormous plain is the Mageddon yielding for us the Armageddon of the Apocalypse. International battles happen in fields, not on mountaintops. The three frog spirits summon the kings of the earth to battle in the plain below Mount Carmel.

Seventh Angel Pours Vial on the Air (Apoc 16:17–18)
[17] And the *seventh angel* poured out his vial upon the air, and there came a great voice out of the temple from the throne, saying: It is done.
[18] And there were lightnings, and voices, and thunders, and there was a great earthquake, such a one as never had been since men were upon the earth, such an earthquake, so great.

The seventh priest-angel pours out his vial upon the air. This act produces a great voice saying, "It is done," and then comes lightning, voices, thunder, and a great earthquake. This mirrors the seventh trumpet, which also triggered lightning, voices, and an earthquake. The earthquake of the seventh plague vial is "a great

213

earthquake . . . such an earthquake, so great" (v. 18). This is the last and final mention of the earthquake in the Apocalypse. As I argued above, the great earthquake is a sign of the resurrection of Christ: "Behold there was a great earthquake. For an angel of the Lord descended from heaven, and coming, rolled back the stone, and sat upon it" (Mt 28:2). The great earthquake in Jerusalem brought an official end to the Old Testament and the law of Moses, as Saint Paul explains:

An Earthquake Begins the New Covenant (Heb 12:26–28)

[26] Whose voice then moved the earth; but now he promiseth, saying: Yet once more, and I will move not only the earth, but heaven also.

[27] And in that he saith, Yet once more, he signifieth the translation of the moveable things as made, that those things may remain which are immoveable.

[28] Therefore receiving an immoveable kingdom, we have grace; whereby let us serve, pleasing God, with fear and reverence.

Saint Paul is teaching the Hebrew Christians that the old earthly temple has been shaken, leaving it useless and empty. He repeatedly instructs them to seek the true temple in heaven, which is served by Jesus Christ, the High Priest. Paul recalls the great earthquake of Christ's resurrection as proof that God "moved not only earth but heaven also" (Heb. 12:26). The outcome is that "receiving an immoveable kingdom, we have grace" (v. 28)—the recurring teaching of the Apocalypse. The great earthquake triggers the reception of the New Testament kingdom.

Jerusalem Shaken into Three Parts (Apoc 16:19–21)

[19] And the great city was divided into three parts; and the cities of the Gentiles fell. And great Babylon came

in remembrance before God, to give her the cup of the wine of the indignation of his wrath.

²⁰ And every island fled away, and the mountains were not found.

²¹ And great hail, like a talent, came down from heaven upon men: and men blasphemed God for the plague of the hail: because it was exceeding great.

This earthquake divides the great city of Jerusalem into three parts. We know the great city is perfidious Jerusalem because it is distinguished here from "the cities of the Gentiles." Babylon is apostate Jerusalem copulating with pagan Rome. "We have no king but Caesar" (Jn 19:15). They rejected their king and husband. Jesus Christ is no longer their king and husband. Their desired husband is the Roman Emperor. As an adulteress, Jerusalem has taken the surname of Rome. The great city is now labeled the "great Babylon." She drinks not the Eucharistic chalice of blessing, but the chalice of the wine of His wrath.

The division of Jerusalem into three parts derives from Ezechiel, who shaves his head and then divides his hair into three parts.

Why God Divides Jerusalem into Thirds (Eze 5:2-11)
A third part thou shalt burn with fire in the midst of the city, according to the fulfilling of the days of the siege: and thou shalt take a third part, and cut it in pieces with the knife all round about: and the other third part thou shalt scatter in the wind, and I will draw out the sword after them . . . This is Jerusalem. (Eze 5:2, 5)

Therefore as I live, saith the Lord God: Because thou hast violated my sanctuary with all thy offences, and with all thy abominations: I will also break thee in pieces, and my eye shall not spare, and I will not have any pity. (Eze 5:11)

The reason Jerusalem is divided into thirds is because the city is unfaithful to God and has defiled His temple.

"And every island fled away, and the mountains were not found" (Apoc 16:20). Islands and mountains are places of refuge and escape. Yet when God's wrath pours out on Jerusalem and the entire world, there is no place to hide. A billionaire's secret island will not hide him. An underground bunker beneath a mountain will not protect him.

Great hailstones fall from heaven, weighing a talent each—one hundred pounds. A plague of hailstones recalls the seven plagues of Moses against Pharaoh and Egypt. Many commentators have noted that the Jewish historian Josephus, in describing the siege of Jerusalem by the Romans in AD 70, relates those Roman catapults sent enormous "stone missiles weighing a talent and travelling two furlongs or more" into Jerusalem. Josephus describes their impact:

> As for the Jews, they at first watched the coming of the stone, for it was of a white color, and could therefore not only be perceived by the great noise it made, but could be seen also before it came by its brightness; accordingly the watchmen that sat upon the towers gave them [the Jewish rebels] notice when the engine was let go, and the stone came from it, and cried aloud in their own country language, the Son Cometh.[169]

Some versions in English will read "the stone cometh," when according to scholars, the Greek read "the Son cometh." Readers want to change "son" to "stone" because they don't understand why first-century Jews would identify talent-sized stones coming into Jerusalem as "the Son cometh." Yet it may very well be that the Jews recognized the destruction of Jerusalem as the coming of the Son of

---

[169] Josephus, *The Jewish War*, book 5, chapter 6 of Josephus' Greek text by William Whiston.

Man, as described by the Prophet Daniel. And they may very well be aware that Jesus Christ described Himself as the Son of Man and told the priests and Sanhedrin that their temple would be destroyed—and Jerusalem with it. Recall that the preterist-futurist interpretation is that these apocalyptic mysteries happened in Rome and Jerusalem in minor ways but point forward to a universal fulfillment at the end of time with the arrival of the final Antichrist.

The Whore of Babylon (Apocalypse 17)

The beast has a consort who is identified as the Great Harlot. She is the Anti-Bride who seduces men and sends them to hell. She stands in contrast to the wise Bride of Christ, who is the mother of the faithful. The Old Testament book of Proverbs often contrasts these two women: Lady Wisdom versus Lady Folly.

Lady Wisdom Is a Dutiful Wife, and Lady Folly Is a Prostitute (Prov 2:16–17, emphasis added)
¹⁶ That thou mayst be delivered from the strange women, and from the stranger, who softeneth her words:
¹⁷ And forsaketh the guide of her youth,
¹⁸ And hath forgotten the covenant of her God: *for her house inclineth unto death, and her paths to hell.*

The Whore Leads to Hell and Is Associated with Wormwood (Prov 5:3–8, emphasis added)
³ For the lips of a harlot are like a honeycomb dropping, and her throat is smoother than oil.
⁴ But her end is *bitter as wormwood*, and sharp as a two-edged sword.
⁵ Her feet go down into death, and *her steps go in as far as hell.*
⁶ They walk not by the path of life, her steps are wandering, and unaccountable.
⁷ Now therefore, my son, hear me, and depart not from the words of my mouth.
⁸ Remove thy way far from her and come not nigh the doors of her house.

Two chapters in Proverbs depict these two women: Proverbs 7 is the Whore, and Proverbs 8 is Lady Wisdom, who is a mother. Proverbs 7 describes how Lady Wisdom protects the man from this Harlot and how the Harlot dresses like a harlot and commits adultery while her husband is away.

The Whore Slays Men and Sends Them to Hell (Prov 7:10, 18-19, 25–27, emphasis added)
[10] And behold *a woman meeteth him in harlot's attire* prepared to deceive souls; talkative and wandering,
[18] Come, let us be inebriated with the breasts, and let us enjoy the desired embraces, till the day appear.
[19] For *my husband is not at home,* he is gone a very long journey.
[25] Let not thy mind be drawn away in her ways: neither be thou deceived with her paths.
[26] For she hath cast down many wounded, and *the strongest have been slain by her.*
[27] *Her house is the way to hell, reaching even to the inner chambers of death.*

Contrast this Whore to Wisdom as a Faithful Mother (Prov 8:1–4, 32–36, emphasis added)
[1] Doth not *Wisdom* cry aloud, and prudence put forth her voice?
[2] Standing in the top of *the highest places* by the way, in the midst of the paths.
[3] Beside the gates of the city, in the very doors she speaketh, saying:
[4] O ye men, to you I call, and *my voice is to the sons of men...*
[32] Now therefore, *ye children, hear me: Blessed are they that keep my ways.*
[33] Hear instruction and be wise and refuse it not.
[34] Blessed is the man that heareth me, and that watcheth daily at my gates, and waiteth at the posts of my doors.
[35] *He that shall find me, shall find life, and shall have salvation from the Lord:*

[36] But he that shall sin against me, shall hurt his own soul. *All that hate me love death.*

The young man must choose between these two women. Lady Wisdom is on high and brings salvation. The apocalyptic Whore seduces and brings down into hell.

Previously, we have discussed the meaning of the "great city" as either Rome or Jerusalem. By reading Ezechiel, we see that the great city punished by God for her marital unfaithfulness is always Jerusalem. How can Rome commit adultery against God if she has never been married to God in a true covenant? Instead, the mystery of Babylon is that the earthly city of Jerusalem (with its temple) is committing adultery with pagan Rome. Earthly Jerusalem becomes the Anti-Church of the Antichrist.

Introducing Great Whore of Babylon (Apoc 17:1–2)
[1] And there came one of the seven angels, who had the seven vials, and spoke with me, saying: Come, I will shew thee the condemnation of the great harlot, who sitteth upon many waters,
[2] With whom the kings of the earth have committed fornication; and they who inhabit the earth, have been made drunk with the wine of her whoredom.

The great city of old Jerusalem was divided up into three parts. Now we see her final condemnation. One of the seven angels says, "Come, I will shew thee the condemnation of the great harlot, who sitteth upon many waters" (v. 1). She sits on many waters, and we have seen that the waters depict the nations. This is confirmed in verse 15: "The waters which thou sawest, where the harlot sitteth, are peoples, and nations, and tongues." She is enthroned over all nations. One might be tempted to see this city as Rome, but Rome was never over all peoples, nations, or tongues. Rome never held domain over the Chinese or Native Americans. Yet, spiritually speaking, old Jerusalem did rule over all nations. The temple was the throne room of God and the place of God's presence on earth. God did not choose many nations to represent Himself. He chose *one nation*, the children of Abraham, and He chose *one city*, the city of Jerusalem. By divine election, Jerusalem and Israel sit above all other nations. And Jerusalem became the unfaithful harlot!

Now comes the condemnation of the Great Whore. Isaias the Prophet foresaw how Jerusalem became a harlot: "How is the faithful city, that was full of judgment, become a harlot? Justice dwelt in it, but now murderers" (Isa 1:21). Jeremias said the same about Jerusalem: "Hast thou seen what rebellious Israel hast done? she [*sic*] hath gone out of herself upon every high mountain, and under every green tree, and hath played the harlot there" (Jer 3:6).

How has earthly Jerusalem played the harlot? "With whom the kings of the earth have committed fornication; and they who inhabit the earth, have been made drunk with the wine of her whoredom" (Apoc 17:2). Isaias and Jeremias describe her as a harlot, but Ezechiel is much more explicit with how Jerusalem has played the whore with Gentile kings by "spreading your legs with increasing promiscuity to anyone who passed by" (Eze 16:25). Then Ezechiel details three affairs she has had with three pagan kingdoms (Egypt, Assyria, Babylon) using explicit language that is shocking to Bible readers:

Ezechiel Uses Shockingly Sexually Explicit Language for Jerusalem (Eze 16:26–29, emphasis added)
[26] You engaged in prostitution with the *Egyptians*, your neighbors with *large genitals,* and aroused my anger with your increasing *promiscuity*.
[27] So I stretched out my hand against you and reduced your territory; I gave you over to the greed of your enemies, the daughters of the Philistines, *who were shocked by your lewd conduct.*

²⁸ You *engaged in prostitution* with the *Assyrians* too, because you were insatiable; and even after that, *you still were not satisfied.*
²⁹ Then you increased *your promiscuity* to include *Babylonia*, a land of merchants, but even with this *you were not satisfied.*

The language is crass. Jerusalem sought "large genitals" (v. 26), and her "promiscuity" is "insatiable" (v. 29). The Great Harlot is "Babylon" because her promiscuity includes Babylonia of old. And most recently she has committed adultery with Rome as her New Babylon: "We have no king but Caesar" (John 19:15). But she is unlike normal harlots. She does not charge for sex. She pays for sex: "Gifts are given to all harlots: but thou hast given hire to all thy lovers, and thou hast given them gifts to come to thee from every side, to commit fornication with thee" (Eze 16:33).

Ezechiel Describes the Perverted Depravity of Her Adultery with Egypt (Eze 23:19–21, emphasis added)
¹⁹ Yet she became more and more *promiscuous* as she recalled the days of her youth, when she was a *prostitute in Egypt.*
²⁰ There she lusted after her lovers, *whose genitals were like those of donkeys and whose emission was like that of horses.*
²¹ So you longed for the lewdness of your youth, when in Egypt your bosom was caressed, and your young breasts fondled.

Earthly Jerusalem, according to Ezechiel, has lusted after her lovers because their genitals were like those of donkeys or horses. Her fornication is akin to bestiality, and now she couples with *the* beast of the Apocalypse. This is why Saint John records that these pagan nations "have been made drunk with the wine of her whoredom" (v. 2).

The Whore Sitting on a Red Beast (Apoc 17:3–4)

³ And he took me away in spirit into the desert. And I saw a woman sitting upon a scarlet coloured beast, full of names of blasphemy, having seven heads and ten horns.

⁴ And the woman was clothed round about with purple and scarlet, and gilt with gold, and precious stones and pearls, having a golden cup in her hand, full of the abomination and filthiness of her fornication.

The woman sits on the seas but also sits on the sea beast, who came out of the sea. The sea beast is scarlet like the dragon. Previously, we were told that the dragon was red, but not that the beast was also red. But it makes sense that the sea beast would be the same color as Satan, the dragon. He is full of blasphemy and has seven heads and ten horns (details from Daniel).

The Jerusalem Harlot is clothed in purple and scarlet, gilt with gold and precious stones and pearls. These details reveal that she is Jerusalem, as Ezechiel describes God adorning Jerusalem as His honorable wife (before she becomes a harlot):

God Clothed & Decorated Jerusalem (Eze 16:9–13)

⁹ And I washed thee with water and cleansed away thy blood from thee: and I anointed thee with oil.

¹⁰ And I clothed thee with embroidery and shod thee with violet coloured shoes: and I girded thee about with fine linen, and clothed thee with fine garments.

¹¹ I decked thee also with ornaments, and put bracelets on thy hands, and a chain about thy neck.

¹² And I put a jewel upon thy forehead and earrings in thy ears, and a beautiful crown upon thy head.

¹³ And thou wast adorned with gold, and silver, and wast clothed with fine linen, and embroidered work, and many colours: thou didst eat fine flour, and honey,

and oil, and wast made exceeding beautiful: and wast advanced to be a queen.

God told Moses that His temple must be decorated with purple and scarlet cloth and gold: "Speak to the children of Israel, that they bring firstfruits to me: of every man that offereth of his own accord, you shall take them. And these are the things you must take: gold, and silver, and brass, violet and purple, and scarlet twice dyed, and fine linen" (Ex 25:2–4). The veil in the temple was blue, scarlet, and violet (Ex 35:35).

She holds a golden chalice in her hand, "full of the abomination and filthiness of her fornication" (Apoc 17:4). She presents an anti-Eucharist to the world. Jeremias describes that "Babylon hath been a golden cup in the hand of the Lord, that made all the earth drunk: the nations have drunk of her wine, and therefore they have staggered" (Jer 51:7).

"Babylon" Written on Her Forehead (Apoc 17:5–6)

⁵ And on her forehead a name was written: A mystery; Babylon the Great, the mother of the fornications, and the abominations of the earth.
⁶ And I saw the woman drunk with the blood of the saints, and with the blood of the martyrs of Jesus. And I wondered, when I had seen her, with great admiration.

As a harlot, Jerusalem has taken the name of her boyfriend. She has taken the mark of the beast "on her forehead." Jeremias even says, "thou hadst a harlot's forehead, thou wouldst not blush" (Jer 3:3). She is stubborn and unashamed. John calls this a mystery. The Greek word for "sacrament" is *mysterion*. She has received the idolatrous sacrament of the beast as her consort. His name is tattooed on her forehead as Babylon the Great. She is the mother of fornications because she is united with idolatry. Ezechiel reveals that Jerusalem of old had melted down God's precious vessels into idols and then spiritually masturbated with them: "And thou tookest thy beautiful vessels, of my gold, and my silver, which I gave thee, and thou madest thee images of men, and hast committed fornication with them" (Eze 16:17).

What is in the cup? The blood of the saints and martyrs of Jesus. Who first persecuted Christians? Jerusalem or Rome? Jerusalem initiated the persecution of the Church, and at the end of time, she will redouble her efforts to stamp out the disciples of Jesus Christ. Jerusalem killed the prophets, John the Baptist, the Son of God, Saint Stephen the deacon, Saint James Greater, Saint James the Lesser, and tried to kill Saint Peter. Jesus Christ says to the inhabitants of Jerusalem, "That the blood of all the prophets which was shed from the foundation of the world, may be required of this generation" (Lk 11:50). Saint John rarely gives his first-person impression, but he does so here: "And I wondered, when I had seen her, with great admiration."[170] As a first-century Jew, Saint John would have been amazed to see that the glorified city of Jerusalem had become the Harlot and Anti-Church. The Bride of God had rejected her Bridegroom. The angel explains the scenario to John:

The Angel Explains the Mystery of the Whore of Babylon (Apoc 17:7–8)

[7] And the angel said to me: Why dost thou wonder? I will tell thee the mystery of the woman, and of the beast which carrieth her, which hath the seven heads and ten horns.

[8] The beast, which thou sawest, was, and is not, and shall come up out of the abyss,[171] and go into

---

170 The original Latin meaning of "admiration" was "wonderment," not "respect."

171 The Douay-Rheims reads "bottomless pit," but the Greek is "abyss." I'll follow the more literal reading as "abyss" as I do throughout the Apocalypse.

destruction: and the inhabitants on the earth (whose names are not written in the book of life from the foundation of the world) shall wonder, seeing the beast that was, and is not.

The angel challenges Saint John. Why are you wondering? The angel then reveals what the vision means. He says the beast "was, is not, and shall come up out of the abyss" (v. 8). This description stands against the description of God as "him that is, and that was, and that is to come" (Apoc 1:4). The angel recognizes the past tense and future tense of this beast, but not the present tense. This likely refers to Satan as an angel, as having fallen through pride, but then arisen one last time from the abyss. It likely refers to the "binding of Satan for a thousand years" in Apocalypse 20:2. Satan is once again active. Christ is resurrected with a great earthquake and binds Satan *for a long time*, and then Satan emerges from the abyss one last time by animating his sea beast as the Antichrist and land beast as the False Prophet. The reference to he who "was, is not, and is to come" likely also refers to the false miracle by which the Antichrist dies by a head wound and rises again to the astonishment of all: he "had the wound by the sword and lived" (Apoc 13:14). Just as Jesus was truly a Jew and truly rose from the dead, so the Antichrist will claim to be King of the Jews and falsely rise from the dead. The Antichrist is a copycat.

The inhabitants of the earth whose names are not written in the Book of Life shall wonder after the beast. This is a wonder of admiration. They love and worship the beast. Note also that the names inside the Book of Life were written at the foundation of the world. Before creation, God knew the names of those who would be with Him forever in Heaven.

The Heads of the Beast Are Seven Mountains (Apoc 17:9–13)

[9] And here is the understanding that hath wisdom. The seven heads are seven mountains, upon which the woman sitteth, and they are seven kings:

[10] Five are fallen, one is, and the other is not yet come: and when he is come, he must remain a short time.

[11] And the beast which was and is not: the same also is the eighth, and is of the seven, and goeth into destruction.

[12] And the ten horns which thou sawest, are ten kings, who have not yet received a kingdom, but shall receive power as kings one hour after the beast.

[13] These have one design: and their strength and power they shall deliver to the beast.

The angel invokes the need for wisdom (as in the case of the mark of the beast) and describes the seven heads as seven mountains. Nearly every commentary on the book of Apocalypse observes that the city of Rome is on seven hills:

1. Palatine Hill (Collis Palatinus)
2. Capitoline Hill (Collis Capitolinus)
3. Caelian Hill (Collis Caelius)
4. Aventine Hill (Collis Aventinus)
5. Quirinal Hill (Collis Quirinalis)
6. Viminal Hill (Collis Viminalis)
7. Esquiline Hill (Collis Esquilinus)

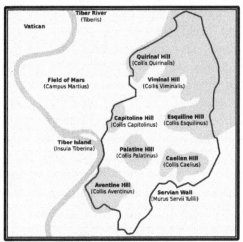

The Seven Hills of Rome

Pagan tradition held that the twin brothers Romulus and Remus built their original settlement upon the central Palatine Hill on April 21, 753 BC. Vatican Hill is where Saint Peter was buried, becoming the devotional center for the Church, but is *not* one of the seven hills since it is outside the walls of Rome.

This proves yet again that the sea beast is Roman. Some have falsely concluded that this means the Great Harlot is Rome and not Jerusalem. Yet this fails to follow the imagery. The Great Harlot rides on the beast. She sits on the beast. Sitting is not geographical. It is political. Jerusalem as harlot has taken the name of Rome and sits upon Rome. The Harlot is not Rome. Otherwise, Rome would sit on top of Rome, and this is ridiculous.

The angel explains that the seven heads correspond to seven kings: "Five are fallen, one is, and the other is not yet come: and when he is come, he must remain a short time" (v. 10). It is natural to turn to the chronicles of the Roman emperors to find these seven kings. Here are the typical lists provided by preterist interpreters of the Apocalypse:

Three Roman Options for the "Seven Kings"
Option 1: Julius Caesar, Augustus, Tiberius, Caligula, Claudius, Nero, Galba

Option 2: Claudius, Nero, Galba, Otho, Vitellius, Vespasian, Titus
Option 3: Galba, Otho, Vitellius, Vespasian, Titus, Domitian, Nerva

None of the three Roman sets of seven kings are satisfying. For Option 1, it must be admitted that Julius was never actually an emperor. Moreover, this list necessitates dating the Apocalypse vision as occurring during the reign of Nero. I sympathize with placing the Apocalypse in late AD 60; however, tradition does *not* place Saint John on the island of Patmos at any time during the reign of Nero (AD 54–68). One positive with Option 1 is that Galba reigned only seven months and seven days, qualifying him as the one who "must remain a short time" as the seventh king.

Option 2 is untenable because it makes Vespasian the sixth king of a "short time," and yet he ruled nine years, eleven months, and twenty-two days. The same goes for Option 3, which makes Domitian the sixth king of a "short time," and yet Domitian reigned fifteen years and four days. Definitely not a short time.

A better solution for the seven kings is found if we turn to the founding of Rome. The three options above look at seven emperors (*imperator*) and not for seven kings (*rex*). As I mentioned above, Romulus and Remus established the first settlement of Rome on the central Palatine Hill. Romulus murdered Remus and became the first king of Rome. Roman history gives the title king (*rex*) to only seven rulers.

1. Romulus the Founder
2. Numa Pompilius
3. Tullus Hostilius
4. Ancus Marcius
5. Lucius Priscus Tarquinius
6. Servius Tullius
7. Lucius Tarquinius Superbus

Moreover, Roman mythology teaches that each of the seven hills of Rome were colonized and annexed to Rome successively during the time of the seven kings:

1. Romulus built on Palatine Hill
2. Later Romulus joined Capitoline Hill to Rome
3. Tullus Hostilius defeated the Albans and annexed Caelian Hill
4. Ancus Marcius annexed Aventine Hill
5. Servius Tullius annexed Quirinal Hill
6. Servius Tullius annexed Viminal Hill
7. Servius Tullius annexed Esquiline Hill[172]

This list of "seven kings" is related historically to the seven hills of Rome. These kings are the founding fathers of Rome, not the emperors. This makes better sense because the angel teaches that there is also an eighth king that emerges and is "of the seven."

Another solid option is to look at the founding kings of Jerusalem. King Saul is the original king, and he was deposed by God for disobedience. God chose King David, who moved the ark of the covenant to Jerusalem. Then his son King Solomon built the temple in Jerusalem to house the ark of the covenant. But there is another major hint in the Apocalypse that we should begin our counting with King Solomon, who reigned over Israel from 970–931 BC—a thousand years (a millennium) before Christ.[173] The only other time the number 666 appears in the whole of the Bible is in reference to King Solomon: "And the weight of the gold that was brought to Solomon every year, was six hundred sixty-six talents of gold" (3 Kings 10:14). King Solomon is the only person in the Bible identified with the number 666, making him the king of 666. The throne of

---

172 Tullius claimed three hills by building a wall around all seven hills.

173 Perhaps the concept of binding Satan for a millennium, a concept within the Apocalypse, relates to this thousand-year interim between Solomon (666) and Jesus (888).

Solomon was also identified as having six steps leading up to it.:

King Solomon's Throne with Six Steps (3 Kings 10:18–20)

¹⁸ King Solomon also made a great throne of ivory: and overlaid it with the finest gold.

¹⁹ It had six steps: and the top of the throne was round behind: and there were two hands on either side holding the seat: and two lions stood, one at each hand.

²⁰ And twelve little lions stood upon the six steps on the one side and on the other: there was no such work made in any kingdom.

In many ways, Solomon is a type of the Antichrist. He is Jewish and truly the Messianic Son of David. When Solomon becomes king, he makes an odd association between himself and his father David: "And now, O Lord God, thou hast made thy servant king instead of David my father: and I am but a child and know not how to go out and come in" (3 Kings 3:7). The Greek Septuagint version of this verse reads *anti David* for "instead of David." This language might have given rise to the notion of Anti-Messiah or Anti-Christ as being the idolatrous son of David who received 666 talents of gold annually.

Recall that the Antichrist will be born of fornication. Solomon's mother, Bathsheba, was married to another man and committed adultery with King David. Solomon grows up to rule over Israel but joins himself to seven hundred wives and three hundred concubines from the nations (3 Kings 11:3). These wives symbolize political alliances since they are described as the princess daughters from Moab, Ammon, Edom, and Sidon. Solomon even married the daughter of Pharaoh in Egypt. He allows his wives to bring their idols and false worship into Jerusalem and Judah:

King Solomon's Wives Pollute Jerusalem with Idols (3 Kings 11:3–11)

³ And he had seven hundred wives as queens, and three hundred concubines: and the women turned away his heart.

⁴ And when he was now old, his heart was turned away by women to follow strange gods: and his heart was not perfect with the Lord his God, as was the heart of David his father.

⁵ But Solomon worshipped Astarthe the goddess of the Sidonians, and Moloch the idol of the Ammonites.

⁶ And Solomon did that which was not pleasing before the Lord, and did not fully follow the Lord, as David his father.

⁷ Then Solomon built a temple for Chamos the idol of Moab, on the hill that is over against Jerusalem, and for Moloch the idol of the children of Ammon.

⁸ And he did in this manner for all his wives that were strangers, who burnt incense, and offered sacrifice to their gods.

⁹ And the Lord was angry with Solomon, because his mind was turned away from the Lord the God of Israel, who had appeared to him twice,

¹⁰ And had commanded him concerning this thing, that he should not follow strange gods: but he kept not the things which the Lord commanded him.

¹¹ The Lord therefore said to Solomon: Because thou hast done this, and hast not kept my covenant, and my precepts, which I have commanded thee, I will divide and rend thy kingdom, and will give it to thy servant.

Verse 5 states that Solomon did not just tolerate false gods but actually "worshipped Astarthe the goddess of the Sidonians and Moloch the idol of the Ammonites."

Solomon built the temple for the first time. So, the Antichrist will be an Anti-David. He will see himself as Solomon building the temple—but for himself to be worshipped as a god. Solomon entered a pact with King Hiram I of Tyre to assist him in building the original temple in Jerusalem. Recall how Ezechiel described Satan as the fallen "prince of Tyre" (Eze 28). This is the Antichrist beast-king and fallen Satan working together.

Another hint of the Antichrist being like Solomon is that King Solomon was the *only* king of Israel or Judah whose kingdom extended so far north it had the Euphrates River as its northern border. The recurring importance of the Euphrates River (sixth trumpet and sixth plague) seems to point to a Solomonic Israel.

Gnostic and rabbinical texts describe Solomon as a magician or sorcerer with power over demons that would do his bidding by bringing him precious gemstones. The Jewish historian Josephus references the legend of Solomon's magic ring, said to allow him to command demons.[174] Likewise, rabbinical literature says that King Solomon received a "seal ring" engraved with the name of God by which he controlled the demons.[175] The ring allegedly was made partly of brass and partly of iron. The brass part commanded good angels, and the iron part commanded evil demons.[176]

The seven kings, then, would be the kings after King Solomon:

1. Rehoboam reigned for 17 years.
2. Abijah reigned for 3 years.
3. Asa reigned for 41 years.
4. Jehoshaphat reigned for 25 years.
5. Jehoram reigned for 8 years.
6. Ahaziah reigned for 1 year. Athaliah (queen mother, widow of Jehoram, and mother of Ahaziah) reigned for 6 years.

---

[174] Josephus, *Jewish Antiquities* viii. 2, § 5.

[175] *Babylonian Talmud,* Gittin, 68a–b.

[176] Joseph Jacobs, "Seal of Solomon," *Jewish Encyclopedia,* referenced 11 April 2022.

7. Jehoash (Joash) reigned for 40 years.

We have a series of seven kings descending from Solomon. The sixth king, Ahaziah, reigned only one year, fitting the identity of the sixth king as ruling for a "short time." These seven kings symbolize the demise of Jerusalem into iniquity and idolatry.

The Ten Horns of Antichrist (Apoc 17:11–13)
[11] And the beast which was and is not: the same also is the eighth, and is of the seven, and goeth into destruction.
[12] And the ten horns which thou sawest, are ten kings, who have not yet received a kingdom, but shall receive power as kings one hour after the beast.
[13] These have one design: and their strength and power they shall deliver to the beast.

Verse 11 reveals that the sea beast Antichrist is actually an eighth king: "And the beast which was and is not: the same also is the eighth, and is of the seven, and goeth into destruction." The Greek word for going into "destruction" here is *Apoleian*, which reminds us of the "king of the Abyss" named *Apollyon* in Apocalypse 9:11. The Antichrist, it seems, is like a founding father associated with these seven founding fathers of Rome. He is like them but separate. He will follow their pattern of introducing sin, idolatry, and immorality into Jerusalem, just as King Solomon of the 666 and his seven kings did.

The seven kings are the seven hills/heads of the beast. But there are also ten horns. These ten horns are also ten kings, but ones that have not yet received a kingdom. They shall receive power to become kings for only one hour—a short time. They will deliver their strength and power to the Antichrist beast. This reference to ten kings derives from the "ten iron toes" of the fourth kingdom (Roman Empire):

234

The Ten Iron Toes of Roman Empire (Dan 2:40–42)

[40] And the fourth kingdom shall be as iron. As iron breaketh into pieces, and subdueth all things, so shall that break and destroy all these.

[41] And whereas thou sawest the feet, and the toes, part of potter's clay, and part of iron: the kingdom shall be divided, but yet it shall take its origin from the iron, according as thou sawest the iron mixed with the miry clay.

[42] And as the toes of the feet were part of iron, and part of clay, the kingdom shall be partly strong, and partly broken.

The description in Daniel is of the Roman Empire breaking into ten pieces. The Roman Empire broke apart into what we today call First World nations. We need not expect them to be *exactly* ten nations. The number ten signifies totality. The ten nations signify all the non-Jewish Gentile nations. They will give their authority to the Antichrist king, who will then rule as the sole "king of kings" on earth. Then they will wage war with the Lamb:

Ten Kings Hate and Burn Whore (Apoc 17:14–18)

[14] These shall fight with the Lamb, and the Lamb shall overcome them, because he is Lord of lords, and King of kings, and they that are with him are called, and elect, and faithful.

[15] And he said to me: The waters which thou sawest, where the harlot sitteth, are peoples, and nations, and tongues.

[16] And the ten horns which thou sawest in the beast: these shall hate the harlot, and shall make her desolate and naked, and shall eat her flesh, and shall burn her with fire.

[17] For God hath given into their hearts to do that which pleaseth him: that they give their kingdom to the beast, till the words of God be fulfilled.

¹⁸ And the woman which thou sawest, is the great city, which hath kingdom over the kings of the earth.

The Lamb is Jesus Christ, who has been killed through the coordinated effort of Jerusalem and Rome. How can they fight Jesus, who is already in heaven? They will attack His Church—the "elect and faithful." The Church of Jesus Christ will win. As the Antichrist pretends to be the king of kings, here we have the Lamb called Lord of lords and King of kings. In verse 15, the angel says that the waters where the Harlot sits are all the "peoples, nations, and tongues." Ultimately the ten horns/kingdoms shall hate the Harlot. They shall hate Jerusalem. They will make her desolate and naked, eat her, and burn her with fire. This happened the first time in AD 70, when Rome turned on Jerusalem, sieged the city, and burned it with fire. Rome even stripped the city of its temple. This will happen again at the end of time with Jerusalem.

Verse 17 explains that the Gentile nations will deliver their kingdoms to the Antichrist until the words of God are fulfilled. Verse 18 explains that the woman is the "great city," and this again confirms the city is Jerusalem: "the great city, which is called spiritually, Sodom and Egypt, *where their Lord also was crucified*" (Apoc 11:8, emphasis added). The great city has "kingdom over the kings of the earth." No city, not even Rome, has had dominion over all the kings of the earth. The dominion here is spiritual—Jerusalem is the only city appointed by God to be the spiritual capital of earth, with His temple as the location of His divine presence on earth.

Babylon the Great Is Fallen
(Apocalypse 18)

The Gentile kings have turned on Jerusalem. She is desolate. She has fallen.

Babylon the Great is Fallen (Apoc 18:1–2)

¹And after these things, I saw another angel come down from heaven, having great power: and the earth was enlightened with his glory.

²And he cried out with a strong voice, saying: Babylon the Great is fallen, is fallen; and is become the habitation of devils, and the hold of every unclean spirit, and the hold of every unclean and hateful bird:

Another angel comes down from heaven with great power and enlightens the earth. He calls out with a strong voice, "Babylon the Great is fallen." This is a quotation from the prophet Amos: "Hear ye this word, which I take up concerning you for a lamentation. The house of Israel is fallen, and it shall rise no more. The Virgin of Israel is cast down upon her land, there is none to raise her up" (Amos 5:1–2).

Jerusalem was a virgin. She became a harlot, marked with the brand of her consort, Babylon. She becomes the home of devils and unclean spirits and unclean birds. Jerusalem should have been a sacred city. Now she is unclean. This cannot be Rome because pre-Christian Rome had always been idolatrous, demonic, and unclean. The scandal is that Jerusalem has become unclean and empty as Christ forewarned: "Jerusalem, Jerusalem . . . Behold, your house shall be left to you desolate" (Mt 23:37–38).

Go Out from Her, My People (Apoc 18:3–8)

³Because all nations have drunk of the wine of the wrath of her fornication; and the kings of the earth have committed fornication with her; and the

merchants of the earth have been made rich by the power of her delicacies.

⁴ And I heard another voice from heaven, saying: Go out from her, my people; that you be not partakers of her sins, and that you receive not of her plagues.

⁵ For her sins have reached unto heaven, and the Lord hath remembered her iniquities.

⁶ Render to her as she also hath rendered to you; and double unto her double according to her works: in the cup wherein she hath mingled, mingle ye double unto her.

⁷ As much as she hath glorified herself, and lived in delicacies, so much torment and sorrow give ye to her; because she saith in her heart: I sit a queen and am no widow; and sorrow I shall not see.

⁸ Therefore shall her plagues come in one day, death, and mourning, and famine, and she shall be burnt with the fire; because God is strong, who shall judge her.

Our Lord Jesus Christ, in speaking about the earthly temple in Jerusalem, says, "Is it not written, My house shall be called the house of prayer to all nations? But you have made it a den of thieves" (Mk 11:17). Jesus drove out the *merchants* from the temple. And here the merchants mourn their ejection. Jerusalem was supposed to be the spiritual house of prayer for all nations. But instead of illuminating the nations, she corrupted the nations. She was a den of thieves. The high priests ran the temple like a business. The nations "fornicated" with Jerusalem. The worst merchant of all was Judas Iscariot. The lyrics of the traditional Tenebrae responsories for Maundy Thursday ("Judas Mercator Pessiumus") recall Judas as the "worst possible merchant":

Original Latin:	English Translation:
Judas, mercator pessimus,	Judas, worst possible merchant,
Osculo petiit Dominum.	Asked to kiss the Lord.
Ille, ut agnus innocens,	He like an innocent lamb,
Non negavit Judae osculum.	Did not reject the kiss of Judas.

Denariorum numero	For a number of coins,
Christum Judaeis tradidit.	He delivered Christ to the Jews.
Melius illi erat,	It would have been better for him,
Si natus non fuisset.	Had he never been born.
Denariorum numero	For a number of coins
Christum Judaeis tradidit.	He delivered Christ to the Jews.

The insertion of monetary exchange within religion breeds corruption and betrayal.

Verse 4 records a voice from heaven saying, "Go out from her," to avoid receiving her plagues. This is the message in the epistle to the Hebrews: "We [Christians] have an altar, whereof they [Jews] have no power to eat who serve the tabernacle" (Heb 13:10). Jerusalem is no longer the great city of God's presence. The temple is empty. Now Christ is the sacrificial Lamb. The true temple and altar are in heaven. The true high priest is in heaven—Jesus Christ. Now we must "go out" from Jerusalem and enter the New Jerusalem, which is in heaven.

Jerusalem's sins have "reached unto heaven," recalling the warning of Christ our Lord about Jerusalem coming to "fill up then the measure of your fathers" (Mt 23:32) in sin. She has mingled blood in her anti-Eucharistic chalice. Her punishment is doubled. Pagan Romans would not be held to this high standard. It is Jerusalem and her priests who have betrayed God, and their punishment is twofold. She glorified herself instead of glorifying God. She boasts "in her heart: I sit a queen and am no widow." The reference here to heart, queen, and widow refers to the fall of Jerusalem in Isaias: "I shall be a queen forever: thou hast not laid these things to thy heart...I shall not sit as a widow" (Isa 47:7–8).

Verse 8 states her plagues, pestilence, mourning, and famine come in one day. Do the seven plagues from the seven vials come all in one twenty-four-hour day? This is apocalyptic language, wherein time is relative and telescoped. The coming judgment is sudden and quick and happens as the Judgment Day of the Lord. Jerusalem was suddenly burned with fire in AD 70. The same will happen again with the Antichrist. The nations will turn on Jerusalem, but the efficient cause is God "who will judge her."

World Mourns the Burning City (Apoc 18:9–16)

⁹ And the kings of the earth, who have committed fornication, and lived in delicacies with her, shall weep, and bewail themselves over her, when they shall see the smoke of her burning:

¹⁰ Standing afar off for fear of her torments, saying: Alas! alas! that great city Babylon, that mighty city: for in one hour is thy judgment come.

¹¹ And the merchants of the earth shall weep, and mourn over her: for no man shall buy their merchandise anymore.

¹² Merchandise of gold and silver, and precious stones; and of pearls, and fine linen, and purple, and silk, and scarlet, and all thyine wood, and all manner of vessels of ivory, and all manner of vessels of precious stone, and of brass, and of iron, and of marble,

¹³ And cinnamon, and odours, and ointment, and frankincense, and wine, and oil, and fine flour, and wheat, and beasts, and sheep, and horses, and chariots, and slaves, and souls of men.

¹⁴ And the fruits of the desire of thy soul are departed from thee, and all fat and goodly things are perished from thee, and they shall find them no more at all.

¹⁵ The merchants of these things, who were made rich, shall stand afar off from her, for fear of her torments, weeping and mourning.

¹⁶ And saying: Alas! alas! that great city, which was clothed with fine linen, and purple, and scarlet, and was gilt with gold, and precious stones, and pearls.

The kings who have fornicated with the Harlot (Jerusalem) begin to weep. They stand far off, afraid to be near her, as they watch the smoke arise from the city. They say, "Alas!

alas! that great city Babylon, that mighty city: for in one hour is thy judgment come" (v. 16). This refers to the original burning of Jerusalem in AD 70, but also to the final burning of Jerusalem at the time of the Antichrist.

After the kings, the merchants weep because their business enterprise has come to an end. Jerusalem was one of the premiere trading cities in the world at the time of Jesus. It is situated on the route between Africa, Asia, and Europe. It has maritime contact with the port on the Mediterranean Sea. This location provided trade with Egypt, Arabia, Persia, Syria, Greece, Italy, and even Spain. Historians recount that Jerusalem had become a center of commerce for gold, silver, gems, linen, wool, silk, perfume, ointments, spices, wine, and fine oils. For example, Mary Magdalene had no difficulty securing expensive spices and ointments in less than a few hours during the narrative of Christ's death and resurrection. Saint John chronicles the list of all the fine items available in Jerusalem. Saint John had lived there and seen it all. All these items are called "the fruits of the desire" and recall the temptation of Adam and Eve who fell into sin after desiring the fruit of the forbidden tree.

One further hint that this great city is Jerusalem is verse 16, which reads, "fine linen, and purple, and silk, and scarlet." The book of Exodus refers more than twenty times to the decoration of the tabernacle as being "violet, and purple, and scarlet twice dyed, and fine twisted linen" (Ex 21:1, 31). The Great Harlot in Apocalypse 17 is wearing these same colors and materials. She is the corrupted priesthood in a defiled temple. A house of prayer is now a den of thieves.

The Great City Is Judged for the Apostles and Prophets (Apoc 18:17–20)

[17] For in one hour are so great riches come to nought; and every shipmaster, and all that sail into the lake, and

mariners, and as many as work in the sea, stood afar off.

¹⁸ And cried, seeing the place of her burning, saying: What city is like to this great city?

¹⁹ And they cast dust upon their heads, and cried, weeping and mourning, saying: Alas! alas! that great city, wherein all were made rich, that had ships at sea, by reason of her prices: for in one hour she is made desolate.

²⁰ Rejoice over her, thou heaven, and ye holy apostles and prophets; for God hath judged your judgment on her.

First, the kings. Second, the merchants. Third come the shipmasters and mariners and those that work in the sea. They also stand far off and weep, watching the burning of the great city. The lamentation over the city by the kings, merchants, and mariners ends with a call to rejoice: "Rejoice over her, thou heaven, and ye holy apostles and prophets; for God hath judged your judgment on her" (v. 20). This city cannot be Rome because Rome did not kill the Old Testament prophets or John the Baptist. Jerusalem killed all the prophets, as well as the Apostle James the Greater and the Apostle James the Lesser. And Jerusalem shall be the center of persecution at the end of time under the Antichrist.

A Great Stone Cast into the Sea (Apoc 18:21–24)

²¹ And a mighty angel took up a stone, as it were a great millstone, and cast it into the sea, saying: With such violence as this shall Babylon, that great city, be thrown down, and shall be found no more at all.

²² And the voice of harpers, and of musicians, and of them that play on the pipe, and on the trumpet, shall no more be heard at all in thee; and no craftsman of any art whatsoever shall be found any more at all in

thee; and the sound of the mill shall be heard no more at all in thee.

²³ And the light of the lamp shall shine no more at all in thee; and the voice of the bridegroom and the bride shall be heard no more at all in thee: for thy merchants were the great men of the earth, for all nations have been deceived by thy enchantments.

²⁴ And in her was found the blood of prophets and of saints, and of all that were slain upon the earth.

A Mighty Angel (Mighty Messenger) takes up a great stone—"a millstone of stumbling"—and casts it in the sea. (For more on the identity of the Mighty Messenger as perhaps being Christ Himself, see the section above on the tenth chapter of the Apocalypse at the sixth trumpet.) This stone is Jerusalem, as foretold by Jesus Christ:

> And Jesus answering, said to them: Amen, I say to you, if you shall have faith, and stagger not, not only this of the fig tree shall you do, but also if you shall say to this mountain, Take up and cast thyself into the sea, it shall be done. (Mt 21:21)

Christ, we know, was talking about the perfidious city on a hill that killed him, not a random mountain. The reference to a millstone recalls also the teaching of Christ: "But he that shall scandalize one of these little ones that believe in me, it were better for him that a millstone should be hanged about his neck, and that he should be drowned in the depth of the sea" (Mt 18:6). Jerusalem being "cast into the sea" is the poetic description of Jerusalem being cast into the nations. She is no longer holy, exalted, or covenantal. She has sunk to the bottom of the sea.

The harpers and musicians will no longer be heard in Jerusalem. This is a reference to the sacred musicians from the tribe of Levi that played instruments at the temple (1 Para 25). The sound of the craftsmen and the mill are also silenced. This refers to the sacred craft of building and designing in Jerusalem, and the mill refers to the ancient memory that the temple was built on the site of an ancient threshing floor and mill (cf. 2 Para 3). The lamps of the temple will no more shine. "The voice of the bridegroom and the bride" refer to the voice of God and His bride, Jerusalem. God will no longer speak in this place. He will speak from within the New Bride and New Jerusalem—the one true Church as the Bride of Christ. The reason for all this is that "in her was found the blood of prophets and of saints, and of all that were slain upon the earth" (Apoc 18:24). This is the open teaching of our Lord Jesus Christ before His crucifixion:

> That upon you [Jerusalem] may come all the just blood that hath been shed upon the earth, from the blood of Abel the just, even unto the blood of Zacharias the son of Barachias, whom you killed between the temple and the altar. Amen I say to you, all these things shall come upon this generation. Jerusalem, Jerusalem, thou that killest the prophets! (Mt 23:35–37)

Wedding Supper of the Lamb
(Apocalypse 19)

Now that the Harlot has been burned for her sins, it is time for God to send out the announcement of the marriage supper of the Lamb to His "New Jerusalem."

Alleluia! Her Smoke Ascends (Apoc 19:1–3)

[1] After these things I heard as it were the voice of much people in heaven, saying: Alleluia. Salvation, and glory, and power is to our God.

[2] For true and just are his judgments, who hath judged the great harlot which corrupted the earth with her fornication, and hath revenged the blood of his servants, at her hands.

[3] And again they said: Alleluia. And her smoke ascendeth for ever and ever.

The great multitude in heaven now praises God after the destruction of the Harlot. They sing, "Alleluia. Salvation, and glory, and power is to our God" (v. 1). The word "Alleluia" appears in the New Testament only four times—and all four times in this nineteenth chapter. This occurrence in 19:1 is the first time Alleluia appears in the New Testament. *Alleluia* is a Greek transliteration of the Hebrew phrase *Hallelu Yah*, meaning "Praise ye Yah"—with *Yah* being the shortened form of Yahweh or Jehovah. Notably, Catholics follow the Greek transliteration and omit the initial *H* and write and pronounce it as it is written here in the Apocalypse: *Alleluia.*[177] Protestants tend to add in the *H* and write and say it as *Hallelujah.*[178]

---

[177] The more recent Greek texts currently have a breathing mark before the initial *A*, but this would not have been present in the ancient uncial versions of the text.

[178] The "Hallelujah Chorus" in Handel's *Messiah* pronounces it with the initial *H*. George Handel was a Protestant.

It may be hard for contemporary readers to hear the saints in heaven *rejoicing* over judgment, but they give the reason why: "who hath judged the great harlot which corrupted the earth with her fornication, and hath revenged the blood of his servants, at her hands" (v. 2). God judges justly, and vengeance belongs to the Lord. They continue to rejoice over the burning of the Harlot.

The Priests and Cherubim Fall Down in Adoration (Apoc 19:4–6)

⁴ And the four and twenty presbyters, and the four living creatures fell down and adored God that sitteth upon the throne, saying: Amen; Alleluia.

⁵ And a voice came out from the throne, saying: Give praise to our God, all ye his servants; and you that fear him, little and great.

⁶ And I heard as it were the voice of a great multitude, and as the voice of many waters, and as the voice of great thunders, saying, Alleluia: for the Lord our God the Almighty hath reigned.

We once again see the throne room of God and the divine liturgy of heaven. The twenty-four priests and four creatures fall down and adore God. There is a call to worship to "give praise to our God" (v. 5). And the great multitude (who are the 144,000) respond with their own "Alleluia" and verse to follow.

The Wife of the Lamb in All White (Apoc 19:7–8)

⁷ Let us be glad and rejoice and give glory to him; for the marriage of the Lamb is come, and his wife hath prepared herself.

⁸ And it is granted to her that she should clothe herself with fine linen, glittering and white. For the fine linen are the justifications of saints.

The great multitude rejoices and announces, "the Lamb is come, and his wife hath prepared herself" (v. 7). In reality the great multitude *is* His wife. She has clothed herself in fine linen, glittering and white. The Catholic Church has traditionally vested her presbyters and clergy in fine white linen garments. Linen symbolizes suffering and martyrdom. Linen is a cloth made by *crushing* the fibers of flax stalks and then combing them to create long soft fibers that are spun into yarns. The final product is "glittering and white." The symbolism shows that the plant is punished in order to produce the fibers. For this reason, the priests of the Old Testament only wore linen in the temple, and the noble wife in Proverbs 31 only wears linen (Prov 31:22). Against the Lutheran heresy of "justification by faith alone," we read that this linen garment of the Church is "the justifications of the saints."

Called to the Marriage Supper (Apoc 19:9–10)

⁹ And he said to me: Write: Blessed are they that are called to the marriage supper of the Lamb. And he saith to me: These words of God are true.
¹⁰ And I fell down before his feet, to adore him. And he saith to me: See thou do it not: I am thy fellow servant, and of thy brethren, who have the testimony of Jesus. Adore God. For the testimony of Jesus is the spirit of prophecy.

The angel instructs Saint John to write a special message: "Blessed are they that are called to the marriage supper of the Lamb" (v. 9). This message is repeated in every traditional Catholic Mass. The presbyter, holding the Eucharist, turns to the people and says, "Behold the Lamb of God. Behold Him who takes away the sin of the world. Blessed are they that are called to the marriage supper of the Lamb." The Supper of the Lamb is at the end of time, but we participate in this supper whenever we attend the Holy Sacrifice of the Mass. Christ the Lamb gives Himself to us when He feeds us with His Body. "These words of God are true."

Saint John falls down before the angel to adore him but is rebuked. The angel is the fellow servant of Saint John and of the brethren. This reveals that human nature has been elevated to dwell with the angels as co-worshipers of God. The angel tells John, "Adore God" (v. 10). The Catholic Church had to formulate this distinction in worship. In AD 787, the Second Council of Nicea taught the important distinction between *latria* as worship of God alone, and *dulia* as veneration of angels, saints, and holy things such as crosses, churches, and sacred images. We do not give the divine adoration (*latria*) to angels, saints, or even to the Blessed Virgin Mary. The Holy Trinity alone receives *latria* (adoration). We do, however, show respect or veneration to holy humans and angels, but it is a lesser veneration given to creatures. The Greek word here in Apocalypse 18:10 is *proskynesai*, but in this context, it refers to the adoration due to God alone.

It is rather odd that Saint John, an apostle who was acquainted with Jesus Christ before and after His resurrection, would be tempted to worship an angel. It is more likely here that John is not mistaking an angel for God. Nor is John tempted to commit idolatry by worshipping an angel in the presence of the Lamb. There are plenty of examples of Old Testament saints bowing down to angels. In the Greek Septuagint, there are even many examples of holy humans performing *proskyneo* for angels. Given these Old Testament examples, perhaps Saint John is merely following what the patriarchs did in the presence of angels: "He ran to meet them from the door of his tent and adored down to the ground" (Gen 18:2).[179] John is saluting one who he perceives as his superior.

The solution is the explanation of the angel: "I am thy fellow servant" (Apoc 19:10). Through the incarnation of

---

[179] For more examples, see also Genesis 19:1, 23:7–12, 27:29, 33:3–7, 37:7–10, 42:6, 43:26–28.

Christ and sacrifice as the Lamb, He has elevated human saints to worship on parity with the angels. Humans are no longer "waiting in limbo" for the Messiah. They are now shoulder to shoulder with the angels in heaven. The Old Testament was mediated through Moses, the priests, and angels. This separation is no longer in place. This is further confirmed by the next verse, which shows heaven now open:

Jesus Christ on His White Horse (Apoc 19:11–13)

[11] And I saw heaven opened and behold a white horse; and he that sat upon him was called faithful and true, and with justice doth he judge and fight.

[12] And his eyes were as a flame of fire, and on his head were many diadems, and he had a name written, which no man knoweth but himself.

[13] And he was clothed with a garment sprinkled with blood; and his name is called, THE WORD OF GOD.

Heaven is open to mankind, and we see Christ riding a white horse. This detail reveals the white horse rider of the first open seal (Apoc 6:1–2) is Christ Himself. This means we are circling back to the first seal. We are back at the beginning of the seven seals—or perhaps we are seeing Christ at the end of his ride after centuries of victory.

This is the Lamb of God riding out at the beginning of the New Testament (AD 33) to spread the Gospel and kingdom among the nations. He is called "faithful and true." His eyes are flames of fire, and he wears many crowns. He has a special name, which no one knows but Christ. This is a mysterious saying, but it likely refers to the reality that no man fully comprehends who Christ is. He is God—beyond our full comprehension. "I am who I am."

His garment is sprinkled with blood. There are two meanings to this. First, the Word was made flesh. The Logos became man and took up the vesture of flesh and blood. But even more, He offered Himself as the Passover

Lamb of Sacrifice. His priestly vestment is gloriously decorated with His own sacrificial blood. There is no need to wash it. This is His glory as sacrificial priest and victim. His name is the Word of God, which is the title Saint John gives to Christ in the opening prologue of his Gospel:

Jesus as Word of God in Gospel of John (Jn 1:1–5, 14)

[1] In the beginning was the Word, and the Word was with God, and the Word was God.

[2] The same was in the beginning with God.

[3] All things were made by him: and without him was made nothing that was made.

[4] In him was life, and the life was the light of men.

[5] And the light shineth in darkness, and the darkness did not comprehend it...

[14] And the Word was made flesh, and dwelt among us, (and we saw his glory, the glory as it were of the only begotten of the Father,) full of grace and truth.

Our Lord Jesus Christ is divine. He is the Word (Logos) of God who was always with God and who is God. The Word was made flesh and dwelt among us to save us. He rides a white horse, and He is followed by armies mounted on white horses:

Jesus Draws a Large Sword from His Mouth (Apoc 19:14–16)

[14] And the armies that are in heaven followed him on white horses, clothed in fine linen, white and clean.

[15] And out of his mouth proceedeth a sharp two-edged sword; that with it he may strike the nations. And he shall rule them with a rod of iron; and he treadeth the winepress of the fierceness of the wrath of God the Almighty.

[16] And he hath on his garment, and on his thigh written: KING OF KINGS, AND LORD OF LORDS.

The armies of the Word of God ride white horses and are clothed in fine linen, as we have seen repeatedly. From the mouth of the Word proceeds a short doubled-edged sword that strikes the nations. John already described this double-edged sword coming from the mouth of Christ in the opening prologue of the Apocalypse (1:16). This sword is the public proclamation of the Word of God who is Jesus Christ. Saint Paul also uses this image of a double-edged sword: "For the word of God is living and effectual, and more piercing than any two-edged sword; and reaching unto the division of the soul and the spirit, of the joints also and the marrow, and is a discerner of the thoughts and intents of the heart" (Heb 4:12). The sword is surgical and reaches down into the soul and spirit.

Jesus the Word rules with a rod of iron, as foretold in Psalm 2 and detailed in Apocalypse 12. He treads the winepress of the wrath of God, a detail we already saw in Apocalypse 14. Written on His vestment and on His thigh is His divine title: "King of kings and Lord of lords." The title is on His thigh where a sword is usually worn by a horseman. But since the sword is in His mouth, the title is on His thigh. This connects his title as King of kings with the proclamation of that message to all the nations from His mouth.

Eat the Flesh of Kings (Apoc 19:17–21)

[17] And I saw an angel standing in the sun, and he cried with a loud voice, saying to all the birds that did fly through the midst of heaven: Come, gather yourselves together to the great supper of God:

[18] That you may eat the flesh of kings, and the flesh of tribunes, and the flesh of mighty men, and the flesh of horses, and of them that sit on them, and the flesh of all freemen and bondmen, and of little and of great.

[19] And I saw the beast, and the kings of the earth, and their armies gathered together to make war with him that sat upon the horse, and with his army.

²⁰ And the beast was taken, and with him the false prophet, who wrought signs before him, wherewith he seduced them who received the character of the beast, and who adored his image. These two were cast alive into the pool of fire, burning with brimstone.
²¹ And the rest were slain by the sword of him that sitteth upon the horse, which proceedeth out of his mouth; and all the birds were filled with their flesh.

"And I saw" once again indicates that John is writing with pen in hand during the vision of the Apocalypse. An angel standing in the sun cries out with a loud voice and invites all the birds to gather for the "great supper of God." We recall that when God made his initial covenant with Abraham, Abraham sacrificed animals and then had to chase off the birds that came to scavenge the sacrifices. Now Abraham, the true patriarch of Jerusalem, does not chase off the birds. Rather, the birds are invited to eat the flesh of kings, tribunes, mighty men, horses, horsemen, freemen, bondmen, and the little and great. Who are these dead corpses? Saint John next sees the sea beast assembled with the kings and their armies and horsemen. And in an accelerated narrative, the (sea) beast and the False Prophet (land beast), who worked signs and seduced those to take the mark of the beast and adore his image, are both thrown into the pool of fire, burning with brimstone. Next, the armies are slain by the sword proceeding from the mouth of Jesus Christ our Lord. Satan is defeated by *preaching*. This narrative is an anticipated conclusion, and the next chapter will rewind the story and then, in slow motion, show exactly how the beast (called Gog) and his army (called Magog) are defeated in the battle of Armageddon.

Gog and Magog at the Millennium
(Apocalypse 20)

The previous chapter of the Apocalypse revealed an accelerated and abbreviated narrative of the final war of the Antichrist and his armies. This chapter provides details of that final battle. This confuses some readers because they think the events of Apocalypse 20 are chronologically *after* the events of Apocalypse 19. This error leads to pre-millennialism, which we will cover in this section of commentary.

Satan Bound in Chains for One Thousand Years (Apoc 20:1–3)

¹ And I saw an angel coming down from heaven, having the key of the abyss, and a great chain in his hand.

² And he laid hold on the dragon the old serpent, which is the devil and Satan, and bound him for a thousand years.

³ And he cast him into the abyss, and shut him up, and set a seal upon him, that he should no more seduce the nations, till the thousand years be finished. And after that, he must be loosed a little time.

The chapter begins with an angel that binds Satan for one thousand years. After this, Satan is released for a short time to persecute Christians and wage the war of Gog and Magog. The confusing part of the vision is that the final war (*after* the thousand years) includes the Antichrist and the False Prophet. Also, during the short time *after* the thousand years, the icon of the beast and the mark of the beast are enforced. When is this thousand-year period in Apocalypse 20, and how does it fit with the previous timeline given in Apocalypse 13 with the sea beast and land beast?

Evangelical Protestant Christians often debate the millennium and the coming of Christ with three various interpretations, which they call premillennialism, postmillennialism, and amillennialism.

- Premillennialism teaches the Second Coming of Christ will come before (*pre-*) the thousand years of binding of Satan. Satan will be bound for a thousand years, and then Christ will return a second time.

- Postmillennialism teaches that the Second Coming of Christ will come after (*post-*) the thousand years of binding Satan. These one thousand years will be a golden age of Christianity on earth, but Christ will remain ruling from heaven (not on earth as premillennialists suppose). After this will come the Antichrist and the coming of Christ.

- Amillennialism teaches that the thousand years is not (*a-*) a literal but symbolic "long time," after which Christ will return.

Postmillennialists and amillennialists agree about Christ returning *once* in the future after the millennium—the difference is that postmillennialists see a future golden age of Christianity lasting about one thousand years, after which Christ comes to judge the living and dead. Amillennialism simply states that from AD 33 until the arrival of the Antichrist (a long time, but not necessarily a thousand years), Satan is bound. In the end, Satan will be released to assist the Antichrist and bring about the Great Tribulation.

The difficulty with premillennialism is that it teaches *two* final comings of Christ: first His earthly return *before* the thousand years, and then another earthly coming *after* the thousand years. In the early church, a form of premillennial theology was simply called chiliasm, from the Greek word *chilias* meaning "thousand." Some Church Fathers subscribed to it, but Saint Justin Martyr explained that the position was contested at his time: "I and many others are of this opinion, and believe that such will take place, as you assuredly are aware; but, on the other hand, I signified to you that many who belong to the pure and pious faith, and are true Christians, think otherwise."[180] Beginning in the AD 300's, chiliasm (premillennialism) had been universally rejected by the Church.[181] Christians in the East and West taught amillennialism—the thousand years was just the long time between the resurrection of Christ (the binding of Satan) and the future coming of Antichrist.

The early church historian Eusebius of Caesarea (d. AD 339) explained that premillennial chiliasm posited a second coming of Christ *before* a millennium and then a third coming *after* a literal one-thousand-year millennium, a notion that originated from the heretic Kerinthus. Kerinthus was the contemporary nemesis of Saint John and died shortly after Saint John around AD 100. Saint Polycarp, a living disciple of the apostle John, related to Saint Irenaeus that Saint John once ran out of a bathhouse at Ephesus without bathing when he was told that the heretic Kerinthus was inside, exclaiming, "Let us fly, lest even the bathhouse fall down, because Kerinthus, the enemy of the truth, is inside!"[182] Irenaeus tells this story only decades after it happened based on a firsthand account, so it is hard to imagine that this odd episode is fictional.

Kerinthus was a Gnostic who taught a heretical version of Christianity that he claimed to have received directly from angels. It might be that Saint Paul was warning against Kerinthus when he wrote, "But though we, or an angel from heaven, preach a gospel to you besides that which we have preached to you, let him be anathema" (Gal 1:8). Kerinthus denied that the true God created the material world. He taught instead that a lower demiurge created the physical universe. He did not use the four canonical gospels

---

[180] Justin Martyr, *Dialogue with Trypho,* cap. 69–88. Some of the early Christian writers that hint at chiliasm are Irenaeus, Tertullian, Commodian, Lactantius, Methodius, and Apollinaris of Laodicea.

[181] The sub-apostolic Epistle of Barnabas is amillennial. The early Egyptian and North African were openly amillennial: Clement of Alexandria (d. c. 215), Origen (d. c. 254), and Cyprian of Carthage (d. c. 258). Augustine and Jerome were also amillennial, and their arguments and reputation solidified the suppression of chiliasm once and for all.

[182] Irenaeus, *Adversus haereses,* lib. 3, 3.4.

but taught instead the unholy Gospel of Kerinthus, which falsely proclaimed that Jesus was a mortal man and not born of a virgin. According to Kerinthus, Jesus was the biological son of Mary *and Joseph* and was temporarily adopted by God for a special purpose. He wrongly taught that the heavenly "Christ" descended on the historical person Jesus at his baptism, remained with him during his three-year ministry, and then left him at the crucifixion.

Saint Irenaeus also tells us that Saint John wrote his Gospel to "remove that error which Kerinthus had disseminated among men."[183] This would explain why Saint John began his holy Gospel with the words, "In the beginning was the Word, and the Word was with God, and the Word was God. . . . And the Word was made flesh and dwelt among us" (Jn 1:1, 14). Saint John definitively refuted the claim that Jesus was just a man adopted later by God for a special purpose. Jesus was God in the beginning with God.

Not only did Kerinthus deny the incarnation of Christ, but he also promoted the idea of a one-thousand-year millennium. Eusebius of Caesarea writes of this in his Church history:

> By means of revelations which he [Kerinthus] pretends were written by a great apostle, brings before us marvelous things which he falsely claims were shown him by angels; and he says that after the resurrection [of the faithful] the kingdom of Christ will be set up on earth, and that the flesh dwelling in Jerusalem will again be subject to desires and pleasures. And being an enemy of the Scriptures of God, he asserts, with the purpose of deceiving men, that there is to be a period of a thousand years for marriage festivals.[184]

---

183 Irenaeus, *Adversus haereses,* lib. 3, 11.1
184 Eusebius of Caesarea, *Ecclesiastical History* III, 28, 2.

This would place the origin of chiliasm, or premillennialism, with the heretic Kerinthus, who ironically, corrupted the Apocalypse of Saint John for his own purposes.

Although many early Christians did adopt the premillennialist interpretation, the Catholic Church definitively settled on the amillennial position. Both the Catholic Church and the Eastern Orthodox Church teach amillennialism and only amillennialism. The premillennialist reading oddly holds that the Antichrist and False Prophet appear both before the thousand years (chapters 13–19) and after the thousand years (chapter 20). How do these two appear in chapter 13 and then *live another thousand years* and show up again in chapter 20? They don't. The chapters of the book of the Apocalypse are not presented in chronological order. It telescopes its message and embeds its visions within visions. The error of the premillennial chiliasts is that they wrongly read chapters 13 through 19 as chronologically preceding chapter 20 in a historical progression, when in fact they describe the same event in different ways. The binding of Satan happened when Christ died on the cross and rose from the dead. This began a long, indefinite period, which John in the Apocalypse calls a thousand years. At the end of this period, Satan is released. He appoints his Antichrist and False Prophet. He makes war on the saints. Let's now look at the rest of chapter 20 using the interpretation of amillennialism—the belief that the thousand years is symbolic and allegorically describing the "long time" between the resurrection of Christ in AD 33 and the arrival of the Antichrist at the end of the world:

Satan Bound in Chains for One Thousand Years (Apoc 20:1–2)
[1] And I saw an angel coming down from heaven, having the key of the abyss, and a great chain in his hand.
[2] And he laid hold on the dragon the old serpent, which is the devil and Satan, and bound him for a thousand years.

Saint John sees an angel coming down from heaven. This sounds like the Mighty Angel who came down from heaven previously. There are three reasons to believe that this might be Jesus Christ, yet again. The first reason is that Jesus Christ described himself as the strong man who binds Satan:

Jesus Says He Will "First Bind the Strong Man" (Mk 3:22–27, emphasis added)

[22] And the scribes who were come down from Jerusalem, said: He hath Beelzebub, and by the prince of devils he casteth out devils.

[23] And after he had called them together, he said to them in parables: How can Satan cast out Satan?

[24] And if a kingdom be divided against itself, that kingdom cannot stand.

[25] And if a house be divided against itself, that house cannot stand.

[26] And if Satan be risen up against himself, he is divided, and cannot stand, but hath an end.

[27] No man can enter into the house of a strong man and rob him of his goods, *unless he first bind the strong man, and then shall he plunder his house.*

The scribes and Pharisees accuse Jesus Christ of being possessed by Beelzebub and casting out demons through the power of Satan. However, Christ explains that this is impossible because Christ first binds Satan and then plunders Satan's house/kingdom. The ministry, death, and resurrection of Jesus Christ binds Satan for "a thousand years"—or a very long time—until the Antichrist emerges. A second reason this angel messenger is Jesus Christ is that He owns the keys of the kingdom and gives them to Saint Peter for the duration of His time in heaven before the Second Coming: "I will give to thee the keys of the kingdom of heaven. And whatsoever thou shalt bind upon earth, it shall be bound also in heaven: and whatsoever thou shalt loose upon earth, it shall be loosed also in heaven" (Mt 16:19). The third reason for seeing this angel messenger as Christ is that Jesus Christ explicitly states that he owns the key to the abyss: "I am the First and the Last, and alive and was dead, and behold I am living for ever and ever, and *have the keys of death and of hell*" (Apoc 1:17–18, emphasis added).

Jesus Christ owns the key and the chain by which he binds Satan and his demons. This is not a future event but a current state of being during the time between the crucifixion and the emergence of the Antichrist. Saint Jude speaks of these chains binding the demons *currently*: "And the [fallen] angels who kept not their principality, but forsook their own habitation, he hath reserved under darkness in everlasting chains, unto the judgment of the great day" (Jude 1:6).

Satan Is Cast into the Abyss (Apoc 20:2–3)

^{2} And he laid hold on the dragon the old serpent, which is the devil and Satan, and bound him for a thousand years.
^{3} And he cast him into the abyss, and shut him up, and set a seal upon him, that he should no more seduce the nations, till the thousand years be finished. And after that, he must be loosed a little time.

Just as Jesus said He would "bind the strong man" (Mk 3:27), so here He "laid hold on the dragon the old serpent, which is the devil and Satan" (Apoc 20:2). Although Genesis never explicitly states that the serpent in the garden was Satan, God reveals here that the snake is the dragon and Satan.

Jesus Christ binds Satan for a thousand years, which is not truly one thousand years but merely a symbolic long time of perfection: $10 \times 10 \times 10$. Satan is jailed in the abyss with a seal over him, that he might not seduce the nations during this length of time of apostolic preaching and missionary success. This is why the twelve apostles and seventy-two elders of Christ are so amazed that they have power over the demons. Their binding has begun already in the life of Christ. After this long period of time, he will be "loosed a little time," and this is the three-and-a-half-year period with the Antichrist as king of the world. How will Satan be released? Will Christ directly release Satan from the abyss? Or will the successor of Saint Peter (who currently holds the keys as Vicar) be the one who "looses" Satan for this final conflict with the Antichrist?

The First Resurrection and a Thousand Years (Apoc 20:4–6)

⁴ And I saw seats; and they sat upon them; and judgment was given unto them; and the souls of them that were beheaded for the testimony of Jesus, and for the word of God, and who had not adored the beast nor his image, nor received his character on their foreheads, or in their hands; and they lived and reigned with Christ a thousand years.

⁵ The rest of the dead lived not, till the thousand years were finished. This is the first resurrection.

⁶ Blessed and holy is he that hath part in the first resurrection. In these the second death hath no power; but they shall be priests of God and of Christ; and shall reign with him a thousand years.

In verse 4, seats are set up in heaven. These are not just chairs. The Greek is *thronos*, or "thrones." Saint John has already seen these thrones established. The twenty-four presbyters already sit on these thrones, beginning in Apocalypse 4:4. This confirms that the Apocalypse is not written in chronological order but in a thematic order. "The souls beheaded for the testimony of Jesus" (v. 4) are those that sit on these thrones. The martyrs of Jesus Christ not only receive thrones but "judgment was given to them" to reign with Christ. Therefore, the twenty-four presbyters wear crowns and dress like priests in linen. They did not worship the icon of the beast or receive the mark of the beast. This shows that the reign of the beast begins in AD 33 but culminates over time and climaxes under the future Antichrist at the end for three and a half years. These martyr saints reign with Christ for a thousand years—the time between the crucifixion and the Antichrist. In the Catholic Church, the book commemorating all the known saints throughout time is called the *Martyrology*, even though not all saints are blood martyrs. It is Catholic teaching that while the blood martyrs go straight to heaven without purgatory, the rest of the non-martyred faithful can and do reign in heaven with Christ and the martyrs, but mostly after some time of purification through fire (see 1 Cor 3:15).

Verse five reads, "The rest of the dead lived not, till the thousand years were finished. This is the first resurrection." The "rest of the dead" could refer to the unfaithful damned who do *not* live for the testimony of Jesus but for the beast. They don't live or rise again until the final resurrection and general judgment by Christ. And then the damned are raised again, only to be sent into perdition. The reference to "first resurrection" refers to the reality of the souls in heaven on thrones with Christ. The first resurrection is the exaltation of souls to heaven, and the "second death" has no power over them. The first death is bodily death. The second death is spiritual death in hell. They are called "blessed and holy," or "blesseds and saints." They are resurrected spiritually, and their souls are saved. But the "second resurrection" will be the final resurrection of their physical bodies at the end of time, after the symbolic millennium. After this length of time between the crucifixion and arrival the Antichrist, then begins the short time of Satan being loosed from his prison.

Gog and Magog as the Antichrist and His Armies (Apoc 20:7)

And when the thousand years shall be finished, Satan shall be loosed out of his prison, and shall go forth, and seduce the nations, which are over the four quarters of the earth, Gog, and Magog, and shall gather them together to battle, the number of whom is as the sand of the sea.

Gog and Magog are mentioned only once in the Apocalypse: here in this verse. This is a reference to the appearance of Gog and the land of Magog in Ezechiel 38–39, beginning with, "Son of Man, set thy face against Gog, the land of Magog, the chief prince of Mosoch and Thubal: and prophesy of him" (Eze 38:2). From this point forward in the Apocalypse, it is a direct parallel with the visions of Prophet Ezechiel:

Visions and Events	Ezechiel's Vision	John's Apocalypse
Resurrection of the Dead	37	20:4–6, 12
Gog of Magog	38	20:7–9
Destruction of Antichrist & Feast of the Birds	39	19:17–21
New Jerusalem Appears	40:2	21:2, 10
New Temple Measured	40–43	21:5–21
Glory of God in New Temple	43	21:22–23
River of Life & Tree of Life	47	22:1–2
Holy City	48:20	21:16
The Lord Is There	48:35	21:22–22:5

Gog is the symbolic name of the Antichrist in Ezechiel, and he corresponds to the terrible beast king in Daniel. Saint John sees Gog and the sea beast as one and the same. Several interpretations have been offered for Gog and Magog. Most suggest that Gog is a leader, and Magog is his people. In Genesis 10, Magog is described as a son of Japheth, who is generally seen as the father of the European peoples. This fits with the apocryphal *Book of Jubilees*, which describes Magog as a descendant of Noah and that a portion of Japheth's land is assigned to Magog.

Many interpreters see Gog as the Antichrist and Magog as the accumulation of vicious peoples, such as the Scythians, Goths, or Saracens.[185] Others, such as Eusebius, say that Gog is the Roman Emperor and Magog is the Roman Empire.[186] The error in all these historical identifications is that Gog and Magog come at the end of time. Also, this terrible army of Magog will be global and not just one tribe, such as the Scythians.

A better solution is provided by Augustine of Hippo (d. 430), who teaches that Gog and Magog are best understood by investigating their original Hebrew meanings.[187] The Hebrew word *gog* means "roof," and *magog* means "from the roof." Gog is both the highest point but also the protection over an edifice. Gog is rightly the chief or king, and Magog are those who come under his roof—under his protection. The Antichrist is the roof under which is collected his kingdom of Magog. This final battle of Gog and Magog is Antichrist against Christ and Anti-Church against Church. Gog is the Antichrist, and Magog is his army as Anti-Church. Magog is not one single nation but the collection of godless people (those of the ten kings)—the ten divided toes (Daniel's vision) of the Roman Empire

---

185 Robert Bellarmine shows this to be the predominant opinion of the Lutheran Centuriators. See *De Pontifice Romano*, Tom. I, lib III.

186 Robert Bellarmine, *De Pontifice Romano*, Tom. Lib. III, cap. 17.

187 Augustine, *De civitate Dei*, lib. 20, cap. 11.

at war with the Church. Their number is that of the "sand of the sea"—a reference to the (defeated) enemies of Joshua in the Old Testament (Jos 11:4).

Some Protestants wrongly believe that Gog is *not* the same person as the Antichrist sea beast. This can easily be refuted in five ways. Let us list the reasons why Gog of Magog is the Antichrist. First, Ezechiel the prophet identifies Gog of Magog as the final Antichrist:

> Thus saith the Lord God: Thou then art he, of whom I have spoken in the days of old, by my servants the prophets of Israel, who prophesied in the days of those times that I would bring thee upon them. And it shall come to pass in that day, in the day of the coming of Gog upon the land of Israel, saith the Lord God, that my indignation shall come up in my wrath. (Eze 38:18)

Gog has been foretold by the prophets, and he will be the one who punishes the land of Jerusalem.

Secondly, Gog receives the exact same punishment as the Antichrist beast: "And I will judge him [Gog] with pestilence, and with blood, and with violent rain, and vast hailstones: I will rain fire and brimstone upon him, and upon his army, and upon the many nations that are with him" (Eze 38:22). Moreover, both Gog and the Antichrist are destroyed by an earthquake (compare the similarities between Ezechiel 39:19–20 with Apocalypse 16:18–20).

Third, the great feast of the scavenger birds eating the dead bodies of the armies of the Antichrist (Apoc 19:17–18) is the same event as the one in Ezechiel 39:1–20, when God calls out to the birds to come and eat the flesh of the dead armies of Gog. There will not be two final flesh feasts by the birds—one of the dead armies of the Antichrist, and another of the dead armies of Gog. Rather, the two accounts are one and the same. Birds eating the dead armies of Gog in Ezechiel is the same event as birds eating the dead armies of the beast in the Apocalypse.

A fourth reason why Gog is the Antichrist beast is that, after he is killed, God's "holy name shall be profaned no more" (Eze 39:7). Both Daniel and Saint Paul say that the Antichrist will be a horrible blasphemer. His death will end all blaspheming and profanity against God. Hence, the death of Gog is the same as the death of the Antichrist.

The battle of Gog is not a different battle than the battle of the beast. Once again, we have circled back or rewound the action to the assembly of the ten kings and ten kingdoms under the Antichrist to battle Christ. The story of Gog and Magog is yet another symbolic retelling of the same event. Gog and Magog are the same as the Antichrist and his ten kings. They fight Jesus Christ not by ascending into heaven, but by killing the Christians on earth who carry Christ within their hearts.

God Destroys the Antichrist and the False Prophet (Apoc 20:8–10)

[8] And they came upon the breadth of the earth, and encompassed the camp of the saints, and the beloved city.

[9] And there came down fire from God out of heaven, and devoured them; and the devil, who seduced them, was cast into the pool of fire and brimstone, where both the beast

[10] And the false prophet shall be tormented day and night for ever and ever.

The Antichrist, the kings, and their armies surround the "camp of the saints, and the beloved city" (v. 8). We know already that the *beloved* city is not the earthly Jerusalem but the heavenly Jerusalem that is above. The Greek word for "camp" here refers to a military camp or outpost. This identifies the earthly church "camp of the saints" as the militant church, which is distinct from the triumphant church in heaven as the beloved city.

Fire comes down from God and devours the enemies of God. Fire falling from heaven invokes the Holy Spirit descending on the Church on Pentecost in Acts 2. Now there is another descent of holy fire, not upon the Church (who already has the Holy Spirit), but upon the enemies of the Church, who are destroyed. The devil is thrown into the pool of fire.

The Great White Throne and Book of Life (Apoc 20:11–15)

[11] And I saw a great white throne, and one sitting upon it, from whose face the earth and heaven fled away, and there was no place found for them.

[12] And I saw the dead, great and small, standing in the presence of the throne, and the books were opened; and another book was opened, which is the book of life; and the dead were judged by those things which were written in the books, according to their works.

[13] And the sea gave up the dead that were in it, and death and hell gave up their dead that were in them; and they were judged everyone according to their works.

[14] And hell and death were cast into the pool of fire. This is the second death.

[15] And whosoever was not found written in the book of life, was cast into the pool of fire.

Saint John then sees a white throne and Jesus Christ sitting on it. The white throne is likely the same as the "white cloud" (Apoc 14:14) that Jesus ascends into and then returns on as the Son of Man riding on the clouds. It may also be the same as the "white horse" (Apoc 19:11) that Christ sits upon. This white cloud/throne/horse is the "right hand of the Father" since Christ is seated on the right hand of the Father.

The face of Christ has long been the focus of pious devotion. Saint Veronica preserved His bloody face on her handkerchief. King Agbar of Edessa allegedly received a miraculous portrait of Christ's face. The Shroud of Turin and its image of the face of Christ is also a popular devotion. In the Apocalypse, the holy face of Christ dissolves creation: "from whose face the earth and heaven fled away, and there was no place found for them." The face of God, who is Jesus Christ, has been the subject of fear for the Hebrews and the desire of those who long to see God "face to face." Every man will be judged simply by looking into the holy face of Jesus Christ. Those burning eyes will reveal all things.

Now that Satan and the Antichrist and the damned are defeated by Christ, the final judgment begins. All the dead "great and small" are assembled before the white throne of Jesus Christ. Books are opened. The context suggests that there are books (plural) that have all "their works" written in them. The damned are judged by those "works" written in the books (plural). All those found in the sea (the realm of the beast) and all those in death and hell (the realm of Satan the dragon) give up all the dead in them. They are "judged . . . according to their works" (Apoc 20:12). Then both "hell and death are cast into the pool of fire" (v. 15). This means that the result of sin as "death and the grave" are now finally abolished. The pool of fire is the second death, and it is much worse than physical mortality. The second death is the everlasting spiritual death in fiery torment with Satan. But there is "another book" (singular), which is the Book of Life. Those who are found in the book are saved and have experienced the first resurrection (souls in heaven) and now receive the second resurrection (their bodies raised up to heaven).

The New Jerusalem (Apocalypse 21)

The appearance of the new heaven and new earth as well as the New Jerusalem are expected because Saint John's Apocalypse follows the flow of Ezechiel's visions. Look at this outline of Ezechiel, and consider the topics and order that we have covered:

> Ezechiel 33: Fall of Jerusalem
> Ezechiel 34: Good Shepherd and New Covenant
> Ezechiel 36: New Heart and New Spirit
> Ezechiel 37: Resurrection of Valley of Bones
> Ezechiel 38: Battle with Gog and Magog
> Ezechiel 39: Gog destroyed and Israel Restored
> Ezechiel 40–48: New Jerusalem[188]

Ezechiel 33 is the fall and removal of old Jerusalem, and Ezechiel 34 brings about the New Covenant—which consists of the seven sealed books that the Messianic Lamb opened already. This leads to the end-times resurrection of the dead (dry bones rise in Eze 37). Then the Antichrist Gog begins his war, and he is destroyed (Eze 38–39). Israel is restored, and a New Temple/Jerusalem (Church) is established (Eze 40–48). Is John copying Ezechiel? No. Saint John is actually receiving the true vision of God for the New Covenant. Ezechiel saw it as the future. John sees it happening. The final two chapters of the Apocalypse illustrate the glory of heaven as the New Jerusalem seen by Ezechiel.

New Heaven, New Earth, New Jerusalem (Apoc 21:1–2)

¹ And I saw a new heaven and a new earth. For the first heaven and the first earth was gone, and the sea is now no more.

---

[188] See the appendix for a thorough side-by-side comparison of Ezechiel's structure to that of John's Apocalypse.

² And I John saw the holy city, the New Jerusalem, coming down out of heaven from God, prepared as a bride adorned for her husband.

When Christ returns and reestablishes His kingdom, it will not be purely ethereal or spiritual. It will be a new heaven and new earth with resurrected real bodies. The Body of Christ was resurrected; the same Body by which He was crucified. It was glorified but it was the same Body renewed. The same is true with all of creation. The old heaven and earth will be renewed and resurrected. It will be the same one but perfected and glorified. The idea of a new heaven and new earth is old and derives from Isaias: "For behold I create new heavens, and a new earth: and the former things shall not be in remembrance, and they shall not come upon the heart" (Isa 65:17).

The Greek word used for "new" heaven and "new" earth and "new" Jerusalem in all three cases is not *neos* (meaning "newly made") but rather *kainos* (meaning "new and improved" or "renewed"). In the final resurrection, the faithful will receive their old bodies renewed—*kainos*. The sea "is now no more," and this is likely because the beast came from the sea.

John testifies, "And I John saw the holy city, the New Jerusalem" (Apoc 21:2). It's not the "great city" of the old corrupt Jerusalem. Now it is the "holy city." John, as he does in his Gospel, testifies as a named witness. Just as the veil in the old temple was ripped from "top to bottom" when Christ died on the cross, the New Jerusalem comes "down out of heaven from God" (v. 2). She, like Christ, comes down. She is prepared as a bride adorned for her husband, Who is our Lord Jesus Christ. The Harlot is killed and burned. This is New Jerusalem, the New Bride.

Behold I Make All Things New (Apoc 21:3-5)
³ And I heard a great voice from the throne, saying: Behold the tabernacle of God with men, and he will dwell with them. And they shall be his people; and God himself with them shall be their God.

269

⁴ And God shall wipe away all tears from their eyes: and death shall be no more, nor mourning, nor crying, nor sorrow shall be any more, for the former things are passed away.

⁵ And he that sat on the throne, said: Behold, I make all things new. And he said to me: Write, for these words are most faithful and true.

Saint John hears a voice saying, "Behold the tabernacle of God with men" (v. 3). Is the tabernacle the New Jerusalem as the Bride, or is it Christ as Bridegroom? This is likely referencing the union of the two. The old tabernacle was where God entered and lived with His people. The one Church is the one Bride of the one Christ. God dwells here and nowhere else. *Extra ecclesiam nulla salus*—"outside the Church, there is no salvation." One must be inside the ark of Christ. One must be inside the walls of New Jerusalem.

"And God shall wipe away all tears from their eyes" (v. 4) is one of the most comforting quotations from Sacred Scripture. Adam and Eve led us into the valley of tears. Now it is finally over. No more death. No more crying. "Behold I make all things new" (v. 5) is the declaration of King Jesus Christ. He uses the Greek word *kaina*, meaning not "created brand new" but "re-created, renewed, and new and improved." Jesus Christ didn't start over with a blank slate. Instead, He perfectly *renewed* what was already sorrowful and broken.

"It Is Done" (Apoc 21:6–7)

⁶ And he said to me: It is done. I am Alpha and Omega; the beginning and the end. To him that thirsteth, I will give of the fountain of the water of life, freely.

⁷ He that shall overcome shall possess these things, and I will be his God; and he shall be my son.

Jesus Christ says to John ("to me"), "It is done." This is an eternal echo of Christ on the cross announcing, "It is consummated" (Jn 19:30). This reaffirms the principle of *kainos* as renewal. Christ on the cross was stricken, smitten, and afflicted. Yet He is the same Christ in the same Body, who in His glory as Messianic King also says, "It is done." This is an eternal antiphon because He next announces: "I am Alpha and Omega; the beginning and the end." Alpha is the first letter and omega is the last letter in the Greek alphabet. Jesus Christ is the Word in the beginning with God and the Word forever.

Jesus Christ in verse 6 states, "To him that thirsteth, I will give of the fountain of the water of life, freely." Saint John knows this teaching already, as he preserved in the fourth chapter of the Gospel of Saint John:

Jesus Promises "Living Water" (Jn 4:10, 14)
[10] Jesus answered, and said to her: If thou didst know the gift of God, and who he is that saith to thee, Give me to drink; thou perhaps wouldst have asked of him, and he would have given thee living water. . . .
[14] Whosoever drinketh of this water, shall thirst again; but he that shall drink of the water that I will give him, shall not thirst for ever.

The "living water" of Jesus Christ is the gift of the Holy Ghost who proceeds from the Father:

"Living Water" Is the Holy Spirit (Jn 7:37–39)
[37] And on the last, and great day of the festivity, Jesus stood and cried, saying: If any man thirst, let him come to me, and drink.
[38] He that believeth in me, as the scripture saith, Out of his belly shall flow rivers of living water.
[39] Now this he said of the Spirit which they should receive, who believed in him: for as yet the Spirit was not given, because Jesus was not yet glorified.

In Apocalypse 21:7, Christ promises all these things to those that overcome the beast. Then Christ affirms his full divinity. Jesus Christ says, "I will be his God; and he shall be my son." A created angel could never say such a thing. Jesus Christ is fully God and fully man.

Jesus Lists Eight Sins (Apoc 21:8)
But the fearful, and unbelieving, and the abominable, and murderers, and fornicators, and sorcerers, and idolaters, and all liars, they shall have their portion in the pool burning with fire and brimstone, which is the second death.

Our Lord Jesus Christ (not John) then lists eight sins that define those who are thrown into the pool of burning fire and brimstone, which is the second death:

1. Fear (the Greek refers to cowardice)
2. Unbelief
3. Abomination (the Greek refers to the abhorrent sexual sins condemned in the Old Testament, such as homosexuality, incest, and bestiality)
4. Murder
5. Fornication
6. Sorcery (the Greek word here *pharmakeusin* refers to pharmaceutical potions used in sorcery and for contraception and abortion)
7. Idolatry
8. Lying

Christ will forgive all these sins to those who repent and turn to Him in faith with baptism and penance. But the damned are unrepentant of the deplorable sins that render them unclean and worthy of hellfire.

New Jerusalem Descends from God (Apoc 21:9–11)

⁹ And there came one of the seven angels, who had the vials full of the seven last plagues, and spoke with me, saying: Come, and I will shew thee the bride, the wife of the Lamb.

¹⁰ And he took me up in spirit to a great and high mountain: and he shewed me the holy city Jerusalem coming down out of heaven from God,

¹¹ Having the glory of God, and the light thereof was like to a precious stone, as to the jasper stone, even as crystal.

One of the seven angels who had vials of the seven last plagues comes to show the Bride of the Lamb to Saint John. This is fitting because this angel oversaw the condemnation and burning of the old earthly Jerusalem. Now he excitedly shows off the New Bride Jerusalem as "wife of the Lamb" (v. 9). He takes Saint John "in Spirit to a great and high mountain" (v. 10). This mountain is the renewed Mount Sion. The mount has been purified of sin. The Holy City Jerusalem is "coming down out of heaven from God" to settle down on New Mount Sion. The holy city has the Shekinah glory of God, and its light is like the precious "jasper stone." This refers to the jasper stone reference in Apocalypse 4:3.

12 Gates & 12 Foundations (Apoc 21:12–14)

¹² And it had a wall great and high, having twelve gates, and in the gates twelve angels, and names written thereon, which are the names of the twelve tribes of the children of Israel.

¹³ On the east, three gates: and on the north, three gates: and on the south, three gates: and on the west, three gates.

¹⁴ And the wall of the city had twelve foundations, and in them, the twelve names of the twelve apostles of the Lamb.

The New Jerusalem has a "wall great and high" with twelve gates guarded by twelve angels. The names of the twelve tribes are inscribed on each of the twelve gates. Presumably these are the twelve names of the twelve tribes listed previously, minus the tribe of Dan for reasons already given. The city is a perfect square with three gates on each of the four sides. The city has twelve foundations with "the twelve names of the apostles of the Lamb" written on them (v. 14). Christ is the foundation *with His apostles.* He built His Church on these twelve.

Saint John Measures the City (Apoc 21:15–17)

¹⁵ And he that spoke with me, had a measure of a reed of gold, to measure the city and the gates thereof, and the wall.

¹⁶ And the city lieth in a foursquare, and the length thereof is as great as the breadth: and he measured the city with the golden reed for twelve thousand stadia, and the length and the height and the breadth thereof are equal.

¹⁷ And he measured the wall thereof a hundred and forty-four cubits, the measure of a man, which is of an angel.

As in Ezechiel, the temple is measured with a perfect golden reed. The city is "foursquare" and has an equal 12,000-stadia length, width, and height—a cube. The length of 12,000 stadia is about 1,500 miles. Clearly these are *not* literal numbers of a literal cubic building. The holy of holies in the old temple was also a perfect cube. The image here is that the entire city is the cubic holy of holies. There are no restricted access areas. Everyone in the city has full access to God within His holy of holies. This city wall measures 144,000 cubits. We know already that this is a holy number: 12 × 12 × 1,000. The number of the Great Multitude in heaven is also 144,000. It's fitting that the wall of the city of the 144,000 Great Multitude would also measure 144,000 cubits.

The Church/Jerusalem Is Made of Precious Stones (Apoc 21:18–21)

¹⁸ And the building of the wall thereof was of jasper stone: but the city itself pure gold, like to clear glass.

¹⁹ And the foundations of the wall of the city were adorned with all manner of precious stones. The first foundation was jasper: the second, sapphire: the third, a chalcedony: the fourth, an emerald:

²⁰ The fifth, sardonyx: the sixth, sardius: the seventh, chrysolite: the eighth, beryl: the ninth, a topaz: the tenth, a chrysoprasus: the eleventh, a jacinth: the twelfth, an amethyst.

²¹ And the twelve gates are twelve pearls, one to each: and every several gate was of one several pearl. And the street of the city was pure gold, as it were transparent glass.

Verses 18–21 list out the precious stones used in the construction of the New Jerusalem. It's made of pure gold and set with twelve precious stones. The streets are pure gold. Each gate is a pearl. Gold, precious stones, and pearls were the costume of the original earthly Jerusalem. Now the New Bride wears the royal family jewels on her wedding day.

God Alone Is the Temple (Apoc 21:22–27)

²² And I saw no temple therein. For the Lord God Almighty is the temple thereof, and the Lamb.

²³ And the city hath no need of the sun, nor of the moon, to shine in it. For the glory of God hath enlightened it, and the Lamb is the lamp thereof.

²⁴ And the nations shall walk in the light of it: and the kings of the earth shall bring their glory and honor into it.

²⁵ And the gates thereof shall not be shut by day: for there shall be no night there.

²⁶ And they shall bring the glory and honor of the nations into it.

²⁷ There shall not enter into it anything defiled, or that worketh abomination or maketh a lie, but they that are written in the book of life of the Lamb.

There is no temple in the New Jerusalem. As we have seen, the entire city is a cubic room like the holy of holies. A temple with graduated access to God based on sacrificial purity is irrelevant in Christ's new city. The Father and the Son *are* the temple. The city also has no sun or moon. The Father and Son are the lamp. The nations are lit by this light, and the kings bring glory to it. This is confirmation that the kings of the world will come to honor Christ: first Armenia, then Rome, and then all the other nations: Egypt, France, Spain, Britain, and so on. The reality of the Church is in heaven perfectly and then progressively over time on earth in history. There is never night nor darkness. Christ is the light of the world. The gates never shut. All are welcome. However, nothing defiled shall ever enter it. This is why baptism is necessary to enter the Church. It cleans the soul and conscience of all sin. Only those in the Book of Life of the Lamb may enter the twelve gates.

The Tree of Life (Apocalypse 22)

The final chapter of the Apocalypse brings us back to the Garden of Eden, with the river of life and the tree of life.

Back in the Garden of Paradise (Apoc 22:1–3)
¹ And he shewed me a river of water of life, clear as crystal, proceeding from the throne of God and of the Lamb.
² In the midst of the street thereof, and on both sides of the river, was the tree of life, bearing twelve fruits, yielding its fruits every month, and the leaves of the tree were for the healing of the nations.
³ And there shall be no curse anymore; but the throne of God and of the Lamb shall be in it, and his servants shall serve him.

Saint John sees a river of water of life. This is not an actual river but the Holy Spirit, as Jesus Christ explained previously in Saint John's Gospel:

The River Is the Holy Spirit (Jn 7:37–39)
³⁷ Jesus stood and cried, saying: If any man thirst, let him come to me, and drink.
³⁸ Out of his belly shall flow *rivers of living water.*
³⁹ *Now this he said of the Spirit* which they should receive, who believed in him: for as yet the Spirit was not given, because Jesus was not yet glorified. (emphasis added)

This river of water of life, who is the Holy Spirit, proceeds from the throne of God the Father and of the Lamb Jesus Christ. The river of life is the Third Person of the Blessed Trinity. The Greek word "proceeding" in Apocalypse 22:1 is *ekporeuomenon.* It is the same word in the exact same grammatical form (letter for letter) as "who proceeds from the Father" (*to ek tou Patros ekporeuomenon*), which is used in the Greek Niceno-Constantinopolitan Creed of AD 381.

Although the original Niceno-Constantinopolitan Creed of 381 did not contain the *Filioque* clause "proceeding from the Father *and the Son*" (emphasis added), the Apocalypse of Saint John does have the Holy Spirit proceeding from the Father and the Son. Unfortunately, this passage is usually neglected in theological discussions concerning the Trinity and the procession of the Holy Spirit from the Son.

Verse 2 oddly presents the one "tree of life" (singular) as on both sides of the river who is the Holy Spirit. How can a tree be on both sides of the river? The prophet Ezechiel describes the same phenomenon but adds a detail that helps us better understand the symbolism:

Trees of Life Seen by Ezechiel (Eze 47:1–2, 6–7)

[1] And he brought me again to the gate of the house, and behold waters issued out from under the threshold of the house toward the east: for the forefront, of the house looked toward the east: but the waters came down to the right side of the temple to the south part of the altar.

[2] And he led me out by the way of the north gate, and he caused me to turn to the way without the outward gate to the way that looked toward the east: and behold there ran out waters on the right side. . . .

[6] And he said to me: Surely thou hast seen, O Son of Man. And he brought me out, and he caused me to turn to the bank of the torrent.

[7] And when I had turned myself, behold on the bank of the torrent were very many trees on both sides.

This passage from Ezechiel is used by the Roman Catholic liturgy from Easter Sunday to Pentecost Sunday. It replaces the penitential antiphon from Psalm 50, "Asperges me." During Eastertide, the Catholic priest sprinkles the faithful with holy water while they chant the passage from Ezechiel:

Vidi aquam egredientem de templo, a latere dextro, Alleluia:

Et omnes ad quos pervenit aqua ista, salvi facti sunt,
Et dicent: Alleluia, Alleluia.

Translation:
I saw water flowing out of the Temple, from its right side, Alleluia:
And all to whom this water came were saved,
And they shall say: Alleluia, Alleluia.

Water flows from the right side of the temple into the world. The temple is the Body of Christ on the cross. The water flows from his right (*dextro*) side: "But one of the soldiers with a spear opened his side, and immediately there came out blood and water" (John 19:34). It is appropriate that John was the only apostle at the foot of the cross and the only one who saw the water flowing from the right side of Christ's open chest. This all happens after "It is finished." Once again, Saint John sees this sacramental reality. It is so important to John that he reaffirms it in his first epistle by stating the flow of water from Christ's side is the river of the Holy Spirit: "This is He that came by water and blood, Jesus Christ: not by water only, but by water and blood. And it is the Spirit which testifieth, that Christ is the truth" (1 Jn 5:6).

Ezechiel's version reveals "on the bank of the torrent were very *many trees* on both sides" (Eze 47:7). It seems that the tree of life has multiplied into many. There may be many trees, but they are participating in the one tree of life. There are twelve fruits, yielding fruits every month. And the leaves (Are they the same leaves used to cover the nakedness of Adam and Eve?) are "for the healing of the nations."

There are two Greek words for "tree." One is *dendron*, and the other is *xulon*. *Dendron* is a living tree, but a *xulon* can mean "tree" or "wood." The word *xulon* is often used to describe large wooden clubs used to beat people. *Xulon* is also used repeatedly in the New Testament to describe the cross that Christ hung upon (see Acts 5:30, 10:39, and

13:29; Galatians 3:13; and 1 Peter 2:24). John is seeing the tree of life as crosses planted on both sides of the river of life that is the Holy Spirit. They are living in that they produce fruit and leaves, but they are also associated with the wooden tree (i.e., cross) of salvation. The curse of Adam upon the earth has come to an end. The throne of God and the Lamb shall be in it, and his servants will serve Him.

They See His Face—His Name on Their Foreheads (Apoc 22:4–5)

⁴ And they shall see his face: and his name shall be on their foreheads.

⁵ And night shall be no more: and they shall not need the light of the lamp, nor the light of the sun, because the Lord God shall enlighten them, and they shall reign for ever and ever.

The references to water and the Holy Spirit remind us of baptism, and verse 4 states that the faithful will see Christ's face, "and his name shall be on their foreheads." This is undoubtedly a reference to the sacrament of holy baptism, which is placed on the forehead along with the mark of the sign of cross in sacred chrism. Verse 5 indicates that night is abolished (just as the seas are abolished). The reason is that both lamps and the sun are abolished because Jesus Christ illuminates all. "Illumination" was an early Christian name for baptism (Heb 6:4), and the baptized are still presented with a burning candle, even today. We worship on Sunday, the first day of the week, because Christ rose on the first day of the week, and he replaces the sun: "But unto you that fear my name, the Sun of Justice shall arise, and health in his wings" (Mal 4:2). Jesus Christ is the *Son* of God and the *Sun* of Justice.

Next, Christ addresses Saint John directly:

Behold I Come Quickly (Apoc 22:6–7)

⁶ And he said to me: These words are most faithful and true. And the Lord God of the spirits of the prophets sent his angel to show his servants the things which must be done shortly.
⁷ And, Behold I come quickly. Blessed is he that keepeth the words of the prophecy of this book.

Jesus Christ assures John the words are "most faithful and true." "The Lord God of the spirits of the prophets" (v. 6) refers to Jesus and either the personal souls of prophets or, more likely, the sevenfold spirit who is the Holy Ghost. Christ has "sent his angel to show his servants the things which must be done shortly." The events of the Apocalypse must be done shortly. As we have seen, the transferal of the kingdoms of the world began at the crucifixion, resurrection, and the ascension of the Son of Man in a cloud. The Apocalypse literally shows us what happens *immediately* after Christ ascends to the right hand of the Father on His cloud. Christ says, "I come quickly" (v. 7), and this refers to the judgment of Jerusalem as Babylon in AD 70, which will happen again under the Antichrist. He gives His lordly benediction to all the faithful who keep the words of the prophecy of the Apocalypse—a unique blessing for which we should strive. Then Saint John testifies:

Seal Not the Words of This Book (Apoc 22:8–10)

⁸ And I, John, who have heard and seen these things. And after I had heard and seen, I fell down to adore before the feet of the angel, who showed me these things.
⁹ And he said to me: See thou do it not: for I am thy fellow servant, and of thy brethren the prophets, and of them that keep the words of the prophecy of this book. Adore God.

¹⁰ And he saith to me: Seal not the words of the prophecy of this book: for the time is at hand.

John falls down *again* to show obeisance at the feet of the angel who showed him all these things. The angel admonishes John not to do this since he and the angel are now "fellow servants." This same thing happened in chapter 19, and we confirmed that John is not attempting to commit idolatry but rather show reverence to a spiritual superior. But as an apostle, John is a fellow servant on par with an angel.

Verse 10 instructs John *not* to seal up the words of the prophecy of the Apocalypse because "the time is at hand" (v. 10). Jesus Christ wants John to publish this book and make it known to the faithful. Christ is seated at the right hand of God, and His kingdom is growing. It will continue until the time of the Antichrist, who will reign for only a short time before Christ returns one final time to judge the living and the dead.

I Am Alpha and Omega, Outside Are Dogs (Apoc 22:11–15)

¹¹ He that hurteth, let him hurt still: and he that is filthy, let him be filthy still: and he that is just, let him be justified still: and he that is holy, let him be sanctified still

¹² Behold, I come quickly; and my reward is with me, to render to every man according to his works.

¹³ I am Alpha and Omega, the first and the last, the beginning and the end.

¹⁴ Blessed are they that wash their robes in the blood of the Lamb: that they may have a right to the tree of life and may enter in by the gates into the city.

¹⁵ Without are dogs, and sorcerers, and unchaste, and murderers, and servers of idols, and everyone that loveth and maketh a lie.

The coming of Christ leads to the separation of two groups. On the left hand of perdition are those who hurt and who are filthy. On the right hand of salvation are those who are just and still become more just and those who are sanctified and become more saintly. Again, Christ says, "I come quickly" (v. 12). Men are judged by Him according to works and not according to faith alone. Again, Christ announces, "I am Alpha and Omega, the first and the last, the beginning and the end" (v. 13). He gives another baptismal benediction: "Blessed are they that wash their robes in the blood of the Lamb: that they may have a right to the tree of life and may enter in by the gates into the city" (v. 14).

Then Christ describes the damned who are outside the City of God: "Without are dogs, and sorcerers, and unchaste, and murderers, and servers of idols, and everyone that loveth and maketh a lie" (v. 15). Previously in Apocalypse 21:8, eight sins were listed. This time He lists six sins: dogs (sodomites),[189] sorcery,[190] unchastity, murder, idolatry, and lying. The two sins not mentioned in this list but listed previously in 21:8 are fear and unbelief.

Jesus Testifies as the Root of Jesse and the Morning Star (Apoc 22:16–19)

[16] I Jesus have sent my angel, to testify to you these things in the churches. I am the root and stock of David, the bright and morning star.

[17] And the Spirit and the Bride say: Come. And he that heareth, let him say: Come. And he that thirsteth, let him come: and he that will, let him take the water of life, freely.

[18] For I testify to everyone that heareth the words of the prophecy of this book: If any man shall add to these things, God shall add unto him the plagues written in this book.

---

189 Deut 23:18 calls male ritual catamites dogs.
190 See the discussion above at Apocalypse 21:8 about sorcery and pharmaceutical potions.

¹⁹ And if any man shall take away from the words of the book of this prophecy, God shall take away his part out of the book of life, and out of the holy city, and from these things that are written in this book.

Jesus Christ testifies to "you" (plural in Greek) about these things in the churches. He confirms He is the root and stock of David. Christ states this to confirm His fulfillment of Isaias's prophecy: "In that day the root of Jesse [David's father], who standeth for an ensign of the people, him the Gentiles shall beseech, and his sepulcher shall be glorious" (Isa 11:10). He is also the bright and morning star. Christ already called Himself the morning star in Apocalypse 2:28 because He is the first one to rise in the morning.

Verse 17 shows the Holy Spirit and the Bride (the Church) saying to Jesus, "Come. And he that heareth, let him say: Come. And he that thirsteth, let him come: and he that will, let him take the water of life, freely." This is the divine invitation to sacramental baptism and reception of the Holy Spirit. The gift is received freely. Salvation in Christ is a free gift: "For by grace you are saved through faith, and that not of yourselves, for it is the *gift* of God" (Eph 2:8, emphasis added).

Verse 18 calls down a curse to anyone who adds anything to the book of Apocalypse. If he does add, God will add the plagues to that man. Verse 19 says any man who takes from this book of the Apocalypse, God shall take him from the Book of Life and out of the Holy City. But since Saint John is the last apostle, and this is the last book written for the entire Bible, we might also confirm that this curse falls on anyone who would add or take anything from the Sacred Scriptures.

The Last Two Verses of Apocalypse (Apoc 22:20–21)

²⁰ He that giveth testimony of these things, saith, Surely I come quickly: Amen. Come, Lord Jesus.

²¹ The grace of our Lord Jesus Christ be with you all. Amen.

The Apocalypse and the New Testament end with these final two verses. Christ reminds us yet again that "Surely I come quickly," and there is an antiphonal response from the Church: "Come, Lord Jesus." The final verse is a simple benediction that the grace of our Lord Jesus Christ would be with you all. The last word of the Bible is, fittingly, "Amen"—the end.

Epilogue:
Choose between Christ and Antichrist

Having read the Apocalypse, you must now choose *daily* who to serve: Christ or Antichrist, the Lamb or the beast.

There is one Jesus Christ and one Bride of Christ. There are not many Brides of Christ. There is only one New Jerusalem. To be saved, you must be *inside the new Jerusalem.* The New Jerusalem is the one, holy, Catholic, and apostolic Church. We enter the New Jerusalem by receiving the mark of His name on our foreheads, by receiving the waters of life, and by dipping our robe into the Blood of the Lamb. All three of these apocalyptic signs refer to the sacrament of holy baptism. We receive His name and mark on our foreheads when we are baptized on the head (either by affusion or immersion). The first century *Didache* document says,

> Now concerning baptism, baptize thus: Having first taught all these things, baptize ye into the name of the Father, and of the Son, and of the Holy Spirit, in living water.
> And if thou hast not living water, baptize into other water; and if thou canst not in cold, then in warm water. But if thou hast neither, pour water thrice upon the head in the name of the Father, and of the Son, and of the Holy Spirit.[191]

The waters of life are the Holy Spirit, and this is why Jesus says, "Amen, amen I say to thee, unless a man be born again of water and the Holy Ghost, he cannot enter into the kingdom of God" (Jn 3:5). And we dip our robes into the Blood of the Lamb through baptism so that we are purified from all sins and made clean. In order to be baptized, you

---

[191] This translation of *The Didache* was originally published in 1885 by Funk & Wagnalls, Publishers (New York). The translation was made by Philip Schaff from the Jerusalem Manuscript of the Didache.

must profess the Apostles' Creed, which summarizes the teachings of the twelve apostles, whose names are upon the foundation of the New Jerusalem.

Through baptism, you enter the city of the new Jerusalem—not the New Jerusalem in heaven, as she is perfect there. We participate in that heavenly city only through our communion with the version of that assembly here on earth that is marred by sinners and our own sin. This community on earth is the Catholic Church, and here on earth, she is occupied by sinners. On earth, in this imperfect state, we are the Church Militant. We fight. For this reason, we receive a second sacrament of Confirmation, or Chrismation, by which we are marked on the forehead as soldiers for Christ and receive the fulness of the Holy Spirit.

We must be fed and consoled in our war here on earth against sin and the spirit of the Antichrist. We weekly assemble on the first day of the week, the day Christ rose from the dead. We come together to witness again the once-for-all oblation of Christ on the cross to the Father. The one sacrifice of Christ is made present to us in the Eucharistic sacrifice. The death of Christ is never repeated, but it is presented to us again and again. We are invited to "behold the Lamb of God" and eat of this perfect sacrifice of His Body and Blood. This is the Holy Sacrifice of the Mass. Just as there are twenty-four presbyters in heaven around the altar of the Lamb, on earth each local church has an ordained presbyter who offers the sacrifice of the Lamb and feeds us with His Body and Blood. We are invited to "lift up our hearts" to perceive this heavenly liturgy with the Lamb upon the altar surrounded by incense, angels, chanting, and adoration.

At the end of the Apocalypse, Christ listed sins that disqualify us from being the heavenly New Jerusalem. If we baptized do fall to these ugly sins, we must restore our baptism, or else we cannot enter back into the New Jerusalem. This restoration happens through repentance in the sacrament of penance. On the evening of the day Christ rose from the dead, He appeared to His apostles and said:

> Peace be to you. As the Father hath sent me, I also send you. When he had said this, he breathed on them; and he said to them: Receive ye the Holy Ghost. Whose sins you shall forgive, they are forgiven them; and whose sins you shall retain, they are retained. (Jn 20:21–23)

The apostles and their successors in the form of the bishops and presbyters can forgive and retain sins through the power of Jesus Christ delegated to them by ordination and jurisdiction. We must repent, confess our sins privately to the presbyter (priest), and formally receive the sentence of absolution from our sins. The priest will also give a small penance to you, which is the way that you show that you are willing to change and walk in the newness of life.

The three remaining sacraments of extreme unction (anointing for extreme illness or death), holy orders (ordaining men to the ministry), and matrimony are covered in my other books.[192] The importance is that you fully hold the one true faith revealed by our Lord Jesus Christ in Sacred Scripture and in Sacred Tradition. You must also be in full union with the one Church (New Jerusalem) established by Jesus Christ and built on his rock:

Peter's Church on the Rock (Mt 16:16–19)

[16] Simon Peter answered and said: Thou art Christ, the Son of the living God.

[17] And Jesus answering, said to him: Blessed art thou, Simon Bar-Jona: because flesh and blood hath not revealed it to thee, but my Father who is in heaven.

---

[192] See especially Taylor R. Marshall's *The Catholic Perspective on Paul* (Dallas, TX: Saint John Press, 2010), chapters 8-9.

¹⁸ And I say to thee: That thou art Peter; and upon this rock I will build my church, and the gates of hell shall not prevail against it.
¹⁹ And I will give to thee the keys of the kingdom of heaven. And whatsoever thou shalt bind upon earth, it shall be bound also in heaven: and whatsoever thou shalt loose upon earth, it shall be loosed also in heaven.

You must be a Christian. You must be baptized. You must be a Catholic. Otherwise, you do not rightly have the mark of Christ on your forehead, nor do you have entry into New Jerusalem, who is the Bride of Christ.

Saint John, Apostle of Love, pray for us.

This book is consecrated to Jesus Christ for the greater glory of God.

Did you enjoy this book?

Please take a moment to offer a prayer for the author.

If you benefited from this book, please share it with family and friends, and please review it on amazon.com.

Thank you!

Dr. Taylor R. Marshall

APPENDIX 1: TIMELINE OF FUTURE EVENTS

Having covered all the sacred verses of Saint John's Apocalypse, you might ask, "So now what? What's going to actually happen next?" There are possible scenarios. If the mystic priest Bartholomew Holzhauser is correct and we are living in the fifth epoch of the Church, then we are living in the age corresponding to the Old Testament age of Babylonian exile and the fifth Apocalyptic church of Sardis. Here is a review of the seven messages and the seven epochs:

Message	Church Message	OT Epoch	Holzhauser Epoch	Holzhauser Dates	Status
First	Ephesus	Adam	Apostolic	AD 33–100	Seedtime
Second	Smyrna	Patriarchs	Apostles–Constantine	100–337	Irrigation
Third	Pergamos	Moses	Constantine–Charlemagne	337–800	Illumination
Fourth	Thyatira	Kings	Charlemagne–Reformation	800–1517	Peace
Fifth	Sardis	Babylonian Exile	Reformation–Restoration	1517–?	Affliction
Sixth	Philadelphia	Restoration from Exile	Restoration	Future	Consolation
Seventh	Laodicea	Christ	Antichrist–2nd Coming	Future	Desolation

Recall that, for Holzhauser, the fifth epoch of Sardis ends with the "Minor Chastisement," which is *not* the same as the Great Tribulation under the Antichrist at the end of time. In the fifth epoch of the Old Testament, Jerusalem and the temple were destroyed, and the Jews were sent into Babylonian exile as punishment for their idolatry. They were allowed to return to Jerusalem under the Persians with Esdras and Nehemias and under the authority of High Priest Jesus and Davidic Prince Zerubbabel.

Holzhauser says that the end of our fifth epoch will end with a Minor Chastisement. After this chastisement, we will experience a restoration of the Catholic Church to her former glory under a holy pope and great monarch.

APPENDIX 2: THE MINOR CHASTISEMENT

If we are in the fifth epoch of the Church, here are the events that we should expect leading up the Minor Chastisement:[193]

Fifth Epoch of Exile Ending in Minor Chastisement

1. The Catholic Church, like the Jews under the Babylonian Empire, will be confused by the introduction of heresy and idolatry. This begins in 1517 under Martin Luther. Christians are separated into thousands of conflicting sects. Like the Jews, the Church will lose her sacred city, her ark of the covenant, and the glories of her divinely ordered worship.

2. According to private revelations, there will be increasing natural disasters and wars.

3. Heresy, schism, and apostasy will increase. The Church will be weak.

4. Civil wars ensue.

5. Natural disasters in the form of earthquakes and floods will afflict humanity.

6. Some mystics say Russia will invade Europe.

7. The pope will flee Rome, go into hiding, and be cruelly murdered.

8. Toward the end of the Minor Chastisement, a saintly pope will be elected.

9. A Catholic "great king" (mystics say he is French) will defeat the Russian invasion against all odds.

10. Somewhere toward the end of this fifth epoch will be the three days of darkness described by Blessed Anna Maria Taigi (d. 1837). Darkness will cover the entire earth, and only blessed candles will provide

---

193 This timeline of the Minor Chastisement is derived (with my modifications) from the timeline on p. xliii in Desmond A. Birch. *Trial, Tribulation, and Triumph: Before, During, and After the Antichrist.* Goleata, CA: Queenship Publishing Co., 1996.

light. Previously, we saw that the fifth vial introduces universal darkness. The fifth vial in Apocalypse 16:10 may very well be the three days of darkness between the fifth and sixth epochs.
11. After the defeat of Russia and the universal three days of darkness, the sixth epoch of peace and consolation will begin.

Sixth Epoch of Restoration, or "Age of Peace"
1. The holy pope will then crown and anoint the great king as the new Holy Roman Emperor of a confederation of Christian nations and societies.
2. Some foresee a Great Council occurring at this time to reform all things in Christ.
3. The Gospel will be preached in the whole world (Mt 24:14; Mk 13:10). Millions will convert to Christ from the various world religions.
4. This state of renewal and spiritual prosperity will last for some time. However, the heart of the people will grow lazy and lax in their love for Christ. Their fire of charity will dim.

Seventh Epoch of the Antichrist
1. The lukewarm Christians (The seventh church epoch of Laodicea is the "lukewarm church.") set the stage for the Antichrist.
2. First, there is the Great Apostasy, in which most of the world will formally reject Jesus Christ as Lord, God, and Savior (Mt 24: 10–12; Lk 18:8; 2 Thess 2:3; 2 Tim 3:1–9) and then the Jewish Antichrist shall appear (2 Thess 2:3–12; 1 Jn 2:18–22; 2 Jn 7).
3. The once-strong Christian Roman Empire that ruled the entire world will at this time cease to exist. The Empire will be divided into ten kingdoms with ten kings, under the power of the Antichrist. Three of these kingdoms will not bow to the Antichrist and will be crushed:

After this I beheld in the vision of the night, and lo, a fourth beast, terrible and wonderful, and exceeding strong, it had great iron teeth, eating and breaking in pieces, and treading down the rest with its feet: and it was unlike to the other beasts which I had seen before it, and had ten horns. I considered the horns, and behold another little horn sprung out of the midst of them: and three of the first horns were plucked up at the presence thereof: and behold eyes like the eyes of a man were in this horn, and a mouth speaking great things. (Dan 7:7–8)

Saint Jerome's commentary on the book of Daniel states that the Antichrist will kill the three kings that "do not bow to him." Perhaps this is the context in which the Antichrist receives a head wound and is healed by the False Prophet.

4. The land beast, or False Prophet, appears at this time and prepares the way for the Antichrist, just as John the Baptist prepared the way for Christ. The False Prophet is the high priest of the cult that worships the Antichrist as God, and worship of his image is made mandatory. The Jewish temple is rebuilt in Jerusalem, and the Antichrist enthrones himself inside of it as God, Messiah, and King of Kings.

5. The Antichrist seizes universal dominion over the entire world and enforces global worship of himself as God and Christ.

6. The two witnesses Enoch and Elias arrive miraculously in Jerusalem. Enoch preaches and converts the Gentiles back to Christ. Elias preaches

and converts the Jews. The Jews entirely convert to Christ at this time, and "all Israel is saved."

7. The Antichrist kills Enoch and Elias and displays their dead bodies in the street for three and a half days. The two witnesses are resurrected to the amazement of all. Their preaching and resurrection trigger a global return to Christ. Apocalypse 11 describes how many gave glory to God after seeing the two witnesses resurrected.

8. Horrified by the world returning to Jesus Christ, the Antichrist as Gog now begins the Great Tribulation of three and a half years, culminating in his Armageddon war against the growing Church, which now contains all the Jews and many of the Gentiles. Perhaps the Church at this time is centered back in Jerusalem. Gog (Antichrist) and Magog (the ten kings) join up to finally extinguish Christianity once and for all. Horrible martyrdom ensues. This is the moment of the greatest and most glorious martyrs in history.

9. The beginning of the three-and-a-half-year (1,290-day) Great Tribulation begins with the abolition of Christian worship, sacraments, and the Holy Sacrifice of the Mass: "And from the time when the continual sacrifice shall be taken away, and the abomination unto desolation shall be set up, there shall be a thousand two hundred ninety days" (Dan 12:11).

10. The ten kings destroy Jerusalem in their wrath against Christ and the Church. Fallen is Babylon the Great.

11. Then there is the death of the Antichrist in Jerusalem

APPENDIX 3: DEATH OF THE ANTICHRIST IN TRADITION

The Holy Bible twice describes the death of the Antichrist. In Apocalypse 20:9: "there came down fire from God out of heaven and devoured" Gog and his armies in the context of battle. Secondly, Saint Paul says the Antichrist is "that wicked one ... whom the Lord Jesus shall kill with the Spirit of his mouth; and shall destroy with the brightness of his coming" (2 Thess 2:8). The Spirit of the mouth of Christ is the Holy Spirit that is also the burning fire on the day of Pentecost. There is no contradiction in saying that Gog is devoured by fire and that Jesus kills the Antichrist with the Spirit of his mouth. The Spirit is the divine fire.

The scholar and mystic Saint Hildegard of Bingen (d. AD 1179) received in a vision from God the details of the death of the future Antichrist. She writes that the crowds will be amazed by the resurrection and ascension of Enoch and Elias. The Antichrist will attempt sorcery to ascend also into heaven like Enoch and Elias. She writes:

> In the sight of the crowds standing around and listening, he [Antichrist] will command the higher strata of the sky to lift him up during his ascension in to heaven, and the words of my loyal servant Paul, who is full of the spirit of truth says "and the Lord Jesus will slay him with the breath of his mouth and will destroy him with his glorious appearance at his coming (2 Thess 2:8). . . . When the son of corruption ascends on high through diabolical trickery, he will be thrust down again by the divine power. The fumes of sulphur and pitch will consume him such that the crowds standing nearby will flee into the mountains for protection. Such abject fear will seize all who see and hear these things

that they will reject the devil and his son [Antichrist] and be converted to the True Faith through baptism.[194]

A similar account of the death of the Antichrist appears in the *Sibylline Oracles* (AD 300's). In an attempt to convert the Jews back to himself, the Antichrist will simulate Jesus Christ's ascension from the Mount of Olives. At that very moment, "the Antichrist will be slain by the power of God through Michael the Archangel on the Mount of Olives."[195] Saint Thomas Aquinas follows this belief when he writes, "For Michael shall kill him on Mount Olivet from whence Christ ascended."[196]

1. After the death of the Antichrist, there is perhaps a short duration of time given for the remaining inhabitants of the earth to repent and accept Our Lord and the message of His Gospel.
2. Then Jesus Christ as Son of Man appears in heaven, coming from the east (Mt 24:30; Mk 13:26; Lk 13:27).
3. Every human person is resurrected in his or her body.
4. Then Jesus Christ judges all resurrected humans from Adam to the last baby born at the Valley of Jehoshaphat (Joel 3:2, 12), which is situated between the Mount of Olives and Mount Sion.

---

[194] Hildegard of Bingen, *Liber Divinorum Operum*, trans. Nathaniel M. Campbell (Washington, DC: The Catholic University of America Press, 2018) in 3.5.

[195] The *Sibylline Oracles* "Tiburtine Sibyl" (late 300's) provides a detailed account of Michael the Archangel killing the Antichrist: "When the Roman empire shall have ceased, then the Antichrist will be openly revealed and will sit in the House of the Lord in Jerusalem. While he is reigning, two very famous men, Elias and Enoch, will go forth to announce the coming of the Lord. Antichrist will kill them and after three days they will be raised up by the Lord. Then there will be a great persecution, such as has not been before nor shall be thereafter. The Lord will shorten those days for the sake of the elect, and the Antichrist will be slain by the power of God through Michael the Archangel on the Mount of Olives."

[196] Thomas Aquinas, Commentary on 2 Thessalonians at 2:8, *Opera Omnia Tomus XIII*.

5. Christ divides humanity: sheep on the right, goats on the left. The just shall be rewarded with the beatific vision, and the wicked shall be cast into the pool of fire.
6. The heavens and earth are transformed into the new heavens and the new earth.

APPENDIX 4: EZECHIEL AND APOCALYPSE COMPARED

EVENTS	EZECHIEL	APOCALYPSE
1. Word Comes	1:1–4, 28	1:9–19
2. The Lord Appears (as Christ)	1:4, 27; 8:2	1:12–16; 5:6
2. Throne Liturgy	1:5–27	4:1–6
3. Four Living Cherubim	1:5–24; 10	4:6–8
4. The Scroll Is Opened	2:9–10	5:1–8
5. Eating the Scroll	2:8–10; 3:1–3	10:8–11
6. Siege of Jerusalem	4:1–8; 5;24	9:4–10
7. Famine	4:16–17; 5:12; 6:12	6:5–6, 8
8. One-Third Destruction	5:2–12	8:6–12
9. Reproach of Israel	5:5–17	18
10. Wrath of the Lord	6–7	6:12–17; 14:7–20

11. Israel's Abominations	8; 16; 20; 22; 33	17:1–7
12. Sealing on Forehead with *T*	9:2–4, 11	7:2–8
13. Image of Jealousy/Idolatry	8:3	13:14
14. The Slaughter	9:5–10; 21	8 – 9
15. Coals from The Altar	10:1–7	8:5–10
16. Restoration of Remnant	11:16–20; 14:22–23; 34:10–16; 36	21:1–7
17. No More Delay	12:17–28	10:1–7
18. False Prophets	13	16:16; 19:20; 20:10
19. Four Judgments/Horsemen	14:21	6:2–8
20. Jerusalem's Fall: The Vine Tree	15	14:18–20
21. Jerusalem as Great Whore	16:22–59; 23	17:3–6; 19:2
22: Jerusalem as Sodom	16:45–56	11:8

23. Treating with Egypt	17:15–18; 23	11:8
24. Lamentations	19	18
25. Destruction of Jerusalem	22:18–22; 23:46–47; 24:2–14	14:6–8; 17:16; 18:10–19; 20:8–9
26. Downfall of the Nations	25–32	10:11; 19:11–15
27. Shepherd Beasts / Land Beast	34	13:11–15
28. Resurrection	37	14:1–5; 20:4–6, 12
29. Gog Battles Jerusalem	38	20:7–9
30. Judgment of Gog (Scavenger Feast)	39	19:17–21
31. New Jerusalem	40:2	21:2, 10
32. Measuring the Temple	40–43	11:1–2
33. The Glory of God in the Temple	43	21:22–23
34. The River of Life and Tree of Life	47	22:1–2

APPENDIX 5: VENI CREATOR SPIRITUS

Veni Creator Spiritus (Come Creator Spirit) is a traditional Christian chant by the ninth-century archbishop Rabanus Maurus of Mainz. It invokes the Third Person of the Trinity as the sevenfold spirit in conformity with the usage of Saint John in the Apocalypse.

Latin text	English version
Veni, creator Spiritus,	Come, Holy Ghost, Creator, come
mentes tuorum visita,	from thy bright heav'nly throne;
imple superna gratia,	come, take possession of our souls,
quae tu creasti, pectora.	and make them all thine own.
Qui diceris Paraclitus,	Thou who art called the Paraclete,
donum Dei altissimi,	best gift of God above,
fons vivus, ignis, caritas,	the living spring, the living fire,
et spiritalis unctio.	sweet unction and true love.
Tu septiformis munere,	Thou who art sevenfold in thy grace,
dextrae Dei tu digitus,	finger of God's right hand;
tu rite promissum Patris,	his promise, teaching little ones
sermone ditans guttura.	to speak and understand.
Accende lumen sensibus,	O guide our minds with thy blest light,
infunde amorem cordibus,	with love our hearts inflame;
infirma nostri corporis	and with thy strength, which ne'er decays,
virtute firmans perpeti.	confirm our mortal frame.
Hostem repellas longius	Far from us drive our deadly foe;
pacemque dones protinus;	true peace unto us bring;
ductore sic te praevio	and through all perils lead us safe
vitemus omne noxium.	beneath thy sacred wing.
Per te sciamus da Patrem	Through thee may we the Father know,
noscamus atque Filium,	through thee th'eternal Son,
te utriusque Spiritum	and thee the Spirit of them both,
credamus omni tempore.	thrice-blessed three in One.

Bibliography

Ante-Nicene Fathers. A. Roberts and J. Donaldson, eds. New York, 1903.

Augustine. *The City of God*. Trans. Marcus Dods. New York: Modern Library, 1950.

Averky (Taushev). Archbishop. Trans. Seraphim Rose (ed.). *The Apocalypse: In the Teachings of Ancient Christianity*. Platina, California: St. Herman of Alaska Brotherhood, 1996.

Bellarmine, Robert. *De Contraversiis I, De Romano Pontifice*, Trans. Ryan Grant. Post Falls, ID: Mediatrix Press, 2016.

Benson, Robert Hugh. *The Lord of the World*. Hawthorne, California: Christian Book Club of America, 1976.

Birch, Desmond A. *Trial, Tribulation and Triumph: Before, During, and After Antichrist*. Goleta, CA: Queenship Publishing Company, 1996.

Boettner, Loraine. *The Millennium*. Philadelphia: The Presbyterian and Reformed Publishing Co., 1984.

Bouyer, Louis. *Eucharist: Theology and Spirituality of the Eucharistic Prayer*. Notre Dame, IN: University of Notre Dame Press, 1968.

Brandon, S. G. G. *The Fall of Jerusalem and the Christian Church: A Study on the Effects of the Jewish Overthrow of AD 70 on Christianity*. London: SPCK, 1968.

Cekada, Anthony. *Work of Human Hands: A Theological Critique of the Mass of Paul VI*. West Chester, OH: SGG Resources, 2010.

Chilton, David. *The Days of Vengeance: An Exposition of the Book of Revelation*. Horn Lake, MS: Dominion Press, 2006.

Chilton, David. *Paradise Restored: A Biblical Theology of Dominion*. Fort Worth, TX: Dominion Press, 1985.

Dix, Gregory. *The Shape of the Liturgy*. New York: The Seabury Press, 1945.

Ferrar, F.W. *The Early Days of Christianity*. Chicago: Belfored, Clarke and Co., 1882.

Gentry, Kenneth L., Jr. *The Beast of Revelation*. Powder Springs, GA: American Vision, 2002.

Gentry, Kenneth L., Jr. *Before Jerusalem Fell: Dating the Book of Revelation*. Powder Springs, GA: American Vision, 1998.

Goodrich, Richard J. *Sulpicius Severus: The Complete Works. Introduction, Translation, and Notes*. New York: Paulist Press, 2015.

Gregory the Great. *Moralia*. Trans. John Henry Parker. London: JGF & J. Rivington, 1844.

Hahn, Scott. *The Lamb's Supper: Mass as Heaven on Earth*. Doubleday: New York, 1996.

Hildegard of Bingen, *The Book of Divine Works,* trans. Nathaniel M. Campbell. Washington, DC: The Catholic University of America Press, 2018.

Hughes, Philip. *A History of the Church*. 3 Vols. New York: Sheed and Ward, 1934.

Hyde, Douglas. "Medieval Account of Antichrist," in *Medieval Studies in Memory of Getrude S. Loomis*. New York: 1927.

Josephus, Flavius. *The Jewish War*. Gaalya Cornfeld, ed. Grand Rapids: Zondervan Publishing, 1982.

Jungmann, Josef. *The Early Liturgy to the Time of Gregory the Great*. Trans. Francis A. Brunner. Notre Dame: University of Notre Dame, 1959.

Knox, Ronald. *Enthusiasm*. New York: Oxford Press, 1950.

Lapide, Cornelius a. *Commentaria in Scripturam Sacram*. L. Vives, 1860.

Manning, Henry Edward. *The Present Crisis of the Holy See: A Warning about Antichrist*. Topeka, KS: Christ the King Library, 2021.

Marshall, Taylor R. *The Catholic Perspective on Paul: Paul and the Origin of Catholic Christianity*. Dallas, TX: Saint John Press, 2010.

Marshall, Taylor R. *The Crucified Rabbi: Judaism and the Origin of Catholic Christianity*. Dallas, TX: Saint John Press, 2009.

Marshall, Taylor R. *The Eternal City: Rome and the Origin of Catholic Christianity*. Dallas, TX: Saint John Press, 2012.

Marshall, Taylor R. *Infiltration: The Plot to Destroy the Church from Within*. Nashua, NH: Sophia Institute Press, 2019.

McDonald, James M. *The Life and Writings of St. John*. London: Hodder and Stoughton, 1877.

Methodius (Pseudo). *Apocalypse*. Trans. Benjamin Garstad. Harvard University Press, Cambridge, MA, 2012.

Miceli, Vincent P. *The Antichrist*. Fort Collins, CO: Roman Catholic Books, 1981.

Shepherd, Norman. "The Resurrections of Revelation 20." *Westminster Theological Journal* 37 (Fall 1974) 1, pp. 34–43.

Suetonius. *The Twelve Caesars*. Trans. Robert Graves. London: Penguin, 1979.

Stuart, Moses. *Commentary on the Apocalypse*. 2 vols. Andover: Allen, Morrill and Wadwell, 1845.

Sweet, J. P. M. *Revelation*. London: SCM Press, and Philadelphia: Trinity Press International, 1979 and 1990.

Thomas Aquinas. *Summa contra Gentiles*. Trans. English Dominican Fathers. London: Oats Burns and Washbourne. 1924.

Thomas Aquinas. *Summa Theologiæ*. Trans. English Dominican Fathers. Notre Dame, IN: Ave Maria Press, 1920.

Victorinus. *Commentary on the Apocalypse of the Blessed John*. Trans. Robert Ernest Wallis. Alexander Roberts and James Donaldson, eds. *The Ante-Nicene Fathers*. Grand Rapids: William B. Eerdmans Publishing Co. 1970. Vol VII, pp. 344–360.

Wallace, Foy E. *The Book of Revelation*. Fort Worth, TX: Foy E. Wallace Jr. Publications, 1966.

Index

Deuteronomy, 32
Dragon, 160, 164, 171, 173
Eagle, 93
Earthquake, 116, 155, 214
Easter, 65, 124, 212, 278
Egypt, 31, 32, 39, 75, 148, 153,
    154, 157, 193, 208, 209, 216,
    221, 222, 231, 236, 241, 276,
    300
Elias, 16, 149, 150, 151, 152, 153,
    154, 155, 166, 173, 178, 179,
    213, 293, 294, 295, 296
Eliseus, 173
Enoch, 149, 150, 151, 152, 154,
    155, 178, 199, 293, 294, 295,
    296
Ephesus, 65, 69, 73, 74, 88, 255,
    290
Esdras, 199, 290
Eucharist, 16, 57, 137, 157, 158,
    188, 224, 247, 303
Euphrates River, 33, 130, 210,
    211, 232
Eusebius, 108, 173, 255, 256, 263
Ezechiel, 16, 19, 29, 38, 71, 89,
    91, 93, 95, 103, 107, 111, 137,
    139, 215, 220, 221, 222, 223,
    224, 232, 262, 263, 264, 268,
    274, 278, 279, 298
False Prophet, 19, 20, 59, 76, 78,
    117, 175, 176, 178, 179, 180,
    188, 206, 211, 226, 252, 253,
    257, 265, 293, 299
Famine, 298
Forehead, 107, 224, 299
Gnostic, 232, 255
Gog, 59, 60, 103, 252, 253, 261,
    262, 263, 264, 265, 268, 294,
    295, 300
Gospel, 12, 46, 59, 91, 108, 116,
    122, 132, 171, 192, 208, 249,
    250, 256, 269, 271, 277, 292,
    296
Gospel of Saint John, 271
Gregory the Great, 45, 52, 91, 151,
    182, 304
Hades, 103
Harlot, 218, 222, 223, 225, 228,
    235, 240, 241, 245, 246, 269
Hell, 103, 127, 129, 218, 219

Heresy, 291
Herod, 82, 165, 170, 199
High Priest, 81, 87, 90, 198, 205,
    214, 290
Holy Spirit, 48, 63, 90, 95, 96,
    111, 112, 118, 143, 163, 188,
    196, 266, 271, 277, 278, 279,
    280, 284, 286, 287, 295
Horse, 101, 102
Horsemen, 100, 299
Idolatry, 16, 59, 78, 272, 299
Irenaeus, 42, 43, 52, 53, 55, 57,
    91, 108, 110, 149, 151, 183,
    184, 185, 255, 256
Isaias, 16, 19, 29, 38, 63, 66, 81,
    94, 107, 108, 109, 116, 122,
    123, 124, 125, 130, 142, 161,
    162, 174, 200, 221, 239, 269,
    284
Israel, 16, 31, 32, 33, 34, 50, 51,
    76, 78, 79, 90, 99, 106, 107,
    112, 113, 120, 137, 142, 150,
    153, 156, 162, 165, 172, 173,
    176, 186, 189, 190, 192, 200,
    201, 203, 206, 212, 221, 224,
    230, 231, 232, 237, 264, 268,
    273, 294, 298, 299
James, 61, 125, 152, 190, 242, 305
Jeremias, 16, 50, 121, 122, 125,
    158, 159, 160, 191, 192, 211,
    221, 224
Jerome, 43, 44, 47, 50, 51, 52, 53,
    57, 84, 91, 151, 255, 293
Jerusalem, 16, 25, 30, 33, 34, 41,
    44, 46, 51, 52, 53, 54, 55, 57,
    59, 61, 66, 68, 71, 73, 80, 81,
    82, 87, 101, 103, 108, 111,
    113, 121, 125, 140, 141, 142,
    145, 146, 147, 148, 152, 154,
    155, 156, 157, 158, 164, 173,
    174, 175, 176, 185, 187, 191,
    192, 193, 194, 200, 201, 204,
    208, 209, 211, 212, 214, 215,
    216, 220, 221, 222, 223, 224,
    225, 228, 230, 231, 232, 233,
    234, 235, 236, 237, 238, 239,
    240, 241, 242, 243, 244, 245,
    252, 256, 258, 262, 264, 265,
    268, 269, 270, 273, 274, 275,
    276, 281, 286, 287, 288, 289,

A Special Thank you to Our Launch Team

I am very grateful to our Launch Team who read the book before publication, gave us honest feedback, suggested improvements, and helped with promotion. Thank you for your time, enthusiasm, and help.

Godspeed,
Taylor

Aames Abanto, Colette Marie Abascal, Cornelius Aben, Sharon Abrahamson, Lisa Abrusia, Adje Accoh, Isaac Acuña, Jessica Adamo, Mark Adams, Amy and John Adams, Ray Adkins, David Emmanuel Agreda, Rudy Agresta, Jose Aguilar, Rudy Aguilar, Edouard Ah-Kye, D.C. Alan, Paul Albares, Paul Albertson, Holly Aleo, Maria de las Victorias Alfano, Joan Alimonti, Patricia Allaman, Carmen Allen, Jonathon Allen, Nelson Almeida, Bernardo Altamirano, Alicia Álvarez, Patricia Anania, Kathy Anastasiu, Kimberly Anderson, Ric Anderson, Jo Reynetta Andonie, Henry Anyikaeme, Jayden Aplin, Enedina Arechiga, Aaron Arehart, Karen Arilli, Maria Cristina Ariza-Gomez, Kristy Armas, Samantha Armentor, MaryAnn Arnaud, Kathy Arno, Julie Arnold, Jonathan Arrington, Marie-Claire Arseneau, Nathene Arthur, Oscar Artola, Antonio Arvesu, Phil Ashford, Jonathan Atchley, Michael Atwood, Louise Aussant, Doug Austreim, Rob Auten, AJ Ayala, Sonia Ayala, Diego Azcuy, Debbie Azevedo, Joseph Azize, Jose Azurdia, Gretchen Babendreier, Jacqueline Badolato, Dawood Badshah, Jerry Baeza, JoAnne Baker, Cristina Baker, Christopher Baker, Trish Baldoni, Suki Baldwin, Jatte Baleyos, Nune Balgomera, Trevor Bantleman, Carlos Baptista, Kristina Baran, Daniel Barbaglia, Kristina Barber, Catherine Barbercheck, Deena Barca, Michele Barczynski, Christina Barela, Pia Barlotta, Jacob Barlow, Marc Barrera, Patrick Barrett, Celestino Barretto, Reniel Barroso, Daniel Barry, Duane Barth, Elaine Bartholomew, Jerrold Bartholomew, Madeline Bauer, Patricia Bautista, Sandra Beattie, Toni Beaulieu, Adriana Beaumont, Tereza Becica, Father Becker, Jonathan Beckett Beckett, Sherrie Bedford, Laurelee Beduhn, Timothy Begley, Sharon Behme, Rory Beirn, Catherine Beirne, Denise Bell, Melinda Bell, Bridgit Bellini, Joshua Belokur, Albert Beltz, Harry Bendelow, Angele Bennett, Robert John Bennett, Coleman Benson, Mary Benson, Ethan Berglund, James (Jimmy) Berkon, Joseph Berling, Jeff Bernard, Leo Bernard, Giovanna Bernardo, Barbara Bertsch, Linda Besink Besink, Kathryn Bevis, Gerard Biagan, Monica Bianco, Sean Binkley, Kelly Birnbrich, Donna Bischoff, Linda Black, Gary Black, Anthony Blacker, Ray Blacklidge, Maria Elvira Blagrove, Jocelyne Blanchette, Donnie Blankenship, Aleksandra Blaszczyk, Mark Bleil, Jenelle Blevins, Bobbi Bloom Bloom, Ronald Boak, Robert Boatwright, Suzanne Boese, Stephanie Bogdan, Amy Bogle, Richard Bole, Anton Bole, Aliziris Bombino, Karen Bonvecchio, Natalie Borda, Mary Bordi, Marita Borer, John Boslem, Jacquelynn Bourdeau, Debbie Bourgault, Eric Boutin, Nicholas Bove, Karen Bowman, Paul Bowser, Karen Boyle, Paul Boyles, Mary Bozman, Rosemarie Brady, Margo Bragg, Aimee Braman, DeAnn Brandel, Jennifer Brechbill, Brian Brecheisen, Michael Breckley, Lori J. Breda, Brendan Breen, Bill Breen, Joseph Bremer, Petey Brennan, Janet Brennan, Rev. Mr. Michael Brescia, Mary Brescia, Gisela Bresler, Thomas Brewer, Linda Brewer, Pamela Briddell, William Bridegroom, Luke Briggs, David Bright, David Brill, Jose Briseno, Deb Britain, Eduardo Brito, Steve Brittain, Marianne Brokaw, Finn Brooke, Marlys Brooks, Annette Brousseau, John Brower, Tom Brown, Paul Brown, Carolyn Brown, Jerry Brown, Dorothy Marie Brown, Frank Brownlow, Nicholas Brueggrmann, Jonathan Brunk, Donna Brunk, Christine Brusnahan, Kate Bryan, Jeff Buchholz, Edward Bucnis, Steve Buda, Jan (John) Bugaj, Roberto Buitron, Fred Bukowski, Jud Bulcroft, Patrick Bump, Fran Burazin, Aisling Burke, Kimberly Burke, Mrs Meredith Burl, Aaron Burns, Tom Bush, Joshua Bussell, Claire Bussell, David Byers, Raymond Byrnes, Lori Byro, Maria Caballero, Eric Cabana, Richard Calderon, Angela Calderon, Marisol Calixto, Suzanne Callahan, Ben Callicoat, Gregg Campayno, Lisa Campbell, Amy Campbell, Kathleen Campos, Miguel Campos, Ela Camps, Jacqueline Candello, Frank Canovatchel, John Cantey, Kamau Canton, Teresa Cantu, Luis

Canuto, Gianluca Caravaggio, Kris Cardella, Teresa Cardinez, Alisa Carraro, Andrew Carson, Kaitlyn Carswell, John Carter, James Carty, David Carusello, Edward Case, Margaret Casman-Vuko, Joe Cassar, Christopher Castagnoli, Armando Castany, Frederico Castro, Michael Cates, Rosalee Cavanaugh, Catherine Cetera, David Chan, Roger Chandler, Lisa Chappell, Don Cheramie, Pascal Chimezie, Alex Choong, Geri Chowning, Matthew Chrisman, Robert Christenson, Samuel Chung, Sandra Cianci, Stephanie Ciccarelli, Erica Cicero, Cindi Cincotta, Francesco Cinotti, Barbara Clark, Father Karl Claver, Fr Cleenewerck, Sean Cloonan, Sonja Cloutier, Betty Cochrane, Linda Cogswell, Thomas Colangelo, David Cole, David Cole, Martha Cole, Erminia Colella, David Coleman, Caleb Colson, Matt Commons, Christopher Conley, Stephen Conlon, Matthew Connor, Paul Conti, Steven Contreras, Dorothy Conway, Linda Coones, Joseph Coote, Patrick Copeland, Sarah Corkery, Christopher Corleone, Eric Cormier, Eric Cormier, John Corso, Gina Coss, Dominic Costantino, Monica Costello, Peter Costello, wayne Costello, Michele Costello, Bradford Cosway, Paul Coupe, Michael Cox, Angela Cox, Larry Crandall, Linda Craven, Barbara Crawford, Wayne Crenwelge, Teresa Crichton, Kristy Crosby, Angel Croyle, Susan Cruickshank, Kenneth Crumpton, Abe Cruz, Daniel Cruz, Carrie Cruz, Tim Cumberland, Katie Cummings, William Curry, Marilyn Curson, John Curtin, Donna Curtis, Cheryl Curtis, William Curtis, Michael Custodio, Cathleen Cutler, Thomas D'Alessandro, Rachel D'Auria, Jeffrey L Dagenais, Gerri Daigle, Suzanne Daly, P Damian, David Danforth, Myron Daniels, Brent Daniels, Henry Darlison, Jack Daugherty, James Davenport, Eugene Davenport, Kevin Davey, Deric Davidson, Oliver Davidson, Mychelle Davis, Ronald Davis, Selina Davis, Sarah Davis, Cameron Dawson, Gail Dawson, Christine Dax, Dominic Day, Peter Dcruz, Yvonne De Garcia, Gabriela De La Fuente, Dawn De La Rosa, Luis De la Serna, Marisu de Leon, Debra De Los Santos, Francis De Lucia, Libby De Mattia, Jason De Neve, Andrew DeCelles, Matthew Decker, Michael DeDecker, Joan DeFeo, Fred DeHerrera, Andrew DeJoseph, Alanna Delagarza, Robin DeLage, Eddie DelaHoussaye, Janice Delamarter, John D'Elia, Catherine Delk, Ric DelValle, Stacey Dennis, Joshua Denny, Michael DePauw, James DeSart, Valerie DeSomber, Prof. Dr. Ingrid Detter de Frankopan, Cynthia Devine, Patricia Devine, Chris Devlin, Marc Devoid, Barbara DeVries, Irma DeWeese, Michael DeWitt, Antonia Dey, Steve Di Mauro, Rick Diana, David Diaz, Oscar Diaz, Nathan Dibley, Brad DiCarlo, David DiGennaro, Catherine DiGiacinto, Joe Dillett, Amado David Dimal, Sean Dineen, Joseph Dionne, Andre Dionne, Michael DiScala, Pam Dittoe, Steven DiTullio, Mark Dixon, Chavel Dixon, Mrs Geraldine Dobson, Daniel Doiron, David Dollman, Jose Dominguez, Brian Domke, Joe Donahay, Deborah Donnelly, Michael Donodeo, Linda Doran, Patricia Doran, Darius Doria, John Andrew Dorsey III, Eugenia Doucette, Brian Downey, Gregory Doyle, Matthias Dransmann, Norla Draper, Andrew Drees, Dylan Drego, Michael Driscoll, Preeti D'Souza, Lisa Dudzik, Dianne Duffin, Collin Dufrene, Eileen Duke, Jake Duncan, David Duncan, Mark Dunn, Jean Dunne, Jane Dunne-Brady, Sandra Dunphy, Chris Dupree, Aaron Durocher, Judita Durovska, Melissa Durow, Adam Durst, Monica Duvall, Brian Dvorak, Pam Dwyer, Kate Dyson-D'Onofrio, Lucia Dziadul, Shawna Dziedziak, Lynn none Eareckson Eareckson, Teresa Earp, William Eaton, Jason Eberly, Elizabeth Ebertowski, Jerry Eckert, Christopher Edmonds, Weston Edwards, Samuel Edwards, Douglas Edwards, Dennis Egan, Georgino El Khoury, Zayda Eleutice, Kelly Elliot, Craig Elliott, Barbara Ellis, Mark Ellwood, Richard Elworth, Enyamu Emmanuel, Thomas Engle, John Engles, David Englestad, Molly Ennis, Laurie Ensworth, Andrea Erickson, Ray Etter, Sue Evans, Pat Evans, Edward Evans, Theresa Evenbly, Lisa Evers, Leslie Ewald, Des Eyden, Anne Fabian, Maryann Fabian, Angela Fairbairn, Linda Fairbanks, Francisco Fajar, Sean Fallon, Randall Farmer, Mildred Farrell, Claire Farrell, Donna Farrell-Pelissier, Leigh Farris, Anna Feher-Holan, Simon Feil, Dr. James Fennessy, Neil Fernandes, Jaime Fernandez, Adan Fernandez, Adrian Fernandez, Monty Fernandez, Victoria Ferraiolo-Madonia, Rick Ferrari, Joseph Ferut, Kurt Finch, Andrea Fisher, Darian Fisher, David Fisher, Jacqueline Fitzwater, Kristi Flanigan, William Flatley, Amy Fleigle, Paul Fletcher, Christiane Flood, Nick Flowers, Kyle Flynn, Francis Fogarty, Marianne Fogelson, Thomas Fohr, Bonita Folvarcik, Tracey Fong, Gabriel Fonseca, Carla

Fontanilla, Martin Forbes, Kimberly Ford, Susan Ford, Dominique Forest, Maria Forte, Patricia Fraide, Philip Francis, Alberto H Francisco, Elijah Frank, Neil Frank, Frederick Frankel, Scott French, Susana Frigenti, Jon Frodin, Howard Fulks, Pamela Fuller, William Fuller, Barbara Fusco, Pat Gabriel, Owen Gagliardo, Jonathan Gagnon, Dcn. Peter Gagnon, Mavourneen Gallagher, Rose Gallardo, Cristina Galliani, Sandra Galliani, Mike Gallico, Jeffrey Galush, Joseph Galvan, Heather Gamble-Smith, Alfred Gambone, Tim Gannon, Ralph Garcia, Julio Garcia, Arnie Garcia, David Garcia (in honor of Theodore Benedict Garcia), Amanda Garcia, Denise Garcia, Anthony Garofola, Ignacio Garro, Susan Gassmann, Louise Gaston, Kathleen Gaudin, Connie Gaudio, Adam Gaulke, Karli Gedmin, Nathan Geier, Teresa Geiselman, Kathleen Gerard, John Germain, Karl Germain, Jeremy Gerondal, Anthony Ghiardi, Anthony Giangiulio Giangiulio, Jennifer Gibney, John Gibson, Alexandria Gibson, Michele Gibson, Laura Giertych, Valerie Giggie, Joshua Gill, Annemarie Gillan, Mary Gillett, Mary Gillmore, Bobbie Gilman, Jim Giordano, Patrick Gnau, Dan Goddu, Amy Goggin, Iris Gomes, Jonathon Gomez, Raymond Gomez, Holly Gomez, Allyson Gomolka, Sergio Gonzalez, Todd Goodman, Sherryann Gordon, Angela Gorenc, Tristan Gorst, Julie Gould, Michelle Gower, Jenna Grable, Zoyla Grace, Reuben Gracia, Jodi Grant, Catherine Grantham, Darren Gray, Linda Graziano, Lois Grebosky, Anne Green, Janet Green, Gloria Greenup, Elizabeth Gregorus, Elizabeth Greiner, Paul Grieco, Denise Griego, Gregory Griffith, Brad Griffith, Briana Grimaldi, Jean Grissom, Robert Groppe, Fred Grube, Veronica Grujevski, Michelle Gudelski, Joseph Guenther, Frank Gunseor, Luis Guzman, Tamara Haas, Connie Hagler, Marie Hajny, Virginia Hajovsky, Alina Halay, Jeremy Halim, Bruce Hamilton, Paul Hammond, Larry Hammonds, Bill Hancock, Elly Hancsak, Scott Handwerk, James Haninger, Melissa Hanks, Sheelagh Hanly, Diana Hanna, Sheilagh Hardy, Jan Harkins, Richard Harmon, Michael Harrington, Melanie Harris, Jonathan Harris, Kevin Harrison, Barbara Harrison, Rebecca Harrison, Chris Harrison, Lisa Hart, Michelle Hart, Mary Harter, Gary Hartley, Vicki Hassessian, Brian Hastie, MaryBeth Hauke, Gerard Havasy, Denise Hawker, William Haybyrne, Matthew Hayes, MaryLynn Haynes, Michele Heath, Karen Hedge, Matthew Heffron, Joseph Helinski, David Helle, Steven Helm, Teresa Hemphill, Roy Henderson, Anthony Henely, MaryBeth Hennessy, Gilbert Herbig, Andrew Herbst, Scott Herby, Jose Hernandes, Emilio Hernandez, Victor Hernandez, Sara Herrington, Donna Hickman, Grove Higgins, Leo Higgins, Stephanie Hill, Kathleen Hill, Carl Hingst, Jannette Hinsley, Dcn. Paul Hiryak, Brian Hnatkovich, Mari Hobgood, Jennifer Hodges, Gary Hoeger, Ian Hoerner, Dana Hoey, Wendy T Hoffman, Linda Hoffstetter, Thomas Hoflich, Dr. David A. Hofrichter, Ryan Hogan, David Hohl, Emma Holland, John Holmstadt, Saclier de la Bâtie Hombeline, Patricia Hooten, Darin Hopegood, Jon Hopkins, Susan Hopkins, Michelle Horner, Kristy Horstkamp, Geraldo Hostin, Richard Housey, Roberta Houston, Carol Howard, Glen Howard, Brandi Howerton, Annette Høyrup, Sean Hudson, Jeffrey Hughes, Mark Hugoboom, Trever Humphres, Dan Hunter, Colin HurlowPaonesssa, Paul Hutchinson, Cindy Hutfles, T.C. Hutzler, Steve Hyatt, Antony Hylton, William Hynd, Eileen Iciek, Raymund Monico III Imperial, Mark Ingoglio, Salvatore Iorfida, Dimas Irusta, Pete Isermann, Maurice Ituriu, Lisa Iuzzini, Anthony Jackson, Kimberly Jacobs, Sydney Jacobs, Nancy Jaeger, Flo Jakobeit, Ewa Jakobson, Arkadiusz Jakubczyk, Sijo James, Daniel Jamieson, Susan Jankowski, John Janney, Stephen Janowski, James Jansen van Vuuren, Heather Jaracz, Jane JarmekClark, Erwin Jaumann, Karlo Jelincic, Tatiana Jenkins, Calvin Jennings, Arthur Jennings, Jeff Jimenez, David Jividen, Peter Johansen, Darryn Johnnie, Michael Johnoff, Judith Johnson, Katrina Johnson, Elizabeth Johnson, Teri Johnson, Bob Johnson, Dale Johnson, Barry Johnson, Ken Johnson, Mary Johnston, Walter Jones, Chris Jones, Kelley Jones, Jon Jonz, James Jordan, Julie Jordan, John Josefsberg, Thomas Joseph, Sharon Joyce, Edith Joyce, Randy Juanta, Chad Judice, Margaret Judy-Kauffman, Claude Julien, Charles Junjulas, Dan Juve, James Kachler, Thomas Kalinosky, Alexander Kalpakgian, Kinga Kaminska, Kathleen Kampa, Rita Marie Kane, Susan Kaness, Karen Karam, Glenn Karhoff, Victor Karlak, Lesley Karran-Seaton, Maria Kattner, Maria Kayser, John Kearney, Nancy Keating, Max Keen, Lawrence Keenan, William Kelim, Todd Keller, Nayhan Keller, Debbie Kelly, Susan

313

Kelly, John Kelly, David Kemp, Adam Kemper, Sylvia Kendall, Christine Kengott, Christine Kennally, Keith Kennedy, Regina M.

Kennell, Garrett Kennell, Joshua Kenney, Rose Marie Kerner, John Kerr, Dolorese Kershaw, Christopher Kertes, Rene Kieda, permanent deacon, Alexander Kilates, Summer Kindle, Luke Kippenbrock, Gary Kirsch, Ed Kise, Joseph Kish, Nancy Kitterman, Maureen Klecker, Joseph Klecko, Clinton Kliethermes, Jessica Klimke, John Klimsak, Aleksandra Kline, Chad Klinger, Lynn Klopstad, Jerry Kluft, Zach Knakmuhs, Stefan Knaperek, Patricia Knotts, Connie I. Ko, Patricia Koch, Joseph Koechl, Steven Koel, Kathy Koenn, Michael Kohut, Lara Komar-Tancock, Wouter Koopmans, John Kopczyk, Patricia Koranda, James Kornmeyer, Georgette Koselke, Konrad Kosiek, Gergely Kosa, Justin Koss, Sunita Kottoor, Emi Koy, Jonathan Krahl, Shobey Day Kramer, Robert Krause, Maureen Krezmien, Gary A Kroeger, John Krol, Karen Kronoveter, Mary Krupa, Krystyna Krupa, Manny Kurian, Diana Kusick, Kenneth Kuzdak, Patricia La La Barbera, Cheryl La Follette, Janet LA Voie, Mike H. Labruyere, Dana LaCombe, Lance Lacroix, Frank Lafleur, Guillermo E. Lainez Z, Karen Lamb, Marianne Lan, Maryann Lanchoney, Juanita Landers, Joe Landreneau, Katie Lane, Micki Lange, Elisabeth Langenkamp, Robert Lapaz, Mark Larkins, Brenda Laronde, Scooby Larson, Miguel Lasaga, Maria Lasaga Callahan, Harvey LaSeur, Larry Laumann, Kathleen LaValley, Mary Lawrence, Michael Lawson, Angela Layfield, Tammy Layton, Asshur Seth Lazar, Thanh Le, Rachel Le Grand, Victoria Leach, Paul Leader, Julie Lebeis, James LeBert, Maurice Lecavalier, Marie Leclair, Thomas Lee, Andrea Lefebvre, Michael Lefort, Jim Lehmann, Donna Lehr, Kimberly Leipham, Angela Lemos, Steve Lenz, Dr. Kathleen M. Leo, Luke Leonard, Michael LeSage, Sandra L Lesperance, Alex Lessard, Kathleen Lesson, Barbara Levins, Chris Levis, CJ Levy, Mark Lewallen, Laurie Lewandowski, Cassandra Lim, Rosario Lim, Julie Linares, David Ling, Cathy Lins, Chris Lloyd, Vincent James Loduca, Lucille Loe, Margaret Loesch, Catherine Loft, Mark Loftus, Joshua Logan, Jim Logue, Rosemarie Loncaric-Spataro, Marie Long, Culm Long, Milt Longworth, Janet Lopez, Elisa Lopez, Dcn. Carl Lordi, Caterina Lorenzo-Molo, Tiffany Loris, Gerrit Louw, Stephen Loyd, Lucy Lozano, Franciszek Luc, Lorretta Lucia, James Lucier, Fiona Lugo, Carmela Lukacs, Stephen Lukic, Jose Luna, Anne Lundt, Jeanne Lupien, Christopher Lushis, Barbara Lydell, Amy Lynch, Michael Lynch, Christopher Lyon, Tonya Lyons, Christina-Maria Mühlberg-Gamper, Taylor Mac Manus, Matthew Mach, Eugenia Macias, Tony Macias, David Mack, Yvette Mackail, Cathy MacMullin, Colm Madden, Yvette Mader, Nicola Maetone, Patti Magnon, Bernadette Maguire, Gerard Maher, Karen Mahoney, Joie Maida, Daniel Maier, Joe Maimone, Michael Maker, Pamela Maliszewski, Bartholomew Anthony Mallett, Jacqueline Manapsal, Greg Mandt, Ann Manhire, Christal Mannikus, Alice Mansell, Denise Mantei, Ann Marcario Bord, Michael Marcin, Debra Marcotte, McGill Maria, Juan Marin, Brian Marks, Patrick Marron, Joy Marshall, Kimm Marshall, Noah Marshall, Michael Marsillo, Jaime Martín Esparza, Phillip Martell, Catherine Marten, Chris Martens, Linda Martin, Valentina Martin, Martha Martinez, Rodolfo Martinez, Andriya Martinovic, Joe Marusak, Tabitha Mason, Abnel Massa, Linda Mastej, Daniel Masullo, Karen Mata, Patricia Mathews, Jennifer Mathews, Carol Mattern, Will Matthews, Cynthia Matthews, Aduzinda Matthews, Judith Maucieri, April Mayer, Mary Mayo, Bridgette Mc Anea, Kevin McAdams, Grace McBride, Mary McBride, John McBride, Thomas McCahill, Michael McCann, Kevin McClements, Thomas McCormack, Aric McCullough, Evan McCutchen, John McDonald, Josh McFall, Tim McFarlane, John McGee, Colette McGirr, Jennifer Mcgovern, Kevin McGowan, Karl McGrath, John McGuiness, Stephen McGuire, Carla McGuirk, Dion McInnis, Kenneth Mckechnie, Paul McKenna, Patrick McKeown, Patrick Mckerry, Harry McKinster, Margie McLeod, Garrett McMillan, Laurie McMurrey, Greg Mcnaughton, Denise McNutt, Clancy Mcquigg, Seth McQuillan, Martina McTaggart, Stephen G. McWade, Anthony McWilliams, Francis A. Meccia, Jorge Medina, Elizabeth Mejia, Miguel Melendrez, James Melfi, Janice Melhorn, Alexander Melhorn, Joseph Melnyk, Richard Melvin, Ana Liza Menguito, Kathleen Merry, Bill Mertka, Sarah Messecar, Walter Metrick, June Meyers, Connie Michaels, Janet Middleton, James Miguez, Vicki Milaitis, Roberto Milian, Tracy Miller, Beth Miller, Linda Miller, Ana Miller, Andrew Miner, Michael Minges, Joshua Minton, Lisa Mione, Anne Miranda, Diana Mirosavljevic,

Timothy Misencik, Rita Misho, Dolores Mitchell, Taylor Mitzel, Carol Mizera-Amick, Cheryl Moir, Doreen Moisey, Erik Mojica, Elizabeth Moldenhauer, Joseph Moless, Alvaro Molina, Jessica Moline, Timothy Moline, Jason Molitor, Suzanne Moltz, Lynn Momboisse, Kathy Monroe, Enrique Montes, Janice Montiel, Connie Montpetit, Robert Moon, Mike Mooney, Joseph Moore, Terrence Moore, Kay Moore, Michael Moore, John Moore, Jorge Mora, Chris Moraes, Teresa Morales, Gabriel Morales, Adriana Morales, Kevin Moran, Crislee Moreno, Angela Moreno, Donald Morgan, Angela Morley, Rob Morris, Derek Morrison, Judith Morrison, Trevor Morrison, Lucy Mosca, Deacon Larry Motyka, Christian Muñoz, Debbie Mueller, Becky Mulkerrin, Kathleen Muller, Christine Mulligan, Daliana Murga, James Lee Murphy, Brian Murphy, Brian Musha, Jon Musser, Felix Mutuc, Madeleine Myers Myers, Lorrie Nantt, Carlos Naranjo, Jorge Narvaez, Chris Nash, Nelson Nazario, Catherine Neal, Darren Neill, Kristina Neill, Erik Nelson, Paul Nelson, Keith A Nelson, David Evan Nelson, John Nelson, Joe Nenninger, Luigi Neri, Regan Neubauer, Darren Neufeldt, Deborah Newell, Raymond Newkirk, Charles S. Newman, Emmanuel Ngabire, Joseph Nguyen, Terence Nicholson, Megan Nicotra, John Niehaus, Allie Niemann, Nicole Amanda Nieto Quiñonez, Katherine Nini, Ryan Nixon, Christopher Nnamani, Joshua Noles, Aidan Noone, Arash Noori, Joseph Norman, Harriet Normoyle Lewis, Vernon Noronha, Jill Novak, Craig Novak, Kathleen Nuttall, Kevin O Regan, Deanna O'Donoghue, Anthony O'Reilly, Norman O'Brien, Ellen O'Brien, Anthony O'Connor, Brian O'Curran O'Curran, Linda Ofstead, Erich Ohrt, Oscar Olague, Loirin O'Leary, Karen Olson, Elaine OMalley, Kathleen Ondracek, Timothy O'Neil, Katherine ONeill, Joanne O'Neill, Brendan O'Neill, Rudy Ong, Greg Onyango, Barbara Opperman, Luis Raul Oquendo, Tony Oquias, Nikki Ormsbee, Diana Orozco, Maria Ortiz, Raymond Ortiz, Joseph Osborne, Aileen Osias, Carol Osteen, John Ostermann, Amanda OSullivan, John Ott, Tim and Elsa Otte, David Owenby, Jeff Owings, Anna Pacek, Paul Packer, Therese Padilla, Ana Padilla, Lupe Padilla, Rebecca Padley, Alan Palacios, Cecilia Palao, Daniel Palese, Janice Palko, Dave Palmer, Tammy Palubicki, Alexander Palyo, Lyndie Panitz, Michael Pant, Eduardo Panus, Judi Paparozzi, Laura Paradis, Mary Parks, Kathy Parlatore, Nanette Parratto-Wagner, Carol Pasaante, Joseph Mark Passante, Patricia Pasternak, Joe Pastorek, David Paterson, Erin Patterson, Mary Ann Pauken, Albin Paul, Joe Paul, James Pavlick, George Paxton, Wendy Payne, Christopher Peacock, Anthony Peacock, Frank Pearson, Leonard Pease, Marco Antonio Pellens, Richard Pelo, Bert Penney, Havilah Pennington, William Penny, James Penson, Brian Perez, Wendell Perez, Daniel Perez, Andrew Perez, Theresa Perkins, Theresa Perkins, Joan Pernicano, Marla Perry, Linda Perry, Valerie Persing, Mitchell Peters, Fran Peterson, Gary Peterson, Pamela Pettibone, Deacon Bernard Pettie, Damian Pettit, Mitzi Phalen, Evan Pham, Wesley Phillips, James N. Phillips Jr., Andrea Phyrillas, George Piccone, Oliver Pickstone, Stanislaw Pieczara, Thomas Piegsa, Tim Pinewski, Maureen Therese Pinho, Pablo A. Pinzón, Carmen Plake, Kyle Pociask, James Pogue, Bridgette Poitras, Steve Pokorny, Matthew Pommier, Jason Ponimoi, Regina Pontes, Ken Popp, Tony Porcaro, Courtney Porter, Christian Porzenheim, Sal Potestivo, Mark Potzick, David Poulin, Jacki Poundd, Vada Powell, Cathy Powell, Robert Powell, Ed Power, Amanda Pozzo, Dolores Priego Porras, Mario Prince, Donna Procher, Jacqueline Pucci-Starks, Stephen Pulkrabek, Beth Pulliam, Gerard Purdue, Kent Purdy, Conor Quincey, Carlos Quintero, Suzanne Radford, Alexander Raemaekers, Daniel Rafferty, Gordon Rafool, Mary Rainey, Michael Rakaczewski, Andrew Ralls, Andrew Ramirez, John Ramirez, Lino Ramirez, Guillermo Ramos, Brian Rankin, Angie Rapelje, Maria Rapp, Joe Rappa, Melko Rasica, Ann Rastorfer, James Rauch, Dr. Antone Raymundo, Brian Reagan, Vinicius Rebuli, Jeff Redecker, Robin Reed, Kim Reed, Maria Reed, William Reedy, Michael Reese, Landon Reffitt, Nathan Reffitt, Danielle Regan, Kevin Reginald, Mark Reid, Marie Philomena Reidy, Jeremy Reidy, Erin Reilley, Anthony Render, Tom Rentz, Rosa Reyes, Paolo Reyes, Rene Reyes, Maureen Reynolds, Damian Rhodes, Gabrielle Rice, Joshua Richards, Frank Riello, Tambra Riggs-Gutierrez, Kevin Rilott, Michael Riopel, Jodie Riordan, Christopher Rissetto, Carrie Ritzel, Dr. Lorena Rivarola-Duarte, Amanda Robben, Aaron Roberts, Chris Roberts, Jason Roberts, O.S.S.M., Jim Robinette, Susan Robinson, Darren Robinson, Rebecca Robinson, James Robinson, Elisha

Robinson, Vince Robles, Natalie Rock, Donna Rock, Ciara Rodgers, Christine Rodrigues, Carlos Rodriguez, Gretchen Rodriguez, Angelica Rodriguez, Luis Rodriguez, Carlos Rodriguez Lampon, Mark Roeckell, Robert Roesser Roesser, Matthew Roessner, Robert Roetting, Mary Rofe, Suzanne Rohe, Marcia Rohrer, Scott Romanoski, Matthew Romeo, Patricia Rondeau, Sandra Rosas, Amy Rose, Bill Ross, Rhonda Rossano, Kathy Rossi, Frances Rotondo, Margaret Roueche, Angela Rousseau, Peggy Rowe-Linn, Scott Roy, Terri Roy, Catherine Royce, Andrea Ruccolo, Jacqueline Rueda, Richard. Ruesch, Michael Ruggiero, Adrian Rusch, Kelly Rush, Bill Rushmore, Brandon Ruth, Ryan Rutkowski, Antonio Ruvolo, Phyllis Ryan, Benjamin Ryan, Thomas Ryan, John Ryan, Federica Sánchez y Carrillo, Bruce Sabatino, Greg Sabourin, Alina Sacerio-Polak, Renate Safford, Andrey Saiz, Saira Saju, Alejandro Salazar Lobos, Carlos Salgado, Jonathan Salmon, Mary Salmond, Sharon Saltzman, Audry Salvador, Amy San Filippo, Al Sanchez, Angelo Sandoval, Maryanne Santelli, Louis Santiago, Catherine Santos, Patricia Santy, Austin Sarabia, Christine Sarracino, Joseph Sarro, Francesco Sasso, Jeremy Sauer, Lori Sautter, Christina Scerpella, Jeffrey Schack, Kevin Schad, Angela Schade, Mary Schaenzer, Bettina Schafer, Mary Schaub, Steven Scheerbaum, Mary Scheetz, Lou Ann Schell, Thomas Schirra, Laurie Schirra, Barbara Schleben, Jessica Schlick, Michael Schmidt, Christopher Michael Schmitz, Ricky Schneider, Richard Schneider, Phil Schofield, Peggy Schoppe, Rick Schrader, Dan Schreck, Jason Schreder, Melissa Schroer, Daniel Schuler, Don Schutt, John Schweisthal, Diane Schwind, Susanne Scott, Michael Scott, Thomas Scott, Cheryl Scott, Paul Sefranek, Gail Seiler, Krystian Sekowski, Robin Sellers, James Senecal, Paul Senecal, Susan Senia, Shelly Senia, Carl Sergeant, Elisabetta Serrani, Paul Serwinski, Kasia Seubert, Donna Seuferer, Michele Severson, Brian Sexton, Paul Sgrillo, Lesa Shackleford, Matthew Shaddrix, Russell Shaffer, Loretta Shalosky, Sean Sharer, Terrance Sharp, Kevin Sharpe, John Sharry, Gary Shash, Genie Shaw, Richard Shea, Robert Shea, Remarna Sheehan, David Sheehan, Elizabeth Sheehy, Jennifer Sheets, Casey Shelton, Josephine Shevlin, Melanie Shiley, Al Shiya, Bernadette Shonka, Carleen Short, Ronald Shpakoff, Kathryn Sibley, Althea Sidaway, Edward Sidleck, Victoria Siedlecki, Armelle Sigaud, Anderson Silva, Douglas Silva, Clarence Sim, Cheryl Simanek, Kristin Simmons, Leila Simonsen, Greg Sipe, Asher Sircy, Annette Skibinski, Carol Slater, Susan Slater, Nathaniel Slattery, Alyssa Smeltzer, Melinda Smith, Eric Smith, Melanie Smith, Amy Smith, Jean Smith, Jimmy Smith, Catherine Smith, Maria Smith, Theron Smith, Julie Smith, Karen Smith, Cillian Smith, Allan Smith, Donna Smith, Mary Smyth, Steve Soldi, John Soley, Jane Somerville, Hugh Somerville Knapman OSB, John Sommer, Julian Sommers, Jennifer Sonnier, Denease Sorapuru, Carole Souza, Caryn Spaniel, Karen Spaziante, Scott Spence, Nick Spicher, Charles Spivak, Jennifer Spurgin, Burke Squires, Zlatko Šram, Pauline Staffa, Sandy Stakes, Susan Stalter, Natalie Stamilla, John Standifird, Anne Standley, Robert Stannard, Laura Stanosheck, Beatriz Stapleton, Beata Stark, Christopher Stark, James Athol Steel, Sally Steele, Jesse Steeves, William Steffen, Eileen Steng, Theresa Stiner, Andras Stirling, Noah Stolly, Vincenzo Stone, William Stowe, Cameron Strachan, Franco Strangis, Teresa Streckfuss, Darwin Stupka, Gustavo Suárez, Sharon Subjak, Susan Sucher, Tessa Sugden, Rev. Billy T. Sullivan, Janet Swallow, Pete Swicker, Corey Swope, Nekeya Sylvester, Mary Syron, Jan Szafranski, Edie Szyperski, Ed Taekema, Franklin Takacs, Jeff Takats, Alice Talbot, Silvana Maria Tanzi Giordano, Joseph Taylor, Maria Taylor, David Taylor Taylor, Colette Tellman, Cynthia J. Tennant, Guadalupe Tenpenny, Mary Tenuta, Maraid Tew, Mark Tezak, Pravin Thevathasan, Sue Thibodeaux, Kevin Thieme, Philip Thoma, Wendy Thomas, Jon Thomas, John Thompson, Dianne Thompson, Daniel Thorpe, Ben & Lola Threinen, David Thrower, Jennifer Tina, Patrick Tina, Betty Tippett, Cindy Titus, Terri Todd, Matthew Toenjes, Joseph Tolin, Jennifer Tompkins, Terrence Tormey, Carlos Torres, J Robert Torres, Cecilia Torres, Natasha Tosic, Joli Toth, Kathleen-Marie Tracey, Nicholas Trandem, Janet Trapp, Jennifer Traughber, Fr. Michael John Travaglione, OFM, Mike Traweek, Susan Treacy, Ernesto Trevino, Mark Trieger, Steve Tristqan, Dave Troupe, Bernardo Trujillo, Lois Tucci, James Tucker, Jayne Tuller, Fr. William Tulua, Jose Tumbaga, Karly Tuttle, Nigel Tyrer, Alan Tyson, Raymond Uherek, Chris Urban, Michael Ursini, Clark Edward Uytico, Lotis Vailas, Oscar Valdez, Tammy Valdovino, Mark Valencia, Jackie

Valentino, Dayle Van Alstine, Teo van der Weele, Martin Van Tassell, Raven Vancil, Paul Vandenheede, Kevin Vanderwater, Brenda VanWeezel, Matthew VanWormer, Gerry Vara, Scott Varga, Gloria Vargas, João Vasconcelos, Jorge Vasquez, Joanne Vavoso, Michael Velosa, David Vermont, Charles Vermurlen, Anthony Vernaglia, Paolo Vetrano, Tonino Vicari, Elisabeth Viegas, Jacqueline S. Villano, Linda Vincent, David Vincent, Ritchie Vincent, Guy Vogrin, Charles Volz, Ryan Vonderhaar, Mark Voorhis, Fr. Chris Vorderbruggen, Morgan W, Matt Waechter, David Wagner, Matt Wagner, Jesse Waitz, Detley Waldrop, Carol Walenga, Heather Walker, Kelliann Wall, Colin Wallace, Robert Wallace Jr., Lisa Wallender, Janet Walmsley-Heron, Brenda Walsh, Catherine Walsh, Christine Walsh, Bill Walton, Catherine Walton, Laurie Walton, Kerry-Anne Walz, Susan Walz, Barbara Wanamaker, Todd Wannemuehler, Joseph Wantz, Teresa Ward, Johnathan Warminski, David W. Warner, Victoria Warner, Michael Warner, John Wasko, Gerald Wassil, Dennis Waszak, Lucille Watson, Gregory Watson, Chris Watts, Deacon Melvin Watts FSSP, Lorain Wauters, Brian Weber, Misty Weber, Tim Weiland, Mark Weis, Genevieve Weiss, Judy Weitz, Ryan Wellman, Marissa Wellman, Ben Wells, Ashley Wells, Jon Wenger, Mary Wermerskirchen, Jillian Wernke, Kara West, Laura Westbrook, Neil Weston, Melissa Wexler, Trish Whitney, Patricia Whittier, Marcel Widzisz, Adam Wiederman, Angela Wies, Gary Wiley, Carson Wilkie, Mike Willey, Fredrick Williams, Kathleen Williams, Rick Williams, Ryan Williams, Deanna Williston, David Wills, Jim Wilson, John Wilson, John Wilson, James Wilson, Steven Windey, Patrtick Winn, Blake Winn, Aaron Winter, Kyle Wirachowsky, James Wiscott, Terri Wise, Carol Wittman, Trinity Wlaschin, Tim Wolfe, Tres Wolfford, Edward Wolski Sr, Maria Woltornist, Douglas Wood, Amy Woodke, Jeffrey Woods, Kathleen Worthington, Evelyn Wortmann, Erika Wright, Susan Wright, Linda Wright, David Wurst, Nicholas Wylie, Lawrence Wynja, Darek Wyrzykowski, Theresa Wyss, Alexandra Yager, Patrick Yanke, Amanda Yates, Debra Yip, Georgette Young, Elisabeth Young, David Yung, Elaine Yuratich, Philip Zanco, III, Omar Zapata, Dominic Zappia, Marilyn Zayac, Richard Zbilicki, Josip Zeko, William Zeranski, Jon Ziegelheim, Thomas Ziolkowski, Mary Zitnik, Craig Zorn, David Zuber, Jaime Zuluaga, Carlos (Rev.) Zuniga, Waldemar Zurek, and Madalene Zwick.